Only My Dreams:
An English Girlhood

Only My Dreams:
An English Girlhood

By HILDA ANN SALUSBURY

Illustrated by Kathy Blankley

ACADEMY CHICAGO PUBLISHERS

Dedicated to Julian and Austen

Published in 1990 by
Academy Chicago Publishers
213 West Institute Place
Chicago, Illinois 60610

Library of Congress Cataloging-in-Publication Data

Salusbury, Hilda.
  Only my dreams.

  1. England—Social life and customs—20th century.
2. England—Biography. 3. Salusbury, Hilda.
I. Title.
DA566.4.S37 1990   942.083   87-19422
ISBN 0-89733-276-8
ISBN 0-89733-275-X (pbk.)

Contents

Editor's Note

Hilda Ann Salusbury was born in 1906 in Great Yarmouth, a fishing port on the Norfolk coast. When she was seven or eight years old the family moved to the adjoining town of Gorleston-on-sea, and that is where the early events of this book take place. The Wood children walked, or sometimes took a bus, to the Edward Orledge School in Yarmouth.

Any modern reader of her story will remark at once upon Hilda Salusbury's apparent basic passivity and her refusal, consciously at least, to blame her father for the direction which her life took. I believe this is one of the notable aspects of this book; it is seldom that we can view first-hand the emotional response of a girl subject to the grimly patriarchal expectations of what was still a Victorian household. That the escape she chose was a life of service as a nurse is not surprising; that she escaped at all is a tribute to her basic toughness and resiliency. Again, that she chose later to apply her training only sporadically should not be surprising: the great achievement of her life she undoubtedly sees as her relationship with her husband and the breaking of the spiral by her children, who both have University educations—and especially by her daughter, who has built a successful career apart from a happy marriage.

—Anita Miller

1. The Family and the Setting

MY mother and father, Grannie and my two sisters and one brother and I all lived in a large old-fashioned house in a small seaside town. My mother, who had a teenaged girl named Violet to help her, had borne four children in four years. I was the eldest.

In about 1910 our street was a mixture of terraced and detached houses, a row of old cottages, shops and three public houses—one doubtful, two smart and respectable. Our street was a turning off the High Street. At the top, the High Street widened into a tramcar terminus—a constant source of entertainment for the neighbourhood children, with its maze of overhead wires from which electricity was conducted by a long arm to the tram. The conductor would gauge just the right moment to swing the arm out to make contact with the wires overhead. According to his skill he would be cheered or jeered by the crowd of small children who never failed to be present when this tricky exercise was performed.

'Garn, Mister, you ain't got no idear . . . Try again, Mister,' they cried when the arm jumped the cable and the sparks flew in all directions. The luckless fellow who hung on the rope controlling the capricious arm which ran around in circles, was in danger of being swung off his feet at any moment. The children loved his predicament. 'Ang on, Mister, or you'll swing for it yet,' they yelled, laughing in delight and running just close enough behind to stay out of trouble. The whole operation delayed the tram and frequently irate passengers would join in the shouting. However, eventually perseverance had to overcome obstacles and the tram started down the street with sparks and crackles, to the loud encouragement of the undersized rabble.

The row of mean cottages running down one side of the street near the tram terminus toward the river were approached through a narrow side entrance. They were one up and one down, and shared an outside toilet at the bottom of the yards. On one side of the cottages was a grey brick public house and on the other a butcher's shop and a general store. There were always dogs and cats around the backs of these commercial premises and small boys baited rats there. This was not unusual at the time.

The general store was called Bussy's; it supplied anything edible in amounts from two ounces to ten tons and most important it supplied it 'on tick' till the end of the week. Most housekeepers in our street would be mortgaged from week to week to the butcher and the grocer. The groceries delivered to our door for the week would cost about nine or ten shillings—about 50 p. English current money and $1.50 American. Food was cheap, but wages were low. Many weekly pay packets held about 30 shillings to feed a family—that would be about £1.50 current or $2.40 American—; and an income of £3.00 a week—about $4.80—was considered affluence. The working class had no modern conveniences; for them living standards were universally low.

When one passed Bussy's, the tone of the street picked up: there were a few semi-detached houses. The people who lived in them had nothing to do with the people in the row cottages; if the children wandered across the class barrier—which they often did—they were hastily retrieved by irate parents amid tears and protestations. After the semi-detacheds, came a higher-class butcher's shop with strings of fresh, succulent, fat pork sausages festooning his window and rabbits hanging upside down in the doorway, their bellies exposed, their eyes glazed. Chickens hung on the walls with elongated necks, their feathers still ruffled from their death throes. Meat was bright red, dripping blood, ready to be hacked off the carcass. This was, of course, in strong contrast to today's plastic-wrapped 'joints', displayed best-side-up or whiter-than-white featherless chickens. All mass produced, ready for the pot. Our joint, a cut off the best topside, never cost more than two shillings and sixpence—15 p. approximately, or 25 cents—and kept a family of six for the best part of a week.

Next to the butcher's, divided from them by one entry wide enough for a horse and cart, were an ironmonger's shop and various small stores; then the street turned off to lead to the beach.

Behind the butcher's and the other premises was the slaughterhouse. We children would watch the reluctant animals being herded up the alley and next day the street would resound to the agonised squeals of pigs and bellow of cattle being killed. The butcher would nonchalantly swill out the yard and entry and a river of blood would run into the gutter in our street.

The other side of the street facing the tramcar terminus was much more select. The corner was dominated by a superior public house with a beer garden; it was popular with visitors from London and the North who flooded the town in the summer, spending money and talking in accents that we called foreign. A pretty little terrace of red brick houses adjoined the pub—they had neat lace curtains at the window and bright polished letter boxes and door knobs. These brasses were polished early in the morning so that they would be seen to be done, not seen being done. We rarely fraternised with the inhabitants of the red brick houses; they were too primly respectable, with their front windows displaying an aspidistra or a photograph of a departed loved one who appeared to watch passers-by with soulful glassy eyes.

After the bright little houses came one or two 'good class' shops, amongst which was a greengrocer. In good weather, this shop gave the street a festive atmosphere; its wares, artistically displayed, spilled out onto the pavement: the best hearted cabbages, the juiciest ripe strawberries, the rosiest apples, flanked by bunches and buckets of flowers, all to be had, courteously, for a few pennies.

Our house had somehow been sandwiched in between the greengrocer's and the newsagent's; it sat back from the street in its own detached front garden in grand isolation. The newsagent's was the corner shop; from there the street branched off to a cul-de-sac of workshops and cottages, its other leg running down to the river. In its day our house had been well maintained, but by the time I was old enough to notice it, it had become sadly neglected. There was a lovely old oak studded door with a heavy wrought-iron knocker, and hanging at its side, a wrought-iron bell which rivalled the church bells when it resounded through the big old house. The foot scraper, supported on each side by wrought-iron lions' heads, also testified to more affluent days. The house was called River House; you could see the river in the distance at the far end of our street.

We shared our back entrance with the newsagent; it was an alleyway which ran across the bottom of our back garden to the back gate. A high fence cut our back garden off from the houses below it. An old couple named Mr and Mrs Piffin kept the newsagent's shop. We children thought they must always have been there, they were so old. Mrs Piffin was a plump round-faced woman who wore her grey hair flattened out round the crown of her head like a pancake, kept in place by a grey hairnet. She was always enveloped from her neck to her ankles in a floral apron, which completely concealed her clothing. Her arms were always bare to the elbow. She had difficulty, I recall, in negotiating the step, up or down, from the hall to the shop; we had trouble restraining our mirth at the sight, but we helped her because she always gave us a few chocolate drops or aniseed balls for services rendered.

Mr Piffin, on the other hand, was energetic, small and wiry; he cycled on his paper delivery rounds like a Grand Prix driver. We felt, with the uncanny instinct of children, that we were not so popular with Mr Piffin as with his wife, and we kept out of his way. He would pop his head over the fence; we suspected that he was standing on a box—and say, 'What you little varmints up to today?'

'Oh, nothing, Mr Piffin,' we assured him, looking at him with wide-eyed innocence. 'Nothing at all.'

The Pippins kept fowl, rabbits and a cat and dog. We always found some entertainment in our back garden, either real or improvised by us. The rabbits got mysteriously out and away, or a chicken flew into our garden or a cat got amongst the chickens.

'Mrs Pippin,' my brother would say in his most polite manner, 'your fence is broken. Would you like me to mend it for you?'

'Why yes, John, how good of you.'

We would all scout round and scrounge some wooden rails from somebody else's fence. Mrs Pippin, well-brought-up and nicely spoken, never suspected us. She would reward us with a nice fresh new-laid egg for tea, or a threepenny bit or sometimes a liquorice stick or sugar mice from the shop.

It was very handy living next door to a little shop which sold practically everything. Our credit was always good there from week to week. I had an unfortunate habit of flicking the tablecloth up when I was setting the table, and catching the gas mantle. Anyone who has had anything to do with gas mantles knows how flimsy they are. Disaster was avoided by my racing round the passage to get another 'on tick'—there was no money to spare for calamities in the middle of the week—and have it 'in situ' before Father arrived home for tea.

Every morning, punctually at eight o'clock, Mrs Pippin delivered my father's *Daily Mail* over the garden wall, with a loud cry of 'Paper oh!' No other word was ever exchanged. Mrs Pippin would hold the newspaper over her head and my father would reach over the wall to take it. This routine took place every morning for nearly twenty years, in all kinds of weather.

The Pippins did not have all that much to complain about from us: their son, about forty years old, was a budding musician—not yet discovered, but still hopeful. His name was Alfred; he had never left home although he married. He brought his wife home to live with his parents. Alfred's incessant piano playing from morning to night would have driven any but a very tolerant neighbour to loud complaints. But my father, luckily, spent half his time in the public library after my mother left, and Grannie was hard of hearing and slept a lot. We children either joined in or disregarded the sounds, if indeed we really noticed them. We had Strauss for breakfast and Sousa's rousing marches for tea. Sometimes my brother took out his violin and joined in for fun.

Alfred's wife was a helpless, neurotic sort. She suffered with her head and, I gathered, never washed her hair. This bright pair contributed nothing to the business. Alfred, who loved animals, tended the chickens and rabbits. During the summer the smell from this miniature farmyard was at times unpleasant. My father would mutter, 'It's not healthy, something must be done. I shall have to tell the Pippins.' But he was basically a man of peace and we suffered their farmyard just as they suffered four lively children living next door.

There were two more shops on the opposite corner to our house, where the street continued down to the river. One was a bakery, the other a fish shop. The delicious smell of home-made bread and rolls straight from the oven would drift in through our windows in the morning and make our mouths water. On Saturday mornings when we did not have to hurry off to school, we always had hot rolls with lashings of fresh churned country butter. No cellophane-wrapped bread or butter can have the taste of these unprotected ones.

Between the fish shop and the riverside where the fish were landed were the fish wharves and curing grounds. We children were forbidden to go in or near the wharves but we frequently disobeyed, because the docks lay on our way to school. As the herring were being landed, we would scramble, slithering around in the mud and filth of the fish dock, to retrieve a string of about two dozen fish. My unsuspecting father often had a meal of fresh herring because of his resourceful children.

The kippers were cured in the traditional way on these docks; split and suspended over a fire of special wood, kept at a specified smouldering temperature, the smoke permeating the fish to turn it a warm golden brown. It absorbed just enough smoke to give it the right flavour and the carefully regulated heat made the fish juicy. Bloaters were cured in much the same way, but were left as nature created them and were not split open. They were smoked less and were more delicate in flavour and color than the kippers. The red herring, a strong-tasting variety of herring much favoured by fishing folk with strong palates, were cured and salted until they were as hard as bricks. Since there was no refrigeration in those days, fish needed brine and smoking: the fish had to be soaked for hours in water to draw out the salt and make them palatable.

It was dispatched from these wharves all over the world in wooden boxes. British Railways, they used to say, 'ran' on kippers; I have heard that Sir Laurence Olivier used to travel by train for the sake of the breakfast kippers. Years ago they were exported in bulk to Russia and were a staple part of the Russian diet. Today the kipper does not have the same status; it is a mockery of its mystic, succulent past.

The early mornings echoed to the clump of the fisher lassies' wooden clogs. For them, all streets led to the fish wharves. In the late autumn, as the mornings got colder and darker, the lassies had to gut herrings by the light of paraffin flares. The huge baskets of herrings, winched from the bowels of the ship, were suspended for a moment in the wintry sky with seagulls and snowflakes hovering round them; in the next second they were tipped, the fish cascading down in a glistening shower into the waiting tubs. Then they were wheeled briskly away to the lassies, who inserted their small sharp knives in the gills of the fish, made a slit and gouged out the inedible gut.

It was done quickly and looked easy, but most of the lassies had cut fingers from the slippery knives, and frozen hands too, because they could not wear gloves while they worked. They had to be tough to survive: they worked standing knee deep in filth and slush, in open buildings like bus shelters, through which blizzards and cruel winds blew from the North Sea. Ill fed and ill clothed, they gutted fish for hours in the light of the paraffin flares, as fast as the trawler fleets could land the baskets. They did not all survive: a season never passed without one or two poor lassies being found by the first light of day, crouched behind a barrel, as dead and frozen as the fish.

The fish shop was white-tiled and the white marble slabs always displayed a tempting array, fresh from the docks. I knew at a very tender age that fish had to be red around the gills to be fresh. Pale around the gills was a dead giveaway, so to speak, no matter how fresh the fish was supposed to be. Today I believe that half the world does not know the taste of fresh fish.

In any case, in our town we had the best of two worlds: the seaside with lovely sandy beaches and towering cliffs and the countryside, with pretty winding lanes for rambles and picturesque Norfolk villages to explore. And we had the river for boating in the summer. In the spring we especially loved the country lanes. We scrambled up hedges and raced across fields, after making sure that there were no cows about. We stumbled and fell and skipped up and away again.

'Oh come on, Laura, don't be a baby,' my brother would scold my youngest sister; she was a little short in the leg and would repeatedly fall and bruise or cut herself. Bravely she choked back her tears and tried to keep up with us.

Startling a rabbit, sending a nesting bird winging skywards, chasing butterflies in the warm sunshine (Grannie never did find out how I bashed the rim of my straw hat), paddling through streams, sometimes stopping to catch a tadpole in a jar, climbing trees . . . The bluebells were a delight. We would gather armfuls to fill the house and to take to teacher. Primroses and shy violets bloomed in the undergrowth, while later in the year the air was filled with the fragrance of honeysuckles and sweet roses.

Often I would lie in the long sweet-smelling grass where poppies bloomed, and just dream in the sun which shimmered over everything and made me lazy. Let my brothers and sisters run about, I would think, drifting off to sleep. What was that song we sang at school? 'Be good, sweet maid, and let who will be clever.' Of course I would be good. I resolved not to slap my little sister any more, not to tease my brother or be bossy just because I was the eldest. And then a voice would call in the distance, 'Come on, Ann! Are you coming?'

Of course there were times when our rambles got us into difficulties; in fact, we flirted with serious accidents or even death. I remember once a gang of rival schoolboys attacked us and encroached on our special tadpole pond which we had discovered and to which we felt we had prior rights. They stole my jar and ran round the pond with it. My brother yelled to me to cut across the pond and head them off. It looked safe enough and shallow, with its coat of green moss. I was soon in the water up to my armpits, and then I found I couldn't move. I was caught somehow in the weeds and undergrowth and sinking into the mud and stagnant water. I screamed and my brother ran shrieking toward a cottage in a nearby field.

A man appeared in the cottage doorway, took in the

situation at a glance and came bounding across the field. He waded in and pulled me out and carried me off. I was shivering and crying, terrified by the realisation that I had almost drowned. The farmer's wife took me from her husband, washed me and dressed me in her children's dry clothes. I remember feeling upset because the clothes were not only too big, they were old and threadbare. None of my own clothes looked like that.

We were all given some milk and sent on our way home. The gang had made off with our tadpoles so we had nothing to show for our adventure.

'What on earth happened to you?' my mother exclaimed when we trooped into the house. 'Where did you get those dreadful clothes?'

My brother was always the spokesman. He explained what had happened, although he did not say that he had told me to cut across the pond. I was scolded for being so simple, but my mother was obviously thankful that I had gotten out alive. On the following Saturday I took a note to the farmer's wife and returned the clothes, nicely laundered. I collected my own, which had also been washed and dried.

On two other occasions my brother was responsible for what could have been a tragedy, but what in any event certainly made me uncomfortable. He liked to invent games of endurance. One of his games involved climbing a tree and seeing who could hang from the topmost bough the longest, while he counted. Since I was the oldest, of course I wanted desperately to win. Once when we were in a sort of meadow I outlasted him by far. He counted to one hundred and still I hung.

'You can come down now,' he said, irritably. 'You're the winner. Come *on*.'

I was triumphant at having won, but I found I couldn't let go. I was paralyzed; I couldn't swing my body back onto the bough. I hung fourteen feet above the earth, practically by my fingertips, gazing fearfully down.

'Come on, silly,' John said, 'don't just hang there.'

'I can't move!' I called.

'Let go the branch and drop then,' he ordered. He was very overbearing.

Something broke my fall: something soft and green and burning. I landed with a thump that shook every bone in my body and brought my teeth together with a click which nearly took off the top of my head. The green blanket enveloped me: it burnt into every uncovered piece of flesh—my face, my hands and arms, my bare legs. I screamed and struggled up. I had fallen into a bed of nettles. They were giant nettles, and vicious little white blisters, surrounded by crimson enflamed patches, were now appearing on my skin. I tore at myself, trying to ease the pain. My sister Alice tried to comfort me as I lay sobbing on the ground: she applied cool dock leaves, a weed, to my swollen face. These were supposed to be a remedy for nettle stings.

Finally my brothers and my sisters half carried and half dragged me home. My mother wept with me as she bathed the affected parts in a bicarbonate of soda and water paste, which eventually eased the itching and burning.

This was an unnerving experience but I did not seem to learn from experience and neither did my brother. We had another similar game, which was hanging over the water from a footbridge. These slipways, as they were called, went over river inlets which were wet or dry docks for small boats under repair. The tide determined the level of the water. One Sunday afternoon when we were playing truant from Sunday school, John said to me, 'Beat you at hanging. Bet you can't hang 'til the water touches your toes.'

'Bet you I can,' I said with bravado. It wasn't a tree, of course, so apparently I didn't sense danger.

We hung side by side gripping the wooden footbridge with our hands. The tide was coming in fast; it all but lapped our feet. My arms began to ache and I started to think about giving up. When the water reached our feet my brother sprang easily onto the footbridge. 'That's it,' he said.

But I could not move. It was the tree all over again. Only this time if I dropped, I would be carried into the river by the current.

'Come on,' John said, 'the game is over.'

I could feel my strength oozing away. My brother lay down on his stomach on the bridge and tried to pull me up, but I was too heavy for him. He shouted for help, but there were few people about on a Sunday afternoon.

'Can you hang on?' he asked anxiously. 'I'll find someone.'

My sisters had begun to run along the quay, shouting wildly for help. Luckily an old man was coming along, out for a Sunday afternoon stroll. My sisters grabbed his hands and pulled him to where I was still hanging. With my brother's help he managed to lift me up; I was quite unable to help myself.

When we got home my mother asked me why my shoes and socks were wet. I gave her an evasive answer about a puddle and she said nothing more about it. But my arms ached for days afterward.

Some weeks later my brother suggested we have some fun on the quayside again. I agreed; nothing exciting was likely to happen at Sunday School. A three-masted schooner was in the harbour. High up in the lookout cage at the top of one of the masts was a man or boy, looking no bigger than a cat from our vantage point below. Some boys were standing around discussing the way the man had climbed the rigging.

'It's easy,' my brother said. 'You just have to mind you put your foot in the right place.'

A big boy smirked at him. 'Like to see you do it, kid,' he said.

'Done!' my brother said cockily. 'Hang around until this chap comes down and goes below and I will show you.'

'Oh, John, come away and don't be silly. If you slip you will crash to death,' I said.

'Girls are always cowards,' my brother said to me and the boys. 'I'll sit up in the Crow's Nest; you'll see.'

I was terrified, but I did not dare go home to fetch my father. Not only would I be considered a spoilsport, but I would have to reveal both that we had played truant from Sunday School, and that we were on forbidden ground. My brother would never forgive me.

The sailor eventually came down easily as he was trained to do and went below decks.

'Now!' called my brother. He leapt over the side of the vessel, ran to the mast and climbed hand over hand up and up as if he were going through the clouds straight to heaven. The boys egged him on. I watched him becoming smaller and smaller until he reached the top and raised his arms, barely visible, above his head—a minute figure in space.

We shouted to him to come down; he had proved himself. But he didn't move. Had he heard us? *'John!'* I called until my lungs felt as though they would burst. 'Come *down!'*

His voice reached us below at last.

'I can't. I don't dare.'

We called again and waited. At last the boys grew tired of it and left. Helplessly I looked up at my brother in his cage. The sun had gone in; a cold wind was blowing off the sea. I shivered. What could I do?

I left my sisters standing crying on the quayside and

clambered aboard the ship, paying no heed to my best clothes and my shoes. I ran along the deck 'til I came to a narrow stairway leading somewhere below.

'Hi there, there's a boy up your mast and he can't get down,' I screamed, hoping someone would hear me.

'Who's up there?' a voice called from below. 'What do you want?'

'Oh, please, Mister, come and get my brother down quick,' I said.

A man dressed like a sailor, wearing a navy wool skull cap on his ginger hair, came bounding up the stairway.

'What's going on?' he asked me.

'He's up there,' I said. I tugged his sleeve and pointed to the mast. I was crying now.

He swore an oath which I did not understand when he saw my brother aloft.

'Who is he, what's his name, what is he doing up there? He'll be starved to death with cold if this wind keeps up.'

'His name is John Wood,' I said.

He looked curiously at me. 'Not Mr Wood's son of Hutchinson's Engineering Works?'

'Oh yes,' I replied eagerly. 'Do you know my Daddy?'

'Indeed I do. Now if you will take me to your father, missy, he can come himself and get his son down, because I don't dare risk it myself.'

I led the seaman to my house—only about ten minutes away. He was very kind and carried my little sister Laura who was frightened and sobbing all the way.

My father was petrified with shock when he learned where his son was on that Sunday afternoon. Luckily he was no mean seaman himself, and had a head for heights. He rescued my brother, who was half dead with cold. The fright was considered an adequate punishment. We didn't play truant from Sunday School for a long time after that.

Of course these disastrous expeditions were not typical. Most of the time we led relatively placid lives, although life became more interesting in the summer, when visitors from London and the Midlands thronged the beaches. Almost every house, large and small, doubled its occupants. Landladies and would-be landladies scrubbed and polished and refurbished their houses for weeks before the invasion. All along the clifftops hotels were painted and cleaned, and staff were engaged for the season of plenty. Our town was considered select as we had no amusement arcade or charabanc parties. But a good deal of the town economy depended on the weather. If it were sunny, one could buy, in numerous stalls erected on the sand, saucers of cockles and whelks, shrimp, oysters and mussels. Some stalls sold jugs of tea (one shilling deposit on the jug) to be carried to the beach for picnickers reclining in deck chairs eating buns and sandwiches along with a certain amount of sand. And there were ha'penny ice cream cornets for sale, and a bright vermilion fizzy drink guaranteed to make any child sick.

Along the water's edge were rows of bathing huts for the modest females who ventured forth in voluminous bloomers or knee-length skirts; the males wore a one-piece garment that stretched from neck almost to ankle. In those days bodies were not exposed to public gaze, or to the sun. Indeed, a great many people did not expose their bodies to the water. Men rolled up the bottoms of their trousers, and women held their skirts surreptitiously to their knees and paddled and splashed like children in the shallow water. That was the general idea of enjoying the seaside. Ladies waded holding their skirts in one hand and in the other an umbrella to protect their complexions from the sun and wind. Modesty was almost an obsession then in the house as well as on the beach. When my father approached, the clothes-horse, which held the family's unmentionable clothing to air in front of the kitchen fire, was hastily removed and hidden to preserve Grannie's modesty.

Fishermen stood in the shallow water with their fragile-looking boats bobbing up and down on the waves beside them and invited the public in raucous voices to 'a lovely seaside ride'. Unwilling donkeys brayed to protest the unaccustomed loads on their backs as they were coaxed and whipped to get moving. Parents dozed happily in their deck chairs while their offspring dug energetically in the sand. We children often contrived to 'find' little Johnny, who had wandered away, or to rescue half-drowned little Mary. Our pocket money was greatly augmented during those long summer months by the rewards we collected for restoring children to their distracted parents.

Sometimes my brother would suggest we go to the circus. We couldn't resist Hardy's Circus which was set up in an enormous tent on the sea front; we loved the tightrope walkers, the bareback riders, the elephant, the snarling tigers—and above all, the ringmaster, resplendent in his wide Stetson hat, red satin suit braided with gold and high black brightly spurred shining boots. He circled his leather-thonged whip over his head and brought it down crackling and whistling at every act, to smack the ground with a resounding swish and hiss. He twirled his long black moustaches, rolled his dark eyes and roared out the next attraction with the voice of a town crier.

The circus presented a challenge to us because the entrance fee was far more than our modest pocket money allowed. Owing to the vigilance of the ticket collector we never saw a show in its entirety all at once, but through perseverance we did see all of it, piece by piece. After all, a canvas tent could not be foolproof. There were also devious ways of getting under the canvas windbreaker surrounding the auditorium where the Pierrot show was given on the beach. Luckily, the wind often dislodged the canvas.

Punch and Judy had the added attraction of being free, and we loved it. Whenever Punch was about to be guillotined, we knew the collection box would be circulated and, although we hated leaving Punch at this crucial point in his life, we disappeared to return discreetly when all danger was past and enjoy the grand finale and join in the shouts of 'Goodbye, goodbye!' which Punch (now revived) and company requested from 'all the nice little boys and girls'.

Every summer a national newspaper sponsored a sand competition: contestants would model in sand shapes which would give the idea that the paper was ahead of the competition in daily circulation. I told my brother I thought we should enter the contest.

'Can you think of anything?' he asked. 'I can't.'

I leafed through the paper looking for inspiration. 'Oh look at this,' I said. 'So-and-So batting, 100 runs not out.'

'What about it?'

'Well, don't you see, the paper could be the batsman and the other papers the opponents trying to beat them. See?'

We worked out the idea and put it into operation. The next morning or so my father picked up his paper, opened it and saw staring at him a picture of his four children; unhappily I, being the tallest, had been beheaded, but the rest of me was unmistakeable. My father was neither proud nor amused; he felt he should have been consulted before his children were exhibited to the world. It was with difficulty that the circulation manager persuaded him to allow us to collect our prizes in a ceremony at the local theatre. 'My children go to bed at a proper bedtime,' he said. 'They are not allowed to stay up at night.'

In the event, however, my father and mother and Grannie accompanied us to the theatre. A box was reserved for us—it was very grand! The prizes were presented halfway through the performance by Elsie and Doris Waters, who were 'doing' the season at the theatre. We were ushered onto the stage. My little sister Laura, overcome, burst into tears and had to be picked up and comforted by the Waters sisters with hugs and kisses. Laura was an appealing child with long eyelashes and dark ringlets hanging to her waist. The sisters kissed us too—much to my brother's discomfort—and handed us money tokens and books. I could not take my eyes off their piano with a picture of the King and Queen painted on it; the sisters always pointed this out during their act to roars of laughter. I didn't think it was funny, and I longed to strike the keys.

We spent happy evenings around the piano in my early childhood, singing old favourites. My mother played and I was learning, and my brother was struggling with the violin. Our favourites were 'Just a Song at Twilight', 'The Bells of St Mary's' and, during the War, 'The Roses of Picardy'. Grannie especially loved 'On Greenland's Icy Mountains'; we had to play and sing it for her every Sunday evening.

Sometimes on Sunday afternoons we would walk along the quay with Father—the only time that place was permissible to us—and cross the river to visit Uncle Harry, Father's brother-in-law, whom we all loved. He had an engineering works. Father and Uncle often toured the works, leaving us to play in the office. My father was a marine engineer and draughtsman and, as I learned later, did work for my uncle in his spare time.

Often I heard them talk in low voices about the likelihood of a war. Uncle Harry thought it would be a flash in the pan, lasting three or four months. But I gathered my father thought it would be more serious and lasting. My father did not trust the Kaiser. I was troubled and frightened by these rumblings of war on Sunday afternoons. In fact the war was to make my uncle a wealthy man and nearly kill my father with overwork night and day on the shipyard. And it was to mark the end of my happy sheltered life.

2. Deserted

IT was during the last summer months of 1918; I had been home from school for three months with a broken arm. My father had not been called up, but he had worked non-stop night and day during the war years. His family life was as shattered as if he had been in the trenches in France. We—his four children—seldom saw him. My mother felt she was neglected and could not accept the situation.

My mother was a gay, restless, lovely creature, always laughing. She filled the house with her friends—mainly soldiers billeted in the town, who flocked to her musical evenings. She was a singer and belonged to a very active concert group organized by Sir Francis Vincent, who lived in a beautiful mansion a mile or two outside the town. My mother welcomed the escape from domesticity offered by the concert group. She was often away at weekend parties at the Manor, or she stayed overnight there for concerts.

Grannie, my mother's mother, lived with us and was the most stable element in our lives. Although she had reared a family of twenty-one, she still, at seventy, had a lot of love to spare for us. We four were the children of her baby, since my mother was her youngest.

I saw and learned a lot during those three months at home, although much of what I heard I did not understand.

'Richard should put his foot down,' I heard Grannie say to an aunt who was always at the house helping my mother with her musical evenings. I wasn't supposed to overhear these remarks.

'Little pitchers have big ears,' my aunt would reply, nodding her head toward me and giving Grannie a warning look. They would either then leave the room, or drop their voices to whispers.

Put his foot down on what? I was mystified, but somehow I sensed that it was my mother that he should put his foot down on.

'You should speak to him, Grannie. Tell him what you suspect. Warn him, then it is up to him.' I overheard that another time.

'No, no, I can't come between a man and his wife. I don't want to make trouble.' Sometimes when they talked like this a troubled tear would steal down Grannie's cheek. 'The War won't last forever,' she said often.

These whispered conversations filled me with foreboding. What was about to happen? I kept thinking my father was going to do something terrible to my lovely mother. But what? And why?

My mother held noisy parties in our big sitting room upstairs. She played the piano and sang, the soldiers joining in, until the early hours of the morning.

One night I had been lying awake listening to the laughter and singing and the constant movement up and down stairs of arriving and departing guests. I decided to have a look at the party. I got out of my warm bed and tiptoed along the cold linoleum on the landing to the sitting room door. It was ajar. I peeped in and saw my mother sitting on a soldier's knee; his arms were round her shoulders, her head rested on his shoulder. She seemed to be crying. I thought I understood. So many went away and never came back.

'Grannie,' I said the next day, 'is Uncle Will going away to the War?' We had so many 'uncles' in those days. 'I saw Mummy kissing him and crying last night.'

'Hush!' Grannie said hastily. 'Don't let anyone hear you talk like that. Promise me you will not tell anyone what you saw. It was very naughty of you to get out of bed. You should have been sleeping. Now you be a good girl and forget all about it.'

'Yes, Grannie,' I said obediently. But I never forgot it, nor did I forget how I had crept back to bed that night wondering why everything had to be so sad, and why people still sang songs and laughed if they were, as I had heard Grannie say, 'facing death tomorrow.'

I wondered why I could not tell my father, but I had promised Grannie to forget it. There was something wrong here, but my daddy would, I felt sure, explain it all to me in his patient way if only I could ask him. My mother entertained the soldiers—he knew about that, and he liked her to sing and be happy. He had to work, but he didn't mind her enjoying herself a little. He would shake hands earnestly with some departing boy, or grown man, and wish him luck. Men didn't kiss goodbye, but I felt my father was just as concerned about them as my mother was.

Finally I dismissed the incident of the kiss as just Grannie's funny way. She was so old—how could she understand?

A week or two after that, my mother's youngest brother, Uncle Billy, came home from the front, on leave. His wife, Aunt Martha, was helping my mother with the cooking; I gathered a party was imminent.

'Martha,' I heard my mother say, 'you'd better be careful now that Billy's home. You know he's not like Richard. You'd better not come tonight to help with the boys.' I think they would have said more, but they noticed me, and dropped the subject.

I wondered what it all meant. Why couldn't Uncle Billy come to the party? Perhaps he wanted Aunt Martha all to himself during his few days' leave.

'Poor Martha,' Grannie said, 'with three girls to provide for on a private's pay. No wonder she was glad to earn a few extra shillings helping your mother. Who could blame her?'

Uncle Billy called to see my father the following evening. We children were in bed. I was awake and I heard raised voices coming from the dining room. I slipped downstairs and sat trembling on the bottom stair, listening. The dining room door leading into the hall was partly open, but they did not see me.

'Get out of my house and stay out!' I heard my father say. I did not remember ever having heard my father shout at anyone like that before. What could it all be about?

'How dare you come to me with your filthy suspicions and lies? If you think you have cause to "beat up" your wife, that's your affair, but nothing justifies a man using violence to a woman. I trust and love my wife. She would not behave in the disgraceful way you talk about. Now leave, and I don't want to see you or Martha here again.'

Uncle Billy came hastily into the hall, and walked to the front door. He opened it and banged it behind him so hard it shook the whole house. Deathly stillness followed. I wanted to go in and kiss my father and make him feel better, but I was afraid. I went back to bed and snuggled under the clothes to shut out the troubled world. Uncle Billy's last words to my father haunted me for days. 'They are a pair of sluts together,' he had said. 'Don't say I didn't warn you. Mine has had her desserts; you must act as you think fit.'

'Sluts!' What could the word mean? He was angry and his tone implied something unpleasant. I had never heard that word before, but people used a lot of funny words during the War. I decided to ask Grannie when she was in a good mood.

Uncle Billy returned to the trenches. A few weeks later I heard the whisper: he had gone over the top and they were all wiped out. Grannie sat rocking back and forth and crying. My mother tried to comfort her.

'What will become of those poor children?' Grannie kept moaning. 'Who will provide for them now? No father. Poor things.' The tears flowed copiously.

What queer expressions they used, I thought. But by listening carefully, I understood. My uncle had been killed.

My mother was greatly subdued by the week's events; the parties became less frequent. She was moody and fretful. Sometimes, sweet and patient, she tucked us up in bed lovingly with a kiss and called us 'her babies'; at other times she sent us off alone with no goodnight kiss and an impatient, 'Get off to bed out of my sight!' I thought she must miss Aunt Martha who never came any more and was sorry that Uncle Billy had been 'wiped out'.

Grannie too did not seem to recover from the loss of her youngest son. I came on her once or twice sitting in her chair near the Grandfather clock, weeping with her black apron over her face. Somehow we seemed to be part of her grief. When she saw me she cried, 'What's to become of you poor children? Oh dear, oh dear,' and wept harder.

'What's the matter, Grannie?' I said. 'We're all right, aren't we?'

'You wouldn't understand,' she said. 'You are too young.'

At night in bed I tried to sort it all out in my mind. Mummy was miserable, Grannie was crying, Father more quiet than usual. All the joy had gone out of the house. It is the War and all the soldiers being killed, I thought. I prayed, 'Please God make my mummy happy again and bless us all.'

Those were sad days. I wished Uncle Billy hadn't come home and upset my father, because that was when it all began. That was when all the fun went out of Mummy's life. That, and when the other uncle I had seen kissing her went away to the front.

She would get a letter from time to time, which made her a little happier. She read it by herself and showed it to Grannie who would scold her and then cry and beg her, 'Forget him.' I wished I were grown up so that I could understand it all.

The children's comic paper *Lot o' Fun* came out on a Friday. My brother and I always raced each other home to claim it first and read the adventures of Dan, who was always being chased and who skidded 'collar-stud over bananaskin' avoiding the grasp of the Law or some worse fate. Even Laura, who was only five, could read enough of it to make sense of it. In those days we had a good grounding in the three Rs at school.

'I'm home first!' I shouted; I burst into the house and

grabbed the paper triumphantly off the hall table. No one answered. There was no welcoming call back. There was no savoury smell coming from the kitchen. The house was unusually still and the doors were all shut as if no one lived there.

'Grannie!' I ran down the hall to the dining room and threw open the door. 'Where's Mummy?'

The diminutive figure was huddled into a chair, with her black apron thrown over her head, moaning and crying.

'Grannie! What's the matter? Aren't you well? Where's Mummy? Is she out? Why are you crying?'

'Oh dear, oh dear,' she moaned, and rocked herself back and forth. 'What will become of you poor motherless children?'

She emerged from the apron with red eyes and swollen face.

'What do you mean? Where is my mummy? Tell me what has happened!' I was now thoroughly alarmed. But I got no reply, only more wailing.

Frantically I ran upstairs. Perhaps she was ill, lying in bed, gasping her last. The bedroom door was wide open; the bed was empty and unmade. The wardrobe door hung disconsolately open and I could see that the wardrobe was empty. Papers lay scattered about, and an old cardboard hatbox. One stocking hung over the back of a chair, and a pair of worn slippers peeked familiarly from under the bed.

I rushed into our bedroom. Three unmade beds met my gaze. Our pyjamas were neatly folded where we had left them in the morning on the bedside chair. I was overcome by a feeling of disaster.

Violet, the maid of all work, would know what was wrong. I raced back down the stairs and burst breathless into the kitchen, where Violet sat dejectedly by the grate. She looked up with her vacant, far-away expression—

Violet's mind was always wandering to her times off with her young man.

'Violet,' I gasped, 'where is Mummy? What are you doing sitting there? Why aren't you getting the tea ready?' Usually she would be clattering about, setting the table.

'Your mum is gone off, run away and left you all, she has.'

'Don't you dare to say such stupid things,' I said. I rushed at her and shook her by the shoulders. She began to cry.

'Leave me alone,' she said. 'Take your hands off me. It's true. Missus has gone off for good; she ain't never coming back. She said so. "Violet," she said, "you will promise me to stay and help Grannie look after the children, won't you?" And with that she went. I don't know what to get you for your tea. Missus didn't say.'

I ran back to Grannie. 'Say it isn't true, Grannie,' I implored her. 'Mummy has been away before but she always comes back. She didn't mean for ever and ever. She couldn't have.'

Grannie shook her head and moaned. 'How will I tell Richard?'

In fact she didn't have to. He had a note which read simply, 'I can't stand it any longer. I am leaving you for good. Ada.'

I wondered what it was she couldn't stand any longer. Were we such naughty children that we had driven our mother away from home? Didn't she love us any more? I decided that she didn't. She doesn't love us, was all I could think, and I was inconsolable. My lovely, laughing mother gone forever. No more parties, no more singing. The joy had gone out of my life and all the love had flown. I wanted to run away somewhere too, and hide.

Since I was the eldest, I enjoyed making myself responsible for the moral behaviour of my brother and sisters. It made me feel important and worthwhile. We shared a huge bedroom: my brother and I each had a single bed, and my sisters shared a double bed. As a penance for misbehaviour I would read a passage from the Bible to them; the Ten Commandments, for instance, which none of us understood, and make them kneel and pray that God would forgive us all and make us better children. At other times, if in my opinion they merited it, I would read them the story of David and the giant Goliath, which my brother loved, or Ruth and Naomi—my own favourite.

Now we had a real problem and we prayed fervently every night on our knees, often shivering with cold, because we had no central heating and no heat at all in the bedrooms.

'Please, dear God, bring our mummy back to us and make her love us again.' After these prayers, my little sister Laura would cry herself to sleep.

In the past the Lord had been very forgiving toward us. I had overcome my parents' opposition to my having a bicycle, with the help of prayer. Once I had lost a threepenny piece and, after pleading to the Almighty for help, had searched diligently on my hands and knees and found it—or one like it—wedged under the skirting board in the bedroom. My faith was boundless. But this time it seemed that God was not listening to us, and after a while our faith was shaken. We felt forsaken.

Life went on sadly without our mother. We went to school as usual. I had to get up earlier now in order to pack a lunch for us all. At that time there were no school dinners. I made sandwiches and packed a cake each and often an apple or an orange as a treat. We had sweets only at the weekend when our pocket money ran to a pink sugar mouse, chocolate drops, aniseed balls or two sticks of liquorice for a halfpenny—all to be savoured

and treasured to the last suck, and remembered long-
ingly until the following Saturday.

At school a room was set aside on the caretaker's
premises in which children were allowed to eat their
sandwiches. It was a narrow room with two long wooden
forms on trestles running its entire length. Since I was
one of the older children, I was often appointed mon-
itor and expected to keep order—a hopeless task among
all those boys and girls of varying ages. Many a battle
was fought and lost over a choice morsel. To this day I
remember the room's stale smell of cabbage water and
the stark bare coldness of it.

In the month of May—May 25th—we always cele-
brated Empire Day. The pupils assembled in the school
playground and had to stand to attention while the Union
Jack was run up the mast in the centre and sing 'Rule,
Britannia' and then march in orderly file into the school.
The senior girls had a Maypole and danced the Maypole
Dance. I was a senior girl.

'Grannie,' I said, 'I must have a white dress for the
Maypole Dance. Teacher said we must all wear white
dresses.'

'You haven't got a white dress,' Grannie said. 'You will
have to tell Teacher.'

'But I must have one,' I said, and burst into tears. I
had a vision of being excluded from the dance round
the Maypole—not threading all those lovely, gaily col-
oured silk ribbons in and out of the intricate patterns
as the dance went on. Everyone in the school would
know why Ann was left out—because she couldn't afford a white dress. The shame of it was more than I
could bear.

'I've got a new white dress,' my best friend said, 'for
Empire Day.'

'So have I,' I lied boldly.

'Believe it when I see it,' she said.

I had to do something about it to save face. I lay in bed brooding about it. Suddenly I had an idea. On the fatal morning I enlisted Violet's help. I did not wear a dress, but I sewed myself into my best white enveloping pinafore over my petticoat.

'You've got a funny dress,' a girl said to me. 'Why hasn't it got sleeves?'

'It's the new fashion,' I answered. 'The summer dresses this year won't have sleeves. So there, Miss Clever!' I tossed my head and walked away from her.

'I don't believe it is a dress at all,' was her parting shot. The other children eyed me suspiciously. Violet's stitches went down the back of the pinafore, holding it together where the two ends met. My bravado won the day. I danced the Maypole Dance and threaded my ribbons with light-hearted abandon.

On Sunday afternoon my father made a noble effort to explain our mother's departure to us. He called us all to him in the 'Holy of Holies'—the sitting room upstairs at the front of the house. The room was gloomy now and little used. The piano stood with its lid closed.

My father cleared his throat and said, 'I want you children to understand that your mother has gone away for good. She will never come back.' He looked at us sorrowfully, each in turn, and controlled his voice with difficulty. My youngest sister Laura, a pretty little thing, raised her huge eyes to Father. Tears overspilled her long black lashes and ran down her full cheeks. She had been my mother's pet, and had been made much of.

'Now don't cry, Laura,' my father said; he took her gently on his knee. 'You will be all right,' he said against the background of Laura's sniffs and gulps. 'But I never want to hear your mother's name mentioned again. She has disgraced us all. You must forget her. All photographs and anything she left in the house will be destroyed. Promise me now that whatever happens, if she writes to you or tries to see you, you will tell me at once.'

By this time we three girls were all crying. My brother kept his manly composure but stood looking steadily at his feet. We all nodded obediently, and Father kissed us each in turn. 'I know I can trust you to carry out my wishes,' he said. 'Your grannie has promised to stay with us. She will look after you. Remember that she and I love you all; I know you will be good children.'

With that we were dismissed. My father went back to his book.

3. The Weekend

DURING my last year of school I had to help Grannie at the weekends. After tea on Friday evening homework had to be done; the four of us sat sudying round the oval mahogany dining table. Then it was bedtime for the little ones. I was thirteen at the time, and considered old enough to stay up later, sometimes to read to Grannie from her favourite local paper. How she loved the Births, Deaths and Marriages columns, and the country news under the heading 'The Fleggs'. This was the name given to a cluster of Norfolk villages where Grannie had spent nearly all her life. She pronounced it 'Flags'.

In the neighbouring town across the river, approached also by a main road and a bridge, was one of the largest open air markets in the country—rows and rows of stalls set out with dairy produce and fresh vegetables; butchers and pork butchers put out their home-made sausages and brawn. Grannie had what she called 'set' the market for a number of years; that is, she was a stall holder and only gave up her place when Grandfather died. She had lived in a country village about six miles away from the town. Twice a week, on Wednesday and Saturday, Grandad used to pile up the horse cart with home-cured bacon, home-grown vegetables, sausages, fresh churned butter and cheese, and the old grey mare would trot them to market.

Grandad was a horse dealer, and no mean vet. Whilst Grannie was busy selling her produce, he was haggling over horses on Norwich Hill, the cattle market. Where Grannie made pence, he made golden sovereigns and would arrive at the stall with pockets bulging with gold and, regrettably, a belly full of beer. On one of these occasions they were home unloading the cart, Grannie told us, and he, being an impatient man, shouted, 'Here, Mother, catch this' and hurled an enormous cabbage at her. It broke her nose, which was crooked forever after.

Grandad had a unique banking system. The sovereigns were counted, entered in a book and stored away in glass dishes in the sideboard. He didn't trust banks, or anyone else. He kept the key to the sideboard on his gold watch chain which looped across his ample middle. Perhaps in those days people were more honest than now; he was never robbed.

After Grandfather's death, when she was living with us, Grannie looked forward to Saturday mornings. We would start out for the market at about nine-thirty in the morning. Grannie would take nearly an hour to get dressed in her best blouse and skirt which reached to her ankles, her black alpaca coat and her black bonnet with an edging of white or purple pleated ribbon sewn in to frame her little face. Two streamers hung down on each side of the bonnet—one black and one white silk ribbon, which she tied securely in a huge bow under her chin. High black button boots, black gloves and an unfurled black umbrella completed the ensemble. She insisted on walking her umbrella, to the impediment of all who came too close.

I was armed with a huge shopping basket, like a butcher boy's, and a string bag. Grannie had her hand-bag, an enormous black leather contraption, shaped like a Gladstone bag and secure enough to carry the Crown Jewels.

We caught the tramcar to the neighbouring town. Getting Grannie settled on board was an achievement. The conductor pulled her up the two steep steps by her hands, and I heaved her from behind. Once in her seat, she proceeded to enjoy herself, nodding and greeting everyone whom she insisted she knew, much to my embarrassment. Since she had lived nearly all her life as the farmer's wife with an imposing establishment on the village green, and had been a devout chapel goer, she probably had at one time known everyone in the town. People were very kind and passed the time of day companionably with her. In those days there was no sense of urgency in everyday life. There was time to spare for a little old lady who looked like a replica of Queen Victoria in her black mourning clothes. Grannie had a presence and a charm all her own.

Getting her off the tramcar at the terminus was just as hazardous as getting her on, but usually willing hands speeded the process, and modesty was preserved—there was never a glimpse of an ankle or a hair out of place.

We alighted at the bridge, a solid relic of a bygone age. It badly needed refurbishment—this was later to be done, and the Prince of Wales presided over the ceremonies. It was reported that the young Prince enjoyed his day in the town. The Mayor at the time had socialist inclinations; he greeted the Prince with a hearty hand-shake and is said to have exclaimed, 'Howdy do, Prince, what do you know?' This set the tone for the day and the Mayor enjoyed himself enormously, forgetting all about previous instructions and rehearsals planned by his 'betters'. In fact, he wined and dined the Prince rather too well at a local riverside hotel. In any case, the beautiful new bridge was declared open, and it graces the town to this day.

The old bridge had to be opened in the centre to allow ships over a certain height to pass beneath it. Each half of the bridge was slowly and painfully winched up, creaking and groaning in protest. It was then in two sections, one on each side of the river, like a sea mon-ster's wide open jaws; the vessel would pass slowly through the gaping chasm while the green sluggish water was churned into lapping waves which settled down again as the bridge slowly closed. Then traffic would flow once more and impatient pedestrians would jostle and push their way over the bridge. An ineffective po-liceman would try in vain to control the mob and the traffic.

If Grannie and I got involved with one of these ex-ercises I was filled with apprehension about getting her safely across the bridge and the wide expanse of quay to the safety of the pavement—although I enjoyed the spectacle of the bridge being 'raised to heaven'. Narrow 'Rows' led from the quayside to Market Square. These were narrow alleyways for pedestrians only. A number of them had one-up-and-one-down houses facing each other on either side for their entire length. The Rows ran in a straight line from the quay to the market, or main shopping centre, and were situated at intervals all along the riverside for about three miles. At some points there was room for only two people to walk side by side between the Rows or to push a barrow; thus light, let alone sunshine, hardly ever penetrated the squalid houses. There was one main road connecting the riverside with the town, but the Rows were a short cut. To this day I can smell their foul garbagy odor. Happily or unhappily most of them were destroyed during Second World War bombings, and they were not rebuilt.

Every Saturday Grannie and I struggled through the Market Row, which was wide enough for a horse and cart—although traffic was prohibited—and on a Saturday it was a heaving, seething mass of humanity fighting their way in both directions. Collisions were inevitable, and tempers were frayed.

The Market Square, with rows and rows of stalls holding produce, was flanked by the magnificent parish Church of St Nicholas on one end and 'live theatre' and hotels at the other. The sides of the Square were bounded by shops; at the far side was the 'Ragged' school. This school fascinated me. It was a huge, grey forbidding-looking structure built of stone, with tall wrought-iron double gates. I had never seen the gates open, or, indeed, any sign of life. The very name 'Ragged' spoke volumes: it was a school for the poor, half-clothed, and half-starved—the underprivileged. It was a blot on the honour and charity of the townspeople. Nobody really cared for the little human wrecks who, deprived of normal sustenance, had nevertheless to know their three Rs. When I mentioned it to Grannie she would shake her head and say, 'The poor bairns, don't bother your head about such things.'

Market Row brought much country custom to the town at weekends. The Row was lined with all kinds of shops except those that sold food. Drapers vied with one another, their windows so crowded with street wear and underwear that it was impossible to notice anything specific. There was no such thing as window dressing as we know it today. Advertising was crude. One draper, where Grannie often purchased a yard of lace or ribbon in order to have an excuse to sit down for a while, had an advertisement which read:

Not too high
Not too low
Just in the middle of the Market Row.

This message was displayed each week on the front page of the local paper. I tried to pace the distance in order to see whether their claim was justified, but I always got jostled and lost count.

At the bottom of the Row was a penny bazaar. The counters were filled with all sorts of domestic requirements from cups and saucers to scrubbing brushes with bristles strong enough to keep the most resistant 'tops' and floors scrupulously clean. All kinds of cleaning aids, in paper bags and glass bottles, could be had for a penny. Odors of carbolic soap, semi-wrapped, mingled with the smell of moth balls. The light glistened on tin cooking utensils—there were of course no bright plastics. There were washing soda and strong ammonia to dispel dirt and grease, and glycerine and rosewater to soften hands which would otherwise be ruined by harsh cleansers. All this and more for a penny an item.

The shops had no security officers, but they had floor walkers or shop walkers who looked after the customers' comfort. Grannie would sail into a shop to spend her one shilling as if it were pounds. A floor walker would greet her with a bow and place a chair for her at the counter, calling 'Young lady, forward please,' whereupon a woman who had given nearly her whole life to the service of the emporium would appear to serve Grannie. These women all wore black, severely tailored dresses and the shop walker was dressed in a black suit and a stiff white winged collar which matched his stiff ramrod back. He bowed from the waist; I almost expected him to click his heels!

Grannie loved all this attention and prepared herself comfortably for a long chat with the assistant—usually a fellow countrywoman whom she had known for years and who could give her all the latest news from The Fleggs, far surpassing the local paper. Sometimes we transacted a good deal of business there: material had to be chosen for underwear and shirts for Father. On these grand occasions the order had to be delivered later in the week by the horse-drawn delivery van, causing quite a stir on our street.

Arriving eventually at the Market Square, we would plunge headlong into the madding crowd, Grannie clinging to my arm with one hand and prodding and manoeuvering with her umbrella with the other. If anyone protested because he had been impaled, she would look at him innocently and be so apologetic that most of the time trouble was averted, although sometimes narrowly. We must have looked an ill-assorted pair, she so tiny and frail and me small and skinny for my age, carrying that enormous basket, big enough almost to hold us both.

We made our way up and down the ranks of stalls, some cheerful with striped canvas awnings and resplendent with the fruits of the earth. We patronised only stall holders whom Grannie knew. She distrusted newcomers; it took years of experience, she said, to 'set' the market.

There was a Mrs Nicholls from Grannie's native village. Grannie had known her when she was a child; she was a friend of her mother. Mrs Nicholls was now a large, raw-boned woman with hips nearly the width of her stall. A spotless white apron covered her voluminous figure; on her head a black straw hat was pinioned to her hair, which was scraped back in a bun, by a huge hatpin. The hat sported a Bird of Paradise, which bobbed up and down when she moved as if it were supervising the operation.

'Here's your bacon, and here's your best butter, and what about a bit of belly pork—it's not too fat this week. Don't forget your sausages, Gran, and eggs is gone up ha'penny a dozen this week, but they're all big and brown.'

She would hand the parcels, wrapped in newspaper, across the stall. 'Here, Ann, hold your basket,' Grannie would scold as I was lost in wondering if Mrs Nicholl's hatpin went through her head and if the Bird would one day chirp. Collecting myself, I would hand over the basket to be tidily laden with the produce. The smell of that delicious home-cured bacon was a dream, and the freshly churned butter needed no colouring when it was spread on the bread or camouflaged with jam. The pork sausages were almost bursting out of their skins with unadulterated meat and the aroma of nutmeg seduced the taste buds. There would be fruit from a special orchard and fresh tomatoes from 'Herbert's' greenhouses.

We walked the ranks of stalls until Grannie was tired, and my basket full to overflowing. The gossip Grannie gleaned would provide topics of conversation for her throughout the ensuing week. Grannie forgot that I did not know these people; however she spoke of them so often that I felt I did know them and listened with interest to the stories of their lives and their ancestry. Grannie, like most old people, lived in the past.

When our purchases were completed I had to get both Grannie and the heavily laden basket safely home again. It was tedious steering Grannie, who was by now much less sprightly than when we had started out, through the crowded Row. There was no time to stop for a rest halfway on the return journey. Willing hands helped to heave her back onto the tramcar again where she collapsed into the first available seat and dozed until we came to our stop, when I would nudge her awake. Luckily our house was only five minutes walk from the tram stop; that was about all Grannie could manage at this point.

Saturday dinner, prepared by Violet, would be ready when we got home. We didn't call it luncheon—that would sound too grand.

Saturday afternoon was the time to do the family baking to last the week. I was now considered old enough to do it, with Violet's help and under Grannie's supervision. The old kitchen range, its flues swept and its exterior black-leaded and shining like a mirror, was stoked up with coal called Best Welsh Nuts. The dampers were set to draw the flames over the top of the oven; a welcoming roar went up, like the roar of a forest fire, but without its danger. The oven door opened to reveal an enormous black cavity. I had yet to learn how to test its heat by inserting my hand; that was an expert procedure which required mature knowledge. By contrast, spitting on an upturned flat iron to see if it was hot enough for ironing required only a strong wrist— mine barely qualified.

Violet had to keep shovelling the coal on the furnace. It gobbled it up, but coal was cheap in those days. The kitchen became hot and filled with steam from the water boiling in the copper, and the smell of hot pastry and fat. The copper was part of the range and had to be filled manually with buckets of water—a tricky process. Violet could tip a bucket up easily without mishap to her strong hands and arms, but I often narrowly escaped being scalded.

Grannie would succumb to the humid warmth and sit dozing most of the afternoon while she recovered from the morning's outing. Occasionally I had to rouse her so that I could ask a question.

'Gran, is it one or two cupfuls for cheesecake mixture?' or 'How much sugar for the lemon curd?'

Everything was measured in tablespoons or cups—no scales to help one in those days. There was dropping consistency, and hand-hot, soft dough and firm dough, and dozens of confusing terms to remember, but I don't recall many failures.

The oven was so accommodating that soon dozens of jam tarts, sausage rolls and fruit pies would be temptingly arranged on cooling racks on the kitchen table. After it was cooled it was stacked away in air-tight tins and stored in the walk-in larder which faced north and was as cool as a refrigerator. The floor was brick and the walls were faced with marble. I do not remember any meat ever spoiling; it was rubbed with brick salt for good measure to preserve it.

The baking was expected to last a hungry family the week. Bought cake was considered an extravagance and a sign of bad housekeeping.

On Saturday afternoons while all this was going on my two sisters and my brother were allowed to go to the matinee at the local cinema. This kept them out of the way. I missed this Saturday treat that I was now too 'grown up' to have. The cinema was called the Coliseum. We had clubbed together to buy liquorice or a few other sweets; the cinema itself took half our allowance of tuppence which we received on Saturdays from my father. It had to last the entire week.

Our penny admission tickets bought us front row seats, too close to the screen. So when the lights went off we crawled on all fours through the gangway, collecting kicks and bruises, until we came to the back seats where we could see better and not be seen. Engulfed in the luxury of red plush seats, we watched Charlie Chaplin's hilarious antics or Lillian Gish being swept helplessly over the rapids—to be continued—accompanied with suitable music on the piano played by a bald pianist who was unfortunately a good target for small boys with pea shooters. I felt aggrieved to be deprived of my Saturday afternoon's entertainment.

At teatime on Saturday we ate any casualties of the afternoon baking, and judgment was passed on my performance. Violet, after helping me wash up, departed in her Sunday clothes for her well-earned evening off, to meet her boyfriend and go to the cinema. She had to be back by ten o'clock. In all the years she was with us, I never knew her to come back late. And she worked very hard. Often after tea, when the little ones were in bed, Violet would sit and rock in Grannie's chair, dozing. Sometimes I found her lying on the hearthrug in front of the fire, sound asleep from sheer exhaustion. All this for five shillings a week and her keep! She was barely literate and I often helped her as she struggled to read her penny dreadfuls.

My Saturday was not yet finished. The huge copper had to be replenished, the damper adjusted to heat the water with the fire which was now burning lazily.

The kitchen glowed in the warm light of the stove: on the big kitchen dresser, the rows of hanging cups and bright plates appeared to dance in the firelight; the odd glasses caught the reflection of the heavy red curtains and glittered like rubies. Before the hearth, on the red brick floor, was a piece rug, manufactured from old clothes stripped into lengths and sewn into sacking with a special needle. These rugs were extremely heavy; it took both Violet and me, each holding an end, to shake our rug. And the porous brick floor had to be scrubbed each week with hot soda water; Violet's hands, which were chapped and burning, never had a chance to heal. I often saw her weep from the pain.

The kitchen table was made of well-scrubbed white wood; six wooden chairs were set around it. Under the window stood an enormous horsehair sofa, stiff and formal, its sausage-like stuffed cushion would not give an inch to any weight, no matter how heavy. Facing the window, between the dresser and the grate, stood Grannie's rocking chair.

It was a plain, simple room but it was cosy. It was always warm because the fire barely went out, night or day, and at a touch of the damper the released flames would leap joyfully up the chimney. On the stove stood a bright copper kettle which usually was boiling merrily away. The kitchen was the heart of the household. It was Violet's domain: here she ate and spent most of her waking moments. Here she cleaned the cutlery and silver, here she ironed the weekly wash, here she helped with the cooking. Here on her knees she scrubbed the floor and polished the steel fender on the hearth and the knobs and trim on the black grate until they shone like silver; so did the brass candlesticks standing with their white wax candles on the tall mantelpiece and the warming pan hanging by the fireplace.

Saturday night was bath night. The big zinc bathtub, which hung outside the back door all the week, was brought in and placed in front of the kitchen fire. This is the cosiest method of bathing I have ever experienced: the warmth from the kitchen fire enveloped and suffused you, while the familiar objects danced in the firelight and the copper kettle sang, ready to 'top up' the water when it was necessary. Who wants cold white tiles or an enormous white enamel bath where the water is cool before a toe is immersed? Give me the kitchen every time, although there is no plug to pull.

The youngest went in first and, as chief bath attendant, I lathered and vigorously scrubbed my little sister, ignoring her complaints. Her long black hair was washed in the bath; we had no shampoo but soap worked adequately with rainwater. She shrieked in agony when her hair was twisted and wrung out. She loved being towelled down in front of the fire. At last, dry and enveloped in a flanelette nightgown, she was finished off by Grannie, who brushed and combed her hair and twisted in into newspaper screws which would ensure an uncomfortable night. But the following morning her resulting ringlets were the glory of the Sabbath!

My sister Alice's turn came. She was not so docile as the youngest and usually half-drowned Grannie with her antics. We did not finish the exercise on friendly terms. But her fair hair suffered the same fate as my other sister's black tresses and eventually the two little girls were escorted to bed by candlelight.

Bathing my brother was an even more exhausting affair. Grannie used to threaten him with 'I'll tell your father!' but she never ever told tales about us, no matter how naughty we were. My brother objected to revealing his manliness and insisted that he could bath himself. His idea was to immerse himself in the water and allow it to do the work with no effort whatever on his part; ears and neck, he thought apparently, somehow cleaned themselves. A battle always ensued and the kitchen was flooded. A sigh of relief, and mopping up operations, followed his departure for bed.

My turn at last! Freshening up the water, I would luxuriate, stretched out in the bath, my toes hanging over the edge, my hair floating round my shoulders. I was a mermaid, splashing around in the ocean one moment, the next caught by a human and hauled onto the ship's deck. A sea captain, no less, would fall in love with me, and just as he was about to make me his own, Grannie's voice would recall me to reality.

'Ann, aren't you ever coming out of that bath? Your father will be home soon.'

I suffered the same punishment with my hair as my sisters did. Sunday respectability demanded it. Finally, the bath had to be emptied, a bucketful at a time, a Herculean effort for me, tipping the water down the sink; the kitchen had to be mopped up and tidied, and the bath hoisted up on the outside hook to face the rigours of the next week's weather and await the following Saturday.

I don't think my father ever did know about my stealthy excursions to the Bottle and Jug on the corner of our street. Father usually went on Saturday night to the cinema and his hour of return was predictable, luckily for Grannie! How I hated going to that den of iniquity. I would prevaricate and dawdle until poor little Grannie was on the verge of tears.

'Ann, it will be too late for you to go for my little drop; if you don't hurry, your father will be home. I can't get through the week without it, you know,' she would wail. 'But there, I'm only a poor old woman, no one cares about me. I would be better off dead.' And she would squeeze a tear from her china blue eyes; it trickled pathetically down her cheek and washed away my resistance.

Timidly, I entered the Bottle and Jug department of the public house. A woman stood against a table; her open-necked blouse gaped to the waist when she bent forward. A man had his arm around her waist in an affectionate embrace; every so often he squeezed her and gave her neck a resounding smack of a kiss, just missing her mouth as she tossed her head in half-hearted protest, exclaiming, 'Give over, Dick, do, what you think you're a-playing at?'

Other men and women sat and lolled about, women on men's laps, barely discernible in the smoke-filled dimly lit room. There was a bittersweet smell of human bodies mingled with the acrid smell of beer and spirits—an odor I find repulsive to this day.

The ribald laughter broke off as I hesitated in the open doorway. All eyes seemed to be upon me; their faces leered into mine, floating in space as they raised their beer mugs in salute.

'Come in, love, shut the door, there's a bloody draught with it open,' said a drunk, lurching toward me. 'Here, have a sip of this; it will bring some colour into your cheeks.'

As I shrank away, Grannie's shawl, which she had thrown over my head and shoulders, slipped away, revealing my hair in paper screws.

'Look at that now,' said the man coarsely. 'All screwed up for the Lord's Day.'

I recoiled, terrified, and the woman disengaged herself and came forward.

'Here, Bill, leave her be, can't you see you are frightening the child?' Turning to me, she said, 'What is it, love, six pen'orth for Grannie? How is the poor old lady? Here, give us your jug, brandy is it, doctor's orders, eh? We know, don't we, Bill?' with a wink in his direction.

'Oh yes please, and could you hurry, I don't want my daddy to know I'm here.'

'Oh no, His Lord High Mightyship wouldn't be pleased to see his daughter in the boozer, I'll be bound!' said another man. A loud burst of laughter followed this, to me, incomprehensible remark. Adults always talked to each other in riddles.

Every night I watched Grannie mix the precious golden liquid with hot water and two lumps of sugar. I saw the brandy, which was stored in a medicine bottle under the head of the bed, gradually disappear and I dreaded having to replenish it again on Saturday night.

I thought I understood at last why I must never mention to my father my nocturnal trips to the 'pub'. Poor little Grannie, who could not afford a doctor on her pension of seven shillings and sixpence a week, did not want to worry my father by telling him she was ill. Her medicine kept her heart going; it was the only thing that kept her alive. I resolved that no matter how much I hated it, it was my duty to fetch Grannie her 'little nip' every Saturday night. Only I could keep her alive.

The following morning, Sunday, we three girls were released from our paper rollers; our hair was brushed and combed around Grannie's finger to form long shining curls which hung almost to our waists. The night's agony was considered to be worth the result.

My father, spruce in his Sunday best—stiff high winged starched collar, dark suit, bowler hat and walking stick, would take his little brood for a long walk which lasted most of the morning. I was now old enough to stay at home on these Sunday mornings and help Grannie prepare the midday meal, but of course I knew what the walks entailed. We always took a route past the cemetery on the outskirts of the town. Occasionally we stopped at the cemetery to put flowers on Grandfather's grave, for Grannie's sake. As the eldest I had the task of arranging the flowers in the cast-iron urn kept on the grave for that purpose.

I felt superior to my sisters and brother, privileged at being able to commune, as it were, with the dead. I would think I wouldn't mind being struck dead arranging Grandfather's flowers and carried to heaven by those beautiful cast-iron hands which supported the urn.

I thought the cemetery, which was full of expensive ornate marble and stone figures lovingly inscribed by relatives, the most beautiful place on earth. I loved all the graves, but admired one in particular, which had a life-sized statue of a big handsome man with a whip in his hand; sprawled across the grave was the figure in stone of a dog who gazed at the man with deep affection. The tablet at the foot of the grave said that the dog had pined away and finally died of grief for his master.

Deeply touched, I often stole a flower from Grandfather's bunch to place on the grave which I learned later contained the remains of Gypsy Randall who had spent all his life on the roads in a horse-drawn caravan. 'More money than sense,' was my father's comment on the striking grave.

Frequently when we played truant from Sunday School we whiled the time away in the churchyard, fascinated by the family graves which had cement structures like little huts built over them, with a large removable ornate concrete lid on top. These were mostly old and in a sad state of disrepair. Where the lids had moved we could see into the vault and frighten ourselves with skulls and bones. We would throw stones in. If they hit the bottom and rattled, it was the Devil speaking to us. If there was no sound it was a good grave; angels might appear or be heard singing. When we tired of this we would play hide-and-seek until the 'goodies' came out of Sunday School and we could go safely home to tea.

On the Sunday afternoon walks my father expected us to be observant and questioned us when we got home about what we had seen. Because of this we were able to store up a good deal of general knowledge. We learned to recognise all kinds of trees and flowers and birds, everything that flew in the air or crawled on the ground, every little animal that scuttled away from us across the fields as we approached. Some Sundays we would tramp for what seemed like miles along the cliffs, which towered over the sandy beach and the harbour and ran into the distance at least eight miles overlooking the sea to the next town but one. The ships out at sea looked like toys from up there; with his mariner's keen eye my father could tell what cargo a ship was carrying when she was only a speck on the hazy blue horizon. As we tramped for what seemed like miles along the cliffs, Father would painstakingly explain that the wind was blowing north or south, or that bad weather was on the way, heralded by the seagulls flying inland from the water, or that varied signs showed that such and such a speck on the horizon was a timber carrier or a fishing vessel. Father carried binoculars; he let us look through them to identify these distant ships. He loved sometimes, too, to get his walking stick and strut ahead with it; occasionally this led to grief and a cut knee, as we hurried to keep up with him.

At the town end of the cliffs were prosperous boarding houses and hotels which did well in the summer season. A boarding school for young ladies commanded a superb view of the harbour. A cousin of mine attended the school there while her parents were abroad; often on Sundays we saw her in the 'crocodile'—a regimented procession—returning from morning services. I valued my freedom whenever I saw her in that crocodile.

After the houses on the cliffs came the tennis courts. The sea below claimed many an ill-aimed shot, especially in windy weather. After that came floral gardens where our pastor preached every Sunday evening during the 'season' for the benefit of the visitors, mostly holiday-makers from the Midlands. Unfortunately, his sermon, like the tennis balls, was often lost to the winds.

A mile or two along the cliff top you could look down on an old wreck which had been nestling for years at the foot of the cliff. When the sea receded it was possible—but dangerous—to paddle out to it. We were warned not to try that, and we only did it once, to be rescued by passers-by. After that we were too frightened ever to make another attempt. To this day the treasures of the wreck remain a mystery.

As we battled along against the strong wind which blows directly off the North Sea, we would come upon a huge concrete jungle, the ruins of Colmans Mustard factory. Under Father's watchful eye on a Sunday we gave it scarcely a glance, but it was an adventure playground on many an occasion during the long summer holiday. The bulk of the mass of cement and iron girders jutted out into the sea. The degree of danger in climbing and crawling over it depended on the tides. A great bulk of concrete, twenty to thirty feet high, sprawled over the sands.

Once my brother challenged my sister Alice. 'Bet you can't climb up and crawl out over the water on that girder.' He pointed to a girder jutting out over the sea with a sheer drop of about twelve feet.

'Easy,' Alice boasted. She climbed up and had crawled along to the tip of the girder when she slipped. Fortunately she was saved because her knickers caught on a projection; the material, happily, was tough. She hung screaming from the girder, spreadeagled, flailing her arms and legs like a crab. My brother, almost always cool in the face of danger, crawled along the girder to her rescue. Bullying her to keep quiet and hold still, he manged to pull her back to safety. After a brief respite, during which they sat like two shipwrecked seamen on the projection, trying to get their breath back, they crawled slowly and painfully back and scrambled down onto the beach. My sister was revived with the last drops of lemonade left over from our picnic.

Grannie viewed the rent in Alice's knickers with suspicion. 'You haven't been climbing on Colman's ruins again, have you? I shall tell your father.' But we knew she wouldn't. My father little suspected how many times we cheated death on those cliff tops and the seashore.

I recall my brother wanting to check the time and speed it would take for a laden push chair to run down an asphalt slope from the top of the cliff to the concrete promenade below. My little sister Laura was the guinea pig. She was strapped securely into the push chair and shoved off at a given signal. The push chair gathered momentum and rushed down the steep slope, toppling over and rolling the last few feet. It was a great experiment for my brother, but near disaster for my poor little sister, who was released, bruised, shaken and bleeding from numerous scratches.

Sometimes when fishing was in season my father would take us for a walk round the quayside and harbour's mouth. Here the hopeful fishermen cast their lines expertly high in the air to drop in the centre of the river, allowing the line to slip quickly through the reel, to be wound back and properly adjusted. There was great excitement when the line jumped and the poor fish was wound in, pierced through the gills and struggling for its life. Occasionally Father would stop to chat about fishing with an acquaintance; I remember hearing Father say what a tragedy it was about Mr Jobling. He had been throwing his line when a strong gust of wind caught him and lifted him off his feet over the quayside into the river. The tide and the currents were strong at the harbour's mouth. He was never seen again.

Mr Jobling had been a jolly fellow. My father had often chatted with him; he had been one of the favoured few who could claim my father's attention at all. Thereafter I shuddered whenever I passed that spot, wondering if Mr Jobling was lying there at the bottom, being eaten by shrimps. I had overheard the men say that they fed on humans. Shrimps were no longer my favourite for teatime, after Mr Jobling had sunk to the bottom of the sea.

After Sunday dinner Father would rest and read lying on the sofa in the front room, which was used only on

Sunday. Grannie would doze in her chair in the dining room, lulled by the ticking of the Grandfather clock and the warmth of a good fire. Violet had the afternoon and evening off to visit her sister. She had no parents.

Sunday evening was the only time we ever had friends in. My father was not a sociable man, although he raised his hat politely to people he knew in the street. Mrs Pippin always said that my father was a perfect gentleman. I think in fact he was the only customer who ever raised his hat to her. But after my mother left he lived in a world of his own, with books and nursing his grief. Consequently we children had very little contact with the social side of the town. Grannie had to be our pattern of womanhood and unfortunately her knowledge of the world was limited. She had spent her life bearing children, twenty-one that she could remember, counting one drowned in the millstream; she loved to relive that accident, telling all the details with wailing and tears. I found this distressing.

In any case the only family my father was friendly with lived in the smart terrace houses at the top of the street, away from the smell of fish and the slaughterhouse. Their name was Millar. Mr Millar was the undertaker whose workshop and yard adjoined the back of our garden, behind a six-foot fence. Mrs Millar was very proper and proud, and there were two daughters, Betty, a little older than I, and Myra, a little younger, who were encouraged to think themselves superior to their contemporaries. I was always jealous of them because they were so fashionably dressed. Myra was dark-eyed and pretty, with an oval pale face framed by naturally curly dark hair. She was in my class at school and she was teacher's pet. She had singing lessons, ballet lessons and piano lessons. She was always chosen first for any activities at school. She was Queen Elizabeth in 'Merrie England' and Maid Marion in 'Robin Hood'. I was sure that I could do as well as she if I only had the chance.

I was having music lessons myself at the time, from a rather broken-down musician who was scraping a living teaching in pupils' houses and playing the piano at the cinema in the evenings. He taught piano to Alice and me, and violin to my brother John. At concerts he had accompanied my mother on the piano.

One day he asked me to sing for him, and joy of joys, he played for me and I warbled my heart out for him.

'You have a good soprano voice,' he said. 'I'll speak to your father and see if you may have lessons.'

He did speak to my father, but Father couldn't agree. The memory of my mother's singing was too fresh; he did not want his daughter to go the same way. Nevertheless my sponsor gave me lessons surreptitiously—half an hour piano and half an hour singing. I was sure now that I had a future and that I would overtake Myra and meet with success.

I sang away to myself when the house was empty and entered a world of fantasy. Sometimes my brother would come home unexpectedly and burst into the room, shattering my dream.

'For God's sake, Ann, can't you stop that awful squalling? I could hear you at the other end of the street.'

I was determined to prove that I had as much talent as Myra Millar. My opportunity came rather sooner than I had expected. A bold notice in the Coliseum caught my eye and my imagination. 'Talent spotting competition,' it said. 'Can you sing? If so, come along to our show tonight and win the chance of a lifetime.'

I scraped up the coppers needed for admission and persuaded Grannie to allow me to go out after my father had gone to the reading room in the public library. It was midsummer, and the evenings were long and light. The cinema was packed because of the summer visitors. I did not know what to expect and I sat through the first part of the programme in trepidation, clutching my copy of 'Rose in the Bud', the song I was going to sing.

At half-time the lights blazed on, the lush red velvet curtains slowly closed across the screen, the stage was revealed before the footlights and the pianist sat expectantly in the pit below the stage. Girls in their uniforms of short red dresses, frill-edged caps and aprons, with a tray suspended from a strap around their necks, paraded the gangways crying 'Ice cream! Chocolate!' at a penny for a tub of ice cream or a bar of chocolate. The air was heavy with cigarette smoke and the odd aroma exuded by a confined mass of people. My eyes watered, my throat felt parched. The ice cream moved temptingly up and down the passages. Oh, for just one penny!

As I sat apprehensively alone, a lout leant toward me and enquired, leering into my face as he put his hand on my knee, 'All alone, are we?' I shrank back into my seat. Luckily at that moment there was a murmur and a stir in the audience. A huge muscular man as broad as he was long, almost, with a voice like a town crier, strode onto the stage, followed by another who was just as dapper but smaller. He had sleek black hair plastered with brilliantine so that it hugged his head like a skull-cap. He was dark and looked Italian. He was wearing a pale beige suit, a pink shirt, a yellow tie and brown shoes and he had a mincing walk.

'Ladies and gentlemen,' the big man bawled, like a ringmaster at the circus, down a huge megaphone which covered his face, 'I would like to introduce you to Mr Lightfoot.'

Here the mincing little man bounced forward and bowed to much applause from the audience, who were very interested in the proceedings.

'Mr Lightfoot has come all the way from London to be with us tonight, to spot any talent in our seaside town. We know we have beauty here amongst our ladies [loud applause]; now we want to find the talent that must be lurking in these lovely creatures. Mr Lightfoot will choose the winner for us and take her back to London, lucky man!' He gave a wink. Laughter and more applause followed this announcement. I was not sure I wanted to go to London with Mr Lightfoot, as much as I wanted to win the competition.

I suddenly realised that the 'beauties' were climbing onto the stage, resplendent in their best dresses and bedecked with jewels. I felt I was at a disadvantage here in my plain blue school dress, but I had pinned my best black ribbon bow on the back of my head; I hoped this gave me a more sophisticated appearance. I took my place in the line of lovelies on the stage, receiving many a disparaging glance from some of the buxom assembly.

The entrants took their turns stepping forward and being introduced by Mr Lightfoot with accompanying suitable remarks. The audience applauded and suffered a shrill soprano rendition of 'Coming Thro' the Rye'. A full-throated lass, representing her native town, gave forth 'Caller Herring' as if she were indeed plying her wares on the fish docks. As the last notes of 'Comin' Home' died away, I heard my name called.

I staggered forward. My dress seemed to have spiralled round my legs. Since I had given my music to the pianist, I didn't know what to do with my hands. I gazed at a sea of upturned faces, all waiting for the sound that did not want to come from my constricted throat. The piano struck the opening chords, the sound of the familiar notes calmed the fluttering in the pit of my stomach and 'Rose in the Bud' blossomed as it never had before. As my voice died away, there was a momentary hush, and then overwhelming applause.

My father was waiting for me. I had won the competition, but he saw the management and explained in no uncertain terms that I was not of age and needed his consent for any undertaking whatsoever. He did not share my enthusiasm for the bright lights. However he could not take away the thrill of that thundering applause for my success. The only person I knew who was impressed with my performance was my music teacher who sympathised with my ambitions.

I now felt I had a reason to think myself level with Myra Millar. I had won a competition—I had sung in front of a seaside cinema audience. I had tasted success!

But when the Millars came to visit us on Sunday evenings and I sang, I received only mild appreciation, although Mrs Millar was kind and Mr Millar was always cheerful—he seemed a happy family man. Betty played and Myra sang to much appreciative applause from their family. No one ever guessed how much I hated my friend on these evenings. She fascinated me with her trained professional manner; I had wanted to take singing lessons too, but my father would not hear of it. Her tongue was too pink, I decided, when she opened her mouth wide, and there was always a smile and a bow at the end as she waited for the applause which she knew would follow. I found her terribly conceited.

'You're only jealous because you can't sing like her and anyway you are not pretty,' my brother teased. How I hated them all. My brother, I imagined, fancied her, with her airs and graces.

One night I was awakened by a loud knocking and then the bell clanged through the house. I listened, trembling. It was our front door; it sounded urgent. Hastily I lit the candle. I crept downstairs, holding the candlestick in one hand, holding to the banister with the other, trying to stop my knees from shaking. The loud knocking sounded again as I reached the bottom of the stairs and hurried along the passage in my white nightgown. I reached the front door, drew back the heavy bolt, turned the key and opened the door on the chain.

'Mrs Millar!' I exclaimed. Through the crack of the door I could see she was in her nightgown, with an overcoat thrown over her shoulders. Myra and Betty were crying and clinging to her. They stood, a shivering trio in the cold night air.

'Call your father,' she gasped. 'Quickly!'

My father appeared on the landing at the top of the stairs as I took the chain off the door and they almost fell into the hall. Mrs Millar ran to my father as he bounded down the stairs. I took Myra in my skinny arms, held her to my flat chest and tried to calm her. Betty stood in silence watching us.

'Oh Mr Wood, something terrible has happened. George has done it!' Mrs Millar cried, clutching at my father and trying to drag him toward the door.

'What is wrong? Done what?' I asked my bewildered father.

'The children!' said Mrs Millar, indicating Myra and Betty. She leant toward my father and whispered in his ear.

'Good God!' my father exclaimed; he looked incredulous. He grabbed his overcoat off the hall stand and shrugged himself quickly into it.

'Ann,' he said, 'take the girls up to bed with you; you will all catch your death of colds down here.'

He took Mrs Millar by the arm and left us, a sorry little group crying and shivering in the vast old hall, dim and wavering in the candlelight.

We huddled together in the bed, all three of us, trying to warm each other by sheer contact.

Myra did not realize what had happened. Her sister

had intercepted her at the foot of the stairs when she came down to find out what was happening. Betty had burst into the kitchen and seen her father lying on the floor in a pool of blood. She stood transfixed with shock and saw her mother's wild look of horror and the blood-stained carving knife on the floor. It was Betty who pulled her mother away and closed the door on the tragedy just as Myra was reaching the last step. Then they fled to my father for help.

Apparently Mr Millar, for all his jaunty cheerful air, was heavily in debt. Only his wife knew it. He could not face up to the threat of bankruptcy. And people did say unkindly afterward, 'They had always carried a high sail!' and, with a knowing nod, 'Pride goeth before a fall.'

At any rate he had the most beautiful funeral the street had ever seen. The hearse was like a mobile flower show. He, having put so many to rest, was sent on his last journey with all the respect due to one of his profession. The church was packed with friends and relations, many of whom were doubtless in his debt and who had thus contributed unwittingly to his premature departure.

A few dissenters complained that Mr Millar should not have had a Christian burial, a suicide was not entitled to it. It was unthinkable, however, that he who had given so many a decorous burial should be dropped unceremoniously into a hole, and the sympathisers and the parson won the day. Honour and Christian charity prevailed.

Grannie was much shaken by this tragedy. She sat moaning with her black apron over her head and shoulders, repeating, 'God moves in mysterious ways.' This was her religious cliché for innumerable occasions.

I felt somehow that the score was settled between our

family and the Millars. My mother was a sinner, but now so was their father. This realisation did not, however, make me happy as I hoped it would. It made me miserable.

4. Leaving School

WHEN my mother had been gone for over a year, it became noticeable that Grannie's condition was deteriorating. She had cataracts in both eyes, mistook her change when she paid tradesmen and became less and less able to run the house. In those days operations for the elderly were not common. I didn't know exactly how old Grannie was, although I tried various methods of extracting this delicate information from her. She had a trite maxim for every occasion and would say, when pressed about her age, 'I am as old as my tongue and a little older than my teeth.'

I was approaching my fourteenth birthday—the school leaving age.

One evening when I went to kiss my father good-night before going to bed, he said to me, 'Sit down, my dear. I want to talk to you.'

I thought I must have done something wrong; my father looked very serious. He was sitting in his red leather armchair by the fire, facing the matching arm-chair which was empty, Grannie having gone upstairs where she waited for me to help her get undressed. The fire was burning low in the grate and the room was dimly lit by one flame of the central gas light suspended over the dining room table which dominated the room. The corners of the room and the fireside were always in shadow. We had no occasional lamps and had to sit at the table to read or write or sew. It was a huge oval table and was of necessity the center of the house. We four children gathered round it to do our homework immediately after tea. After they had done their work to my father's satisfaction the two younger children went to bed. As the eldest, I was the last to go to bed; I had various duties to perform before retiring, apart from my schoolwork.

Therefore it was with some trepidation that I sat down on a hard dining room chair to listen to what my father had to say. I remember gazing at the highly polished red linoleum on the floor and wondering why the black design on it was called a 'Turkey' pattern.

'Ann,' my father's voice recalled me. 'I am sorry, my dear, but I am afraid you will have to leave school at the end of this term.'

'Oh,' I gasped in dismay, 'I couldn't, Daddy. Miss Hunt is going to put me in for a scholarship for teaching. She says I should get a grant from the Education Authority; it won't cost you anything.'

Miss Hunt was my teacher. I adored her and the thought of going against her wishes or disregarding her advice was unbearable.

'You will have to forget all that. I and your sisters and brother need you at home here. Your Grannie is getting too old to cope with the housekeeping. You will have to take charge of everything. Grannie will help you, and Violet will still be here—for a time at least.'

My dreams and ambitions came tumbling down.

'I can't,' I said, bursting into tears. 'What will I tell Miss Hunt? She will be angry with me.'

'Don't worry,' my father said. 'Leave that to me.'

'Oh! I don't want to be a housekeeper. I want to be a teacher,' I said, between sobs.

'Now stop crying,' my father answered gently. He looked at me earnestly. 'I need your help, you are all I've got, the only one who can help me at the moment. Your sisters and brother need you too. It won't be so hard as you think. I'm sorry I can't let you go away to a training college. What would I do without you?'

I left school at the end of the term and took over the awesome housekeeping duties under Grannie's super-vision. She was very reluctant to relinquish her author-ity. As time went on, when she was in one of her 'moods', she was definitely aggressive and obstructive towards me.

'Now,' said my father on the first payday. He handed me three one pound notes. 'Here is your housekeeping allowance and here, on this sheet of paper is a list of your responsibilities. Remember, this money has to last the week, that is all there is. Don't get into debt, don't try to buy what you can't afford. Grannie will advise you on the food purchases.'

I was overwhelmed. Three pounds all at once seemed such a lot of money. And it was: money went a long way in those days. The grocery bill for the family would come to only about ten or twelve shillings.

'Now, missy, let me see, the best end of topside, isn't it?' the butcher would say, cutting off a huge, lovely red juicy-looking chunk of meat with just the right amount of fat encircling it, for our weekend joint. I would usually pay half a crown for it; it never varied within a copper or two. It was the only joint we ever had; no other cut was right for my father.

Every Sunday luncheon he carved the joint and remarked on its quality or the excellence of my culinary efforts. Woe betide me if it was overcooked and a little dry, or underdone and too moist, so that the red blood ran as the knife slipped through it. My tender years and lack of experience were no excuse: my father demanded perfection. My tears, which came easily in those days, often flowed over my roast and two vegetables as a result of my father's frank criticism. Of course he meant well, and, as Grannie used to say, 'his bark was worse than his bite'.

Not long after I left school Violet gave her notice. She said she was 'heartbroke' at having to leave us children but she had to better herself and she didn't want a living-in job no more, because she was courting and needed her evenings free. I gathered she was going to live with her sister and would go out to work daily. My father was paying her five shillings a week, and she could get seven and sixpence at her new place. So Violet left, with many hugs and admonitions to the little ones to be good children.

This put the heavy burden of 'maid of all work' on me. Grannie was by now quite helpless and completely incapable of doing any household chores.

From time to time my Aunt Martha used to come and help to clean and tidy us. She was the widow of my mother's youngest brother, and was living in very straitened circumstances. For reasons I could not understand at the time, my father had forbidden her to come to the house. I knew it was somehow because of the 'goings-on' before my mother's departure. Father held

Aunt Martha partly responsible for my mother's behaviour and was highly suspicious of the motives behind her visiting us.

Grannie used to say to me, 'She is my daughter-in-law and I have a right to see her.' I thought that made sense. She would continue, 'Don't you tell your father that Aunt Martha has been here this afternoon.' In this way I was, against my will, coerced to deceive my father. My loyalties were severely strained. I loved both Father and Grannie and I couldn't bear to see Grannie weep, which she seemed to do a good deal these days.

After Violet left, Aunt Martha came at least once a week. Sometimes she would help out and sometimes she would make tea and she and Grannie would sit and chat most of the afternoon. I would sit in the kitchen with a beloved book for an hour or two on my own. I was forgotten, I'm sure, because Grannie couldn't bear to see me sitting idle with a book. She always found me some hateful sewing or silver-polishing to do. She considered reading a waste of time. My brother was a great reader and loved to use big words. She would taunt him with being 'dictionary learnt'.

Aunt Martha would leave hastily just before the 'little ones' got home from school, in case they should see her and forget and tell Father. She was always saying mysterious things to Grannie, like, 'I will tell her how they are,' and 'Her heart aches for the little one. I'll tell her what you said.'

Grannie seemed to expect a lot of me, without considering my age. She kept me running about constantly, and waiting on her. I think that because of her age she forgot the present, and thought that she was still living on her farm with daily help and a family of growing daughters to assist her. She had had a washerwoman then, who stood all day at a washtub for sixpence and her meals.

I could imagine what it had been like. On beautiful summer days the clothes would flap and billow on the line stretched out across the field; the sheets billowed like tents in the wind and the sweet scent of the dew-laden grass bespattered with buttercups permeated everything. On such days as this the woman would gather a great armsful of fresh washing and fold it all neatly, ready for ironing the next day. She would leave the house, with rough red hands and arms, tired from a hard day's work, but with a sense of accomplishment and also possibly a basket of fresh vegetables and fruit to augment her sixpence.

I could not find the experience rewarding; I was too small physically. Washerwomen were few and far between in the towns and laundries were also scarce—and expensive. I missed Violet: she was a tall, strapping girl who could easily lift a bathful of water and clothes out of the sink and set it on the floor, and effortlessly carry huge buckets of cold water to the copper. This lifting and carrying exhausted me. Violet could turn the clothes through the old wooden rollers of the mangle almost casually, while I, pulling with both hands on the handle, would be lifted off my feet. Violet had both the knack and the strength. I had neither.

Kindling the copper was a dangerous, tricky business. The grate was a hole in the brick structure containing the copper, about a foot from the floor, into which paper and sticks were strategically placed. If the wind was blowing from the right direction, a merry conflagration, helped along by some coal, was soon under way. Grannie warned me not to use paraffin in the copper hole, but somehow the sticks, bought at a half-penny the bundle, never burnt for me. What with carrying huge buckets of water across the scullery, half drowning myself in the process, and struggling with the fire, Monday mornings did not go well. Notwithstanding Grannie's warning, I often threw paraffin up the copper hole, when all efforts failed to ignite the dying embers. I occasionally lost an eyebrow when the resultant explosion hurled me halfway across the scullery; it went off with a whoosh! like a petrol bomb.

But the means justified the end for me; the water in the copper would soon be boiling, filling the scullery with warm steam, which ran down the walls in rivulets and filled the house with a damp, earthy vapour. The scullery window, jammed hard by years of neglect, refused to open; it was too chilly with the back door open, so the steam did not escape.

The smell of common soap and wet soiled linen mingled with the steam as I plunged the garments into strong, near-boiling soda water. By the end of the day my hands and arms looked like a joint of red, raw meat. I put glycerine and rosewater on them, and they seemed on fire; my eyes teared with pain. By the end of the week my hands were just beginning to recover some semblance of whiteness—then it was time for another dose of hot water and soap.

One Monday morning I was struggling with the voluminous underwear Grannie discarded every week when there was a knock at the back door. I opened it with some difficulty; my hands were wet and slippery.

'Mother!' I gasped.

All the emotion pent up for over a year broke loose. I was in my mother's arms, sobbing wildly. Her tears mingled with mine; she hugged me and stroked me.

'Don't cry, my love. Please don't cry. I can't bear to see you cry so.'

'Mummy, I'm not really crying. I'm just so happy you have come back.' I began to laugh hysterically and hugged her tightly. She would never leave us again, I was sure. I pulled her by the hands through the kitchen into the dining room. I threw the door open with a bang.

'Grannie, look who is here! Mummy has come back,' I cried.

There was a deadly hush. Grannie had been dozing in her armchair, nodding in time to the ticking of the Grandfather clock in the corner. A fire was blazing in the hearth next to her chair. She looked up.

'Ada. So you have come,' she said. She did not seem surprised, and I had a feeling she was expecting my mother. Mother rushed across the room, fell onto her knees and buried her face in Grannie's lap, sobbing uncontrollably.

'There, there, my baby,' Grannie said, stroking her hair and kissing the top of her head. 'It will be all right. Don't cry.' Now Grannie herself was crying.

I stood watching this drama, transfixed. I didn't think that 'grown-ups' ever cried like that.

And Grannie called my mother her 'baby'. That was because Mummy was Grannie's youngest child. Grannie seemed to have forgotten all her bitterness; there was no talk of the dreaded horsewhipping which she had threatened would happen to my mother. Oh, I did hope my father would forgive her too, for running away. I could understand her running away to have a rest from all that washing and cooking and housework. But she had come back.

'Ann, go and put the kettle on,' Grannie said, 'and make your mother a cup of tea.'

When I returned with the tray and teapot my mother was sitting beside Grannie, holding her hand.

'Ann,' she said, 'I have brought you a new dress.' She held up a woollen jumper and skirt for me to try on.

'It's lovely,' I said. I walked about wearing it, feeling its softness. I had not had anything new for a long time.

'You must tell your father Grannie bought it for you.' my mother said.

'But she didn't.'

'Now do as I say and things will be all right,' she said. 'You are growing up and must learn to be discreet. It's not wise to tell your father everything. He doesn't understand—he thinks in his own way.'

To me this was very confusing, but I certainly wanted the new dress and as Grannie explained later it was only a 'white lie' which could not harm anyone. I was to learn that Grannie could fit several degrees of lying into her moral code, which did not measure up at all to my father's standards.

My mother said it was time for her to leave.

'Aren't you going to stay to see Daddy?' I was dismayed.

'Not this time, Ann,' my mother said. She gave me an odd look. 'You are such a child,' she said. 'I wish I could tell you more. Take care of your little sisters and your brother and kiss them for me.'

I noticed suddenly how sad she looked. I had never seen such unhappiness as showed in her face and her wide eyes. She had no trace of the laughter and gaiety I remembered so well. I wanted to ask her if she still played the piano and sang, but I was afraid she would start crying again.

Grannie composed herself before my father came home and made me promise to say nothing about the visit. To this day I don't know whether he ever found out about it, but I was troubled by the burden of guilt I shared with Grannie.

Some weeks later I said, 'Grannie, is Mummy coming home? Where has she gone again? Why couldn't she stay here that day?'

'Don't ask so many questions! I can't tell you what I don't know myself. She might come home. It depends on your father's attitude.'

I longed to talk to my father and plead with him to let her come back. After this conversation I often found Grannie rocking back and forth, crying into the large black apron which she always wore. She threw it over her head and shoulders as if she wanted to shut out the world. Later when I was living abroad I discovered that Greek and Cypriot peasants behave this way. They cover their heads—or more precisely, bury their heads and shoulders in their garments when they mourn their dead or departing relatives. I have seen women do this at airports when the plane is taking off. But in those days I never saw anyone but Grannie behave so. She retreated into her world of darkness under her black apron at times of duress, laughter or tears.

'Why do you cry so much, Grannie?' I asked anxiously, peering under the apron. 'Are you ill, have you got a pain?'

'Oh, dear, Oh, dear! What will become of you poor motherless children,' she wailed behind her screen, 'when I am gone?'

'Gone, Grannie, where are you going?' I cried in alarm.

'I am only a poor old woman, I must go when the Good Lord calls me,' she answered sadly.

This was a new idea. I had never thought of Grannie as having to go anywhere, much less being 'called', as she put it. Surely God would not take her away from us, if, as they said, He knew and saw everything. He must know how much we needed her. I questioned Grannie about this.

'God moves in a mysterious way,' she said piously.

For a long time I was troubled by the thought of Grannie being called. I would drop what I was doing and peep into the dining room to see if she was sitting in her chair by the fire. Every day I would ask her if she felt all right. I would awaken in the night to find her sound asleep beside me, and then go back to sleep, reassured. I fancied somehow that she would be spirited away from us. I wanted to ask my brother for advice—he knew a lot of things—but I was afraid he would laugh at me. He didn't have much imagination.

Aunt Martha continued her furtive visits to Grannie, always leaving before my father came home. She was a kind person and would have done more to help physically with the house if she could. All she could offer was work; she had no money.

Once when the door was left slightly ajar, I heard Grannie say, in a trembling voice, 'Well, Martha, it's final. She won't come back now. How could she accept such conditions? Are you sure that is what the letter said?'

My aunt murmured something I couldn't catch and then Grannie burst out, 'How could he be so cruel, how could he refuse for the sake of the children? He must know that no woman could live with her husband under such conditions. He is a brute with no feelings—to pretend he loves her—he pretends, but it's all self-pity. Oh dear, oh dear!'

Grannie collapsed into loud wails of grief. I knew she was hidden behind her black curtain.

How dare they call my father a brute! I burst into the room. 'But he isn't a brute,' I insisted, 'he isn't cruel, he isn't! He is the best father in the world.'

My aunt and Grannie looked startled at my sudden intrusion. 'We may as well tell her,' Aunt Martha said to Grannie. 'She will have to know some day.'

She turned to me. 'Ann, listen to me. Your mother wants to come home, she misses you all and wants to be with you again. She has written to your father to ask him to forgive her and take her back for the sake of you children at any rate. He will agree to take her back only as a housekeeper, not as his wife. He can never forgive her for what she has done to him. He is a very proud man, your father. And he will not agree under any circumstances to a divorce.'

I ran upstairs and threw myself on my bed in a paroxysm of grief and despair. I hadn't completely understood what my aunt had said, but I knew that my beautiful dream—that we would all live happily together again—was over.

I saw the years ahead of me: washing, cooking, cleaning. No fun, and no future. I wept bitterly in pity for myself and because my mother was lost to me forever.

5. The Blow

GRANNIE went to the country to stay for a week or two with her daughter. I missed her company and her guidance; running the house myself was a heavy responsibility. My father was normally a gentle man: I don't remember hearing him raise his voice or his hand to any one of his four children except under great provocation. But he was a punctual man and hated unpunctuality in other people; he regulated his day-to-day habits by the clock. 'Watch the clock,' he would say to us, and woe betide us if we were unmindful.

The Grandfather clock struck one. It stood tall in its corner near the chimney breast, lording it over the low

73

chiffonier and Granny's empty red plush armchair. Hastily I poked the fire into a cheery flame with the shining brass poker and spread the spotless white damask cloth over the bright polished oval mahogany dining table. I heard my father's footsteps coming down the back garden path as I was setting the cutlery in place.

'The dinner not ready, Ann?' my father asked.

'Oh yes, Daddy,' I said cheerfully. I reached the cruet off the sideboard.

'It is not ready. It should be on the table waiting for me to serve,' he said.

I was not a mature housewife and I knew nothing about the devious ways to soothe a ruffled male. I answered airily, 'It won't take many minutes,' and slipped past my father, through the door to the kitchen and into the scullery. This was a bare, cold, stone-floored room with a small open basket type of iron fireplace. The grate was suspended about eighteen inches from the floor, between two pillars which were called 'hobs'. On one of them a saucepan was boiling merrily. Next to the fireplace was the brick copper where we boiled the weekly wash every Monday morning. The only furniture was the old wrought-iron mangle and a white wood drop-leaf table and wooden chair. The table was scrubbed every day with hot soda water; it was as clean as the scrubbed porous brick floor. Under the window next to the back door was a porcelain sink with a cold water brass tap—polished daily. There were two doors on the wall opposite the fireplace: one opened into the coal house and the other into the pantry. Coal was carted into the coal house in hundred weight bags, on the coalmen's backs, all up the back passage, along the path past the neighbors' back gardens, down our garden path and across our scullery through the back door. When I expected the coalman I saved myself a lot of work by laying a carpet of newspapers over the scullery floor—otherwise I would have to get down on my hands and knees after he left and scrub the entire floor. However this would not prevent the coal dust from seeping into the pantry, amidst the crockery, which consequently had to be washed along with the shelves, under Grannie's strict supervision. The poor coalman was not very popular.

On this day we were having steamed steak and kidney pudding for our dinner. My father followed me into the scullery and watched as I lifted the delicious-smelling pudding by the steaming hot cloth which was secured under the rim of the basin, its ends drawn up and knotted on top.

'You are only about to dish up,' my father said in an accusatory voice. 'You are very late today. What have you been doing all the morning, not to have the meal ready?'

I did not notice the tension in his voice.

'It isn't very late, it is nearly ready,' I said.

'You are not ready,' my father said again.

'Well, it's cooked,' I answered, with all the defiance of my fourteen years. I took the steaming hot cloth triumphantly off the pudding and deposited it on a dish to take it to the dining room.

Something struck me forcibly on the side of my head and nearly burst my eardrum. The blow was so hard it sent me reeling across the scullery to crash into the floor at the foot of the mangle. I lay flat on the cold bricks unconscious.

I came to my senses drenched with cold water which my father had splashed on my face to revive me. He was patting my hands and calling my name, wiping the water off my face. I was shivering with cold. I opened my eyes to see my father's stricken face. The anger was gone; his dark eyes were full of remorse and concern.

'Here,' he said, 'drink this,' He was offering me some pale yellow liquid in a small glass. I sipped it, my teeth chattering. It rushed through my body like fire and I felt suddenly warm. I put up my hand and felt a huge bump, too tender to touch, on my temple. It throbbed and I winced with pain. Father bathed it carefully with ice cold water from the scullery tap. We had no ice.

'Now,' he said after a while, 'do you think you can manage a little dinner?' He helped me to walk, very unsteadily, into the dining room. Somehow I managed to sit at the table, still sniffing.

After dinner, before Father left for the works, he said, 'I think, Ann, you should rest this afternoon after you have done the washing up.' He patted my head and kissed me good-bye. The pat made me wince; my bruised head was so sore. The kiss was as near as this proud man could get to saying he was sorry.

As soon as my father was out of earshot I left the washing up. I did not clear the table. I put on my hat and coat and set out for the neighbouring town to see my aunt. She was my mother's sister, and I was very attached to her. I gathered she was not a favourite with my father, although he was good friends with her husband, Uncle Henry, who was a dear, much loved by everybody.

I must go and see my Aunt Nancy, I told myself. She will know what to do. I had only a sixpenny piece in my purse; it wasn't really mine, it was housekeeping money. I dared not spend two pennies on the tramcar fare to take me the long way round and over the bridge to my aunt's town. To take the ferry involved a walk of several miles along the riverside—a daunting feat in my unsteady state—but it would cost only a halfpenny to cross the water by ferry.

I didn't feel like walking but I had to talk to someone. I cried as I stumbled along up the hill to the High Street through our town and down to the river, and along the river bank to the ferry. The little rowing boat, tied to the landing stage, bobbed up and down on backwash from passing craft and from the tide.

'Hurry along, missy, if you want this ferry,' the 'old salt' cried, when he saw me waving to let him know I was coming. He eyed me a bit suspiciously as I stumbled aboard, and gave me a helping hand. 'Steady there,' he said. Normally I would have jumped laughing into the little 'cockle shell'.

We rowed placidly across the wide expanse of water separating the two towns. I trailed my hand in the cool, refreshing water, feeling a little better. The tide was low, the steps to the quayside were wet and slippery. 'Be careful how you go; them steps is slippery, missy,' the boatman said. He put a steadying hand on my elbow to help me over the gap between the boat and the step. Mistiming could easily end in a disastrous plunge into the river; so could a slip on the step. I murmured my thanks gratefully and gave him the halfpenny fare. His face had as many weather-beaten wrinkles as the river had ripples.

I walked the two miles along the quay and riverside to the fashionable part of town where my aunt and uncle lived in an imposing house. Before he retired Uncle Henry had been a partner in a marine engineering firm which had made a fortune during the War. My father had been only an employee with his big shipyard so he had of course not enjoyed the kind of success Uncle Henry had had. My aunt was very conscious of her new wealth and consequent social position; this probably accounted for my father's obvious dislike of her.

I climbed the steps between the two pillars and pulled the bell near the front door. The maid of all work, in her white apron and cap and black afternoon dress, opened the door. She took one look at me and dashed back to call my aunt.

'Why Ann, what on earth has happened to you? You're

as white as a sheet!' She began to guide me into the sitting room.

'Oh Auntie,' I said, bursting into a paroxysm of tears, 'Daddy knocked me across the scullery.'

'Henry!' said my aunt. 'Just look at this poor child. Richard has been knocking her about.'

My uncle was in poor health. He lay under a rug on a maroon plush sofa in front of a roaring fire. He felt the cold badly. He raised himself on one elbow and said, 'Come over here, child, and tell me what this is all about.'

I was so abandoned to my grief that I was almost inarticulate but as I unfolded the sad tale my aunt kept saying, 'The beast, the brute!' over and over again. She was the kindest of creatures, but she loved to dramatise everything and make it sensational.

'He nearly killed her,' she said. 'Just look at this bump. It's in the most dangerous spot it could possibly be. Oh, he is not fit to have the care of children; you must never never go back to him; you must stay here with your uncle and me.'

She tried to comfort and console me, and gave me tea and lovely hot crumpets, toasted on the end of a long fork in front of the glowing fire. I was soothed by the love and warmth and cosiness.

My aunt was house proud. The whole house was furnished on a lavish scale. The dining room was large and lofty and tastefully furnished with a big mahogany dining table and bureau bookcase, very fashionable then. The dining chairs were all pushed in under and round the huge table. The warm carpet matched the rich maroon chesterfield suite and the heavy damask curtains. The room was large enough to accommodate comfortably all this furniture.

Having been fussed over, fed and listened to, I suggested it was time I was getting home.

'No, you can't go, Ann. I can't let you go, you poor

child—to be knocked about by that terrible father of yours.'

'Auntie, please,' I implored her. 'It wasn't as bad as that. My Daddy is not terrible—he only knocked me across the scullery because I answered him back. I said the dinner was ready when it wasn't—well, not quite,' I added. 'I must go home. My sisters will be home from school and there will be no one to get tea for them.'

My aunt was about to speak; my uncle stopped her.

'Be careful, Mother,' he said. 'And listen to me. Ann, come here. Of course you must go home; we know your father loves you all and would not harm any one of you. He did not mean to hurt you—he lost his temper. Now, stop crying,' he said as he saw I was in tears again. 'You must try to understand and not make him angry with you—he has a lot to bear.' To my aunt he said, 'Mother, wrap some cakes for the children and give them to her to take home.' He pulled me down to him and, patting my face kindly, he pressed a sixpenny piece into my palm. 'No walking home, you go on the tramcar.'

I left my kind aunt and uncle, Aunt Nancy muttering about men sticking together and saying, 'Now if your father touches you or as much as lays a finger on you, come to your uncle and me immediately. Remember that!'

I felt somewhat better going home than I had before I left home; I managed to have everything ready for the evening meal in spite of my throbbing head.

'Ann,' my father said, 'what did you do this afternoon?'

'I went to see my Aunt Nancy,' I stammered in confusion, knowing that he wouldn't be pleased about it. He looked at me sadly. 'I could wish, my dear, that you hadn't done that,' he said gently. He seemed to have trouble controlling his voice, and I thought I must have made him angry again. I wanted to cry. Why did I always say or do the wrong thing?

That night I could not get to sleep. I thought about my father's anger. Why had he lost his temper? Was it my fault? Uncle Henry said he had a lot to bear. What was it? How could I help if grown-ups insisted on talking in riddles? What a disappointing day it had been—everything went wrong. But the steak and kidney pudding was lovely, I knew, and it was hardly touched.

I made up my mind that I would never leave my father, whatever he did to me. I felt sure that it wouldn't have happened if Grannie had been there. She would only be gone three weeks and she had been away two weeks already. Next week she would be back and we would all be happy again. I couldn't manage everything all by myself. I needed my dear little Grannie.

6. Intrigue

ALTHOUGH my father had made it clear to everyone that my mother's name was never to be mentioned, Grannie spoke to me about her when we were alone. She received letters from her which Aunt Martha read to her on her weekly visits. And the odd parcel was delivered to her by the mid-morning post.

Once a week in the afternoons Aunt Martha called on Grannie. As they sat together Grannie cried over my mother and forgave her or condemned her as the mood took her. She kept all the letters and Aunt Martha read them to her so often that she must have known them all by heart. In the parcels were mostly sweets or hair ribbons or some other little gifts for us girls. Of course I knew where these little treats came from, but they were always given with strict instructions. 'Ann, don't tell your father,' and 'Don't say anything about your Aunt Martha being here this afternoon.'

I couldn't see why my father disliked Aunt Martha so much. She had three little girls of her own, our cousins, and, although they lived close by in a back street called 'Drudge Road', we seldom saw them. Our Grannie was their Grannie too, but they visited her by stealth and never when my father was at home.

Aunt Martha was always kind and helpful to me. 'Not much of a life for you, Ann,' she would say. 'You're missing all your youth, growing up.' I didn't quite understand this talk—how could I stop growing up? I would call to see her every week when I was shopping for Grannie or to give her some message that Grannie gave me to pass on to her in strictest secrecy. Grannie loved mystery and created intrigue out of the most innocent situations.

Aunt Martha was a 'drudge'—her road could have been named after her. As I approached the little house, two up and two down, plus a scullery or wash house, I could smell the boiling suds and clothes in the copper and see the steam billowing out the open scullery door. Aunt Martha took in washing to augment the pitiful pittance the country gave her for the loss of her husband in the War. When she wasn't washing she was out at the 'big house' cleaning, for a copper or two per morning. On her way home she would buy fish and chips for the children's dinner. I envied my cousins this 'high living'. My father would not allow such a delicacy in our house.

On wash days, three afternoons a week, after having been out cleaning all morning, Aunt Martha would be at the sink, her arms plunged up to the elbows in hot soapsuds and strong soda water guaranteed to take the skin off the hardiest hands and arms. She would be scrubbing, scrubbing and rubbing the soiled linen on a ridged dubbing board with the energy of an Amazon, her arms red as beetroot from the hot water, her wrists red raw.

The Dolly peg was another form of torture. It was a long length of wood, pronged at one end, which was plunged into the washing container standing on the floor, and manually rotated among the immersed clothes. I could never summon enough strength to turn this instrument, but Aunt Martha spun it round and backward and forward with apparent ease and expert gusto. She churned the clothes like a dairy maid churning butter; however, the smell was less pleasant.

The room leading from the wash house was the 'living' room. It was always festooned with clothes in the various stages of their tortuous ritual from wash tub to neatly folded and ironed finality. In bad weather it was as wet inside the house as outside, in spite of a cheery kitchen fire which did its best to dry the suspended garments and dispel the vapour.

In spite of all this Aunt Martha's kitchen was somehow cosy. She would find time to make a cup of tea and when not too 'behindhand' as she would say, read the tea leaves—sometimes my future was going to be better, and sometimes there was trouble ahead. She was an expert cook; she could make a little go a long way. Her rock buns were always delicious.

I would sit contentedly beside Aunt Martha's kitchen grate, munching her buns, drinking her tea, watching her ply the iron, while creases miraculously disappeared from shirts as they were expertly ironed, folded and packed in a laundry basket ready for collection. I ignored the steam running down the walls in little rivulets; an occasional drop of water would splash like rain from a dripping garment on the line strung across the kitchen from the huge built-in dresser. Drops would fall onto the kitchen table, kept scrupulously scrubbed white, or onto me as I sat there. But the kindness and comfort outweighed the discomfort. I never heard Aunt Martha complain of her lot. She did her best and accepted her role in the scheme of things.

I would leave her damp world and return to Grannie with a message that Aunt Martha would pop in one afternoon if she could spare the time, to have a chat and read to her, which I knew meant a session with 'The Letters'. Grannie looked forward to these visits as if Aunt Martha were Royalty.

I often wondered why Aunt Nancy in the neighbouring town, who was Aunt Martha's sister-in-law, never spoke to her. I could not understand why Aunt Nancy, as Grannie said, 'looked down' on Aunt Martha. Aunt Martha could not help being poor. Aunt Nancy would sometimes send Aunt Martha her cast-off clothes, as a great favour. I was usually the carrier of these charitable donations. She did not know these children, who were her nieces. The older I grew the more I found myself puzzled by grown-up behavior. My own father and my aunt would not recognize these three little girls whose father had died for his country, yet everyone talked about creating a land fit for heroes—only live ones, it seemed.

Uncle Henry, who had amassed a huge fortune from his flourishing marine engineer and boiler works, had been exempt from war service. Uncle Henry was a simple man with a memory like the memory of the proverbial elephant; his nickname was 'Old Data'. He never needed a diary: it was all stored away 'up top'. He made the money and my aunt and her three daughters spent it. My uncle's portrait hangs in the local marine gallery. To his family's disgust he was depicted in his boiler suit, with the added humiliation of holding a spanner in his hand. The picture of him in my aunt's drawing room was much more to her liking: he was wearing full Masonic regalia.

When Aunt Martha came to visit, always careful to leave before Father came home, she would say to me, 'Ann, your mother sends her love and hopes you are well and looking after the little girls and your brother.'

Sometimes my emotions would get the better of me, and I would burst out tempestuously, 'I don't want her to send me her love. Tell her to come home and look after her children herself; it is her job—not mine.'

I would run from the room amid all the talk of 'She should have done this' or 'He should have done so and so,' with accompanying tears from Grannie. I hated it all; I felt humiliated and deceived. When I was in this mood I wouldn't accept the little gifts she sent me. I was fighting against my imprisonment, the waste of my youth, my frustrations.

The summer came and with it shops along the sea front came to life with all their tatty, useless gifts. Hotels and restaurants reopened, bravely bedecked over all in gleaming fresh paint. All these places required seasonal staff; Aunt Martha forsook the Dolly tub and the wash tub, for higher, better employment with doubtless better pay. The little house was locked up all day, and the children were at school or being minded by a neighbour. The copper no longer belched forth its steam, the kitchen fire was dead. The clothes lines, free from their duties, danced and gyrated in the wind in the little concrete backyard. The kitchen looked unfamiliar through the clear kitchen window, shining bright in the summer sun and free from vapour. The sea breezes once again blew unchallenged round the house.

Grannie fretted at not seeing Aunt Martha, whose working hours left her no time for visits. I tried to cheer her up: I read the 'Deaths, Births and Marriages' column of the local paper over and over again until I felt I knew all the people mentioned. But it was the drama of the letters that Grannie missed. She could not tempt me to read them to her. She would get the box in which she kept them and turn them all over uselessly and give me appealing, pitiful looks. I felt sure she must know them all by heart already, she had heard them so many times. I longed for the Season to finish so that Aunt Martha would resume her drudgery at the washtub and her weekly visits as well.

It was a beautiful summer but the weeks dragged by gloomily.

Then one morning I heard a letter drop on the mat with a heavier thud than usual. Luckily Father had already left. I ran through the hall and picked it up. It was addressed to Grannie in my mother's round bold handwriting. I was seized by panic and began to tremble. Oh, what should I do? I held the letter against me as if it were a secret clutched close to my chest. Should I give it to Father to deliver to Grannie? No, that would be courting trouble. Should I hide it until Aunt Martha came to visit Grannie again? Should I take it straight away upstairs to Grannie who would cry and implore me to read it to her? How persuasive she could be, how she could bribe me, how easy it would be to give in. I did so need a pair of stockings—mine were laddered beyond repair. Why was life so difficult?

I dashed upstairs. Grannie was sitting up in bed having her first cup of tea. I handed her the letter without a word. Peering at it she said, 'It is from your mother, child. Open it and read it to me.'

I stood motionless, fighting my conflicting emotions. I longed to read it. But I had promised my father most solemnly that I would never read a letter, never write, never have any communication with my mother whatsoever.

'I can't, Grannie,' I cried in anguish. 'You know I promised never to read her letters.'

'You must,' said Grannie. 'There is no one else to read it to me. Come now, be a good girl, you won't be the loser. I will see you are rewarded. And don't worry about your father. He'll never know.' She held the letter out to me coaxingly.

'No, Grannie, I can't. It wouldn't be right. Daddy might ask me and I would have to lie to him.'

'I tell you he won't know—and what harm is there in a white lie to make your poor old Grannie happy?' She started to weep copiously. 'No one cares about a poor old half-blind woman,' she cried. 'I shall end my days in the Workhouse, my days will end in shame.'

Now the Workhouse was, as I thought in my ignorance of the world, the most dreaded of institutions. Grim tales were told of its inhumanity. No old person ever came out alive. And no one, according to Grannie, had a respectable burial. 'Just wheeled out on a cart or barrow and put in a hole,' she would declare. If ever she wanted to frighten me she had only to mention the Workhouse. Children who today are put 'in care' would in her day have been put in the Workhouse to work at a very tender age.

I jumped up and knelt on the bed, took my little Grannie in my skinny arms and rocked her soothingly to and fro.

'There, there, Grannie,' I wailed, weeping with her, 'No one will take you from us to the Workhouse. I will read your letter to you just this once.'

The Workhouse had won, as it always did and would, as she very well knew. Her tears quickly stopped as she listened to the letter relating the doings and comings and goings of her wayward daughter.

There was a ten shilling note in the pages. 'Now,' Grannie said, 'You shall have a whole shilling from this for yourself for reading to your poor old Grannie, and another shilling when you answer it for me. Was it worth making all that fuss about and upsetting yourself?'

The first letter was the hardest to resist. Others followed. I read and answered them. Grannie was not in the least troubled with conscience and felt happy in her false security.

If only I could justify my actions to myself. At night I would lie awake and hear my father, unable to sleep, walking about the house in his squeaking slippers. He had a lot on his mind—so too had I. If only I had the courage to go to him and confess my wickedness. He would surely understand that I was no match for Grannie and forgive me.

I opened my box with the seashells all around the top of the lid; I kept my hair ribbons in it. There were no less than three lovely new lengths: a black shiny satin, a soft pale blue watered silk (very fashionable) and a flaming scarlet silk which fell into folds and tied handsomely in a huge bow on the back of my head in a most becoming manner. In addition to this I now had two pairs of artificial silk stockings. All this was my reward from Grannie for being, as she said, 'a sensible good girl'. Gazing at my spoils with tears trickling down my cheeks, I lost all the joy of possession. I thought I knew how Judas, whom we heard so much about at Sunday School, felt with his thirty pieces of silver. I would have done anything to undo what I knew to be my wrongdoing.

I remember now Grannie's maxim which I think she applied to my father. 'If you have a good husband blind him in one eye. If you have a bad'un, blind him in both.' I never discovered to which category my father belonged, but then Grannie could change her mind according to her whim or to changing circumstance.

One morning the postman, for some reason, was early. The expected letter dropped with a sickening thud on the hall door mat. My father, who was about to leave the house, picked it up. As he looked at it the blood drained from his face. He stood absolutely still staring at the familiar writing. Suddenly he clutched the banisters and raced upstairs straight into Grannie's room without a knock or any other warning and closed the door behind him.

I listened at the foot of the stairs. I felt weak and sank onto the bottom stair, straining to hear. I expected Father to shout at Grannie—voices raised—but all was deathly quiet. Tears—perhaps of relief—were trickling down my face onto my clasped hands, unheeded. The silence was oppressive and ominous. Whatever my father was saying to Grannie, he was saying with restraint.

He came slowly, almost blindly down the stairs, not noticing me, crouched against the banisters. He staggered up the hall like a drunken man and let himself quietly out the front door.

I raced up the stairs to Grannie. She was hysterical, crying in what I thought of as her feeble, helpless voice.

'He has taken my letter,' she cried. 'He wouldn't give it to me. He says I must go away for a while, until he decides whether I can live here with you dear children, whether he dare let me stay to influence you against all his expressed wishes. He made it sound as if I was a criminal, instead of a poor old woman trying to do her best for four helpless, deserted children.

'Oh dear, what shall I do? What a cruel, wicked man your father is!'

That was too much for me.

'Grannie,' I cried, 'you know my Daddy is the best in the world. He is not cruel, he is not wicked!'

'Then why does he want to send me away from you all?' she cried, the tears chasing down her cheeks, which were pink despite her years, her eyes glistening china blue, moist and innocent. Who could stay cross with this little Dresden china figure?

'Come, Grannie darling, stop crying. I don't think Daddy will send you away from us. You must just obey his wishes, that's all. He isn't really hard at all,' I said. But I did not realize how hurt and angry my father was.

After this incident, so far as my father was concerned, I was sent to Coventry. He looked at me without seeing me, and ignored me unless it was absolutely necessary to speak to me. He bade me good-night stonily in response to my warm, eager good-night kiss. I tried to talk about the letter but he was too disappointed by my deceit to discuss it. He was polite to me, as if I were a servant in his house.

No punishment could have hurt me more. I cried myself to sleep. I fretted by day and lost my appetite. I adored my father: to be in disgrace with him was sheer torture for me. If I tried to speak to him he didn't hear, looked through me or answered only 'Yes' or 'No'.

Grannie pleaded headaches which she said were helped by copious nips from a medicinal liquid kept under her bed. As far as I could see, this liquid refreshment made her look flushed and only heightened her antipathy to my father. After she had been hiding in her bedroom for a week, my father summoned me to him.

'Ann,' he said, 'I wish you to take your Grannie to your Aunt Nancy next week and explain that I must review the conditions under which she can return here, if ever at all.'

'But Daddy,' I said, 'we cannot manage without Grannie. And oh! I love her and she doesn't want to go. Please don't send her away.'

My father looked at me coldly.

'You will do as I wish,' he said. As I made for the door, he added, 'I think I am the best judge of what is the right course for all of us.'

A week followed of preparations for Grannie's departure to live with her wealthy daughter. Her best black had to be brushed and hung on the line to air in the sun, and hopefully for the wind to blow away the smell of mothballs. This chore was particularly trying to me because I had an allergy to moth balls. My eyes would stream and I would sneeze violently. Grannie's blouse had to be refurbished: I expertly sewed round the inside of the neck half a yard of white frilling purchased at the haberdashery for a penny. Her bonnet of black silk fashioned on a buckram shape had to have new white silk ribbon pleating round the brim, to frame her little face, and the long white streamers had to be washed and ironed to tie, together with the black ones, under her chin. Her pension of five shillings, bestowed on the elderly by David Lloyd George, had to be transferred.

I collected this handsome sum for her every week after she had made her identifying X. It kept her in luxuries: toilet requisites like Icilma for her pink and white skin, Violet powder, often used as a quick substitute for a wash, and a little Mirchum or Yardley's Lavender Water to help the illusion of a wash. Then there was the medicinal nip from the local, and finally a tin of red salmon for Sunday night tea.

What was left went to bribe us children to run errands for her or hide little indiscretions committed during the week either by her or by me. It was a very happy arrangement for all concerned. My brother, being a boy, and Grannie being pro-male as most women were in her day, usually wheedled more than his fair share of coppers out of Grannie for his hare-brained mechanical experiments. I am sure David Lloyd George would have been most upset if he had known the uses that some of his generosity was put to. I occasionally came in for a major share to buy a pair of artificial silk stockings which, as we have seen, helped in my downfall. These stockings were an indistinct beige color, with cotton toes and heels. The artificial silk was coarse and shiny and reached to just below the knee. From there up the stocking was cotton stretching up the thigh to be secured by clumsy metal suspenders from an uncomfortable corset, or by wide elastic garters guaranteed to encourage varicose veins. For all this one's legs, because of the shiny texture, looked as if they were encased in glass. These stockings were a luxury and of course a status symbol. Mercifully, dresses at that time were below the knee and if one sat decorously not a hint was visible of the hideous cotton tops. The drop-waistline then in fashion made things a little difficult because it was inclined to pull tight around the wearer's bottom when she was sitting down.

Grannie had none of these problems. She was Victorian in her dress to her dying day. She wore only black out of respect for the memory of Grandfather, who had been a drunk and knocked her around, but who was now a dead Saint. In those days liquor was cheap and men drank heavily. Grannie wore black from her high-necked blouse to her ankle-length skirt. Her little feet—size two—were always encased in button boots. On the subject of her underwear I will draw a veil—suffice it to say that it made her look buxom, but divested of the layers of it she was tiny with a wasp waist in spite of having given birth to twenty-one children.

On the occasions when Grannie visited her daughter, she did not travel by tram as if she were going to market, but in style in a hansom cab. Mr Palmer, the local cabbie, made his living, for better or worse, with his grey mare and black hansom cab—open in summer, closed in winter. The Cabbie sat high up in front, his broad back to his customers. This Cabbie was so broad that he had almost as much difficulty in heaving himself off and on his seat as he had in getting Grannie settled. He would push Grannie none too gently from behind as she negotiated the three steep steps into the cab, fussing over whether modesty was being outraged by the exhibition of an ankle or an inch of leg. After he had disposed of her, he grasped the sides of the cab and heaved himself laboriously into his seat. With what breath he had left, he would shout, 'Whoa up there!' and crack his whip. I sat beside Grannie and, because of the length of her proposed stay, this time her tin trunk was on the opposite seat.

We bowled along the highway, Grannie bowing and waving as if she was Royalty. The break in routine had momentarily revived her spirits; she appeared to forget that she might be trotting out of our lives. Small boys appeared from nowhere and cheered the old lady. They always loved to see a horse-drawn cab.

The drive was pleasant on a nice day, along the High Street with shops interspersed with chapels of all denominations, and one or two prosperous merchants' big houses set back from the road in their own grounds. The High Street rose gently to meander through smart terraces of houses standing high on one side of the road with an uninterrupted view of the river. Beyond, between the river and the North Sea, was a stretch of land called the Denes. I believe it is now a racecourse.

As we clip-clopped along this stretch of gently rising road with its uninterrupted view of the North Sea, I was reminded of a Zeppelin raid which took place near here during the War. The Zeppelin was shot down in flames over the water; crowds had gathered, attracted by the sound of gunfire, to watch the battle. I wondered how men could set fire to each other and laugh and cheer at each other's agony.

Another mile and we came to the Halfway House. Here Mr Palmer paused to refresh his horse and himself, probably with the tip that Grannie gave him in advance in order to take priority over his other customers whenever she needed him. My aunt would give him the standard amount when he delivered Grannie—not knowing, of course, that the 'old rascal' had already drunk his first tip. Grannie and I would sit patiently waiting outside the Halfway House—so called because it was situated about halfway between the two seacoast towns.

Grannie would look shocked if the Cabbie offered to fetch her a drink. A surreptitious nip in the bedroom for medicinal reasons was one thing; drinking for pleasure on the public highway was quite another matter. It was years before the nicety of the matter resolved itself for me.

The road now ran level for almost three miles with the river, past an ugly enormous gasworks which exhaled its obnoxious smell for miles around, and timber yards which stretched from the Halfway House all along the quayside to the town bridge which spanned the river connecting the two towns. Huge stacks of timber from Norway, Sweden and other foreign countries were offloaded on the quayside and stacked in identical lengths to form huge cubes and pyramids, yellowish-brown and with sawn ends exuding the indescribable sweet scent of new hewn wood. On our walk home from school along the riverside (a forbidden route) these timber stacks provided a wonderful playground for us. The odd lengths jutting out afforded steps for climbing to the top: the gaps were a challenge to long jumpers and a loose plank made a super see-saw. Climbing or playing there was extremely dangerous, but an irresistible challenge. My brother was winded from a fall on more than one occasion, and he sustained abrasions, bumps and bruises.

'Oh hurry, hurry, Mr Palmer!' Grannie was terrified when we came to the bridge that we should be dropped through the gap into the water or taken up skywards when the bridge went up. And this time we just made it. The men were dragging the heavy chain across the margin to stop any more traffic passing. A ship was toot-tooting and whistling in impatience, its gigantic funnels reaching nearly as high as the upturned bridge. It would pass through and tie up the other side of the bridge to do whatever it had set out to do, and then turn about under the bridge again and thence up the river and out into the North Sea. People cheered as the ship passed through, either in relief because the bridge would slowly wind down so that its two sections would meet and clinch, or in admiration for what was in those days an impres-sive engineering feat.

We didn't stop to cheer or admire. After the bridge the river front was not commercialised except for sea-sonal catering for small pleasure craft. Our horse clip-clopped through the crowds along the quayside, across the Town Hall square, through the banking zone, past the smart shops and into the street leading directly to the sea front, where visitors flocked in their thousands from the Midlands, the North and London, to be housed, fed and entertained. Some would have their annual total immersion.

The road along the sea front was wide and compar-atively new. Tram cars ran its full length on rails which added to the hazard of our progress. The Cabbie had to keep a tight rein on the mare, who whinnied from time to time in protest at the weight of traffic and the general level of noise. We hugged the kerbside and jogged along at a leisurely pace. Grannie, enjoying the sea air and the sights, was in no hurry to arrive at her destination.

Hotels and boarding houses lined the route facing the sea; ice cream parlours, mostly owned by Italian experts in the field, dance halls, ballrooms, and amusement arcades abounded. The Old Hippodrome drew crowds in wet or fine weather with its circus and the theatre held its own with much loved musical comedies of the day like *No No Nanette* and *Rose Marie.* People had to go out and look for entertainment in those days.

Ornamental gardens, concrete slopes and paths led down to the wide stretch of inviting golden sand where deck chairs were hired out at a penny an hour. Woe betide you if you were caught cheating the Corporation; honesty was indeed the best policy then. There wasn't an inch to spare on the sands: parked at the water's edge were beach cabins, from which the population emerged covered in beach attire from neck to toe; only the arms and legs to the knee could be bared. Sweethearts could lie side by side, but at a respectable distance from each other. No contact was made, at least in broad daylight.

We jogged past the magnificent pier jutting well out into the sea. An impressive glass floral hall, like the Crystal Palace, was on the pier; tea dances were held here during the week and dances once a week. Romances blossomed there to the strains of 'The Sheikh of Araby'; the heavily scented air from the massed flowers added to the heady atmosphere.

Finally we went at right angles to the sea down the avenue where my aunt lived, as befitted her station in life, in a magnificent stone Victorian house. Between pillars an imposing flight of concrete steps led to the front door.

The door was opened by the little maid-of-all-work in her afternoon black, with frilly white apron and cap. She left the Cabbie, who had pulled the bell, standing on the step while she went through the hall to inform her mistress.

'Mother dear! How are you?' my aunt gushed. 'Do let me help you down.'

Grannie prepared to negotiate the three tricky steps from the cab to the pavement, her progress hampered by her umbrella, which she refused to relinquish. The Cabbie stood by, waiting patiently. He looked capable of picking Grannie up bodily, running up the steps and depositing her in the hall. My aunt assisted Grannie up the steps, and called back over her shoulder imperiously, 'Bring the luggage, Mr Palmer, please!' But Mr Palmer could not leave his horse. So Lizzie, the maid, and I remained with the horse, while Grannie and her tin trunk containing all her worldly possessions were duly installed in the house. I was to return alone with the Cabbie, so as not to waste the return fare.

'Aunt,' I said timidly, 'my father says you will have to keep Grannie this time until he decides whether he can take her back or not.'

'Oh, that's disgraceful,' my aunt said. 'After all she has done for you children, he has no right to turn her out like this. He is a cruel man.'

'Oh no, he isn't,' I cried, in defence of my father. 'Grannie and I deceived him and made him angry. He will have Grannie back, I know he will.'

My aunt looked hard at me. 'You don't understand,' she said. 'Now stop crying and kiss Grannie good-bye; the cab is waiting.'

I clung to Grannie and she to me. She kept telling me to look after the little ones and come to see her next week. She slipped a silver sovereign into my hand.

I kissed my aunt who stood on the doorstep watching my departure. I sobbed all the way home. I didn't notice the crowds and the gaiety of the sea front which Grannie and I had shared a short while before. I felt bereft of love. What was my life going to be like, with a father who had withdrawn his tenderness, understanding and affection from me, and sent my dear little Grannie away with her wealth of love for us all?

I arrived home to an empty house; the fire was nearly out. I set the tea table and awaited the family.

'Did you give your aunt my message?' my father inquired coldly.

'Yes,' I whispered, barely restraining my tears. That night I went to kiss my father good-night, but he averted his face. I was still unforgiven. A curt 'Good-night, Ann' was my dismissal.

Oh, please God, let my daddy love me again and send my Grannie back to us, I prayed fervently, while I was sobbing myself to sleep.

When Grannie went for her prolonged holiday I had been out of school for a year. During that period I had only sixpence a week pocket money, out of which I had to save enough to buy my clothes. My wants were very limited, since I had no friends and seldom went anywhere. My clothes now consisted of my cousins' cast-offs adapted to my skinny underdeveloped figure. I hadn't a nice coat and I had fretted all spring about how I could get one before another winter. I was determined that I was not going to wear the hideous khaki nursing sister's coat discarded by my father's sister after the War. It was serviceable, warm and well-cut—virtues which seemed disadvantages to me, especially since I hated its style and color.

Finally I hit on a solution. I could earn the money by getting a summer job. I had discussed it with Grannie and she had agreed that she and Alice, the sister next to me in age, could manage for at least the school summer holidays. It was another little secret Grannie and I shared; not a word was breathed to anyone else, least of all my father. One morning by first post, the notice arrived informing me that I had the job I had applied for as a waitress in the cafe. My sister had just started her summer holidays. I showed her the letter.

'What shall I do?' I asked her. 'What will Father say, will he let me go?'

Alice was always the most practical of us.

'Of course you will have to go,' she said. 'You have given your word.' And she gave me an assurance that she would be all right and could manage. 'You will have to show Father the notice,' she said, 'when he comes home.'

'Father,' I said, in considerable trepidation, 'I have got a job as a waitress on the sea front.' I pushed the notice in front of him.

He looked startled, and read the notice. He looked up. 'Well, you have arranged to do this work. No doubt your Grandmother had a hand in it. Now you must honour your word.'

'But I thought Grannie would be here to look after things. How can Alice manage on her own?'

'You should have thought about that, and consulted me before you undertook this,' my father said reproachfully. As I was about to speak again, he stopped me. 'Your sister will manage. I have nothing more to say to you.'

Alice wasn't very pleased. 'Some holiday for me,' she said ruefully.

I bribed her with sixpence a week out of my earnings. And to my brother who was home from boarding school on holiday I promised threepence a week if he would help my sister to wash up and run errands. He agreed readily.

I had to have a black dress. The restaurant supplied black and white checked aprons which had to be laundered fresh each day. The tables had black and white checked tablecloths to match. It was a clean, spruce restaurant. I rummaged through Grannie's drawer, looking through the few things she had left behind. Her black aprons were there, because Aunt would not allow her to wear anything so undignified as an apron. I made myself a short-sleeved magyar dress out of one of these black sateen aprons. Luckily I had black shoes and I bought a pair of black lisle stocking for threepence; later I graduated to black artificial silk after I earned my first two days' tips.

It was sheer luxury to have a bed and bedroom to myself now that Grannie was gone. I could have the window open at night, which Grannie never could abide on account of the draught. I opened up the chimney breast and took out all the newspaper packing which stopped the air flow. The room smelt fresh and clean. Bottles were retrieved from under the bed and thrown away, along with odds and ends of bronchial mixtures and cough elixirs. I scrubbed and polished the linoleum, laundered the curtains and nets and cleaned the bed-spread. To me the room was fresh and beautiful. No odour reminiscent of poor little Grannie lingered, and not a trace of her belongings except for the clothes she had left behind bundled into the bottom drawer in the chest, in case she came back to us and asked for them. With the window open the room was noisy: there were barnyard noises from Piffins next door and the early cock crew right under my window. But I was so exhausted with my daily work that these things did not disturb my sleep.

I soon discovered that being a waitress was no picnic. It seemed as though the entire population of the Midlands and London hissed 'Miss! Miss!' at me from early morning until late at night. The early morning bathers, stalwarts all, came shivering and with teeth chattering, calling for hot drinks, after their struggles with the North Sea waves before the sun—if any—had had a chance to take the night chill off the water. The breakfast queues were impatient; everyone was starving because the un-accustomed sea air gave them an appetite; the mid-morning revellers were parched and eager for cool drinks and buns. By lunchtime the crowds for sausage and mash and fish and chips took the place by storm. Tables were too close together; chairs were too skimpy for their occupants. A waitress, I learned, had to be a cross between a juggler and a contortionist with a saintly disposition, and to be quick with it, too. Forgetful children left spades and pails in odd places for unsuspecting waitresses to trip over—which could mean, I learned very early in my career, the loss of half a week's wages in damages. The wages were poor, but the tips were good, especially for girls quick on their feet, like me. I was a fast learner and soon discovered how to deal with situations. Grannie's devious approach to unpleasant dilemmas served me well. 'Miss! Miss!' rang in my ears at night when I was trying to relax.

'What you doing tonight, Miss?' some lout would ask, trying to slip an arm about my waist.

I soon learned not to shrink away from these advances, which only made the applicant bolder, but to answer tartly: 'Busy serving louts like you.' That soon dampened their ardour!

I learned to stack cups and saucers professionally so that they would not fall off a tray. I learned how to scrape butter on and off bread economically, to slap the minimum of filling into a sandwich to ensure my employer's continued prosperity, and how to handle a boiling tea urn and fill small teapots from cauldrons without endangering my own and others' lives. I learned to anticipate a customer's wishes before a word was spoken, to tot up as quickly as any racecourse bookie, and to disregard headaches, fatigue or aching feet and hunger. Our mealtimes were chaotic: snacks snatched on the premises according to the demands of the trade. We never sat down to eat or drink. Speed was the essence!

When the shop closed, the floors had to be swept, a task often enlivened by the surreptitious discovery and pocketing of the odd coin. Tables had to be re-set for breakfast the following morning and the kitchen left tidy with everything in its place.

It would normally be ten o'clock before I got home; I had left the house at seven a.m. It was a long day for anyone, much more an inexperienced fifteen year old. All through those long two months my father scarcely spoke to me. I fretted and felt the lack of his esteem and affection. I didn't take to being in disgrace. Alice was really too young to talk to seriously. I missed my Grannie and her misguided advice.

One night toward the end of the two months, I came home particularly footsore, tired and disheartened. As I plunged my feet into the soothing bowl of hot water my sister had ready for me, and looked at my swollen ankles, I wondered if I had ruined my feet for life. My back felt bent in two and ached from carrying the heavily laden trays. No contender for the walk from Lands End to John O' Groats could have more aching feet. The hunchback of Notre Dame could not have felt more humped.

'Am I straight?' I asked Alice, bracing myself.

'Of course, silly,' she replied. 'You're quite normal.'

She dried my feet for me and rubbed them with methylated spirits to harden the skin. Any little scratch on my feet stung and made my eyes water. My arms felt too heavy to raise so that I could pull my dress over my head; I thought my wrists would snap at any moment. My sister helped me to undress and get to bed. She brought me a glass of hot milk to soothe me to sleep. 'You will feel better in the morning.' she said.

I hobbled to work the next day and struggled some-how through the next week, which was my last. I took my last week's pay, together with my tips—a princely sum to me—and said goodbye to my boss and work-mates with very few regrets. I had achieved my object, but at what cost! I felt I would never be in one sound piece again. I made one resolve—never again to be a waitress!

My sister and I walked boldly into the town's most fashionable ladies wear shop. I will never forget it: the little round gilt chairs which looked too delicate to hold a human being, the lofty ceilings and cornices and friezes picked out in gold against white walls. There were beau-tiful full-length cheval mirrors surmounted by golden birds with outspread wings. The departments were sep-arated by golden Corinthian pillars. The tall windows were draped with cream satin curtains looped back half-way down their length by gold cords. The wall-to-wall carpeting was cream-colored to match the curtains.

The assistant eyed Alice and me a little suspiciously; we were not her usual type of clientele. She had a su-perior manner.

'I would like to try the coat with the fur collar in the window,' I said firmly.

'But we 'ave plenty of models in the salon,' she said. She had a foreign accent. No, I said, they would not do. I had set my heart on the one on display on the elegant wax figure in the window.

She said she would 'ave to see the shop walker, an imposing figure in pin-striped trousers and a tail coat with a white carnation in the buttonhole. He looked as if he were just off to a wedding. He came forward to speak with the assistant, never once condescending to look at Alice or me. By this time we had sat down very gingerly on the fragile-looking gilt chairs. I exchanged a glance with Alice, who had a sense of humour all her own. I think the situation was beginning to capture her imagination. I was a little nervous about her; she was quite capable of deliberately disturbing the decorum of the shop. Finally the shop walker said loudly, 'Well, if Madam insists' and walked away, with his nose in the air. I loved being called 'Madam'. It made up for all the indignities of the hissed 'Miss! Miss!'

As we sat on our spindly chairs my sister whispered to me that it was like being in church. Secretly I agreed with her but I tossed my head in what I thought was a sophisticated gesture, and said, 'Shh, silly!'

The coat was even lovelier than I had dared dream. I snuggled into its warmth and stroked the fur collar, which hugged my neck and shoulders. I felt the soft silk of the lining. All the world would recognise it when I wore it because it had been in the shop window and it was the best coat in the shop. Alas, it was a little too long and too wide in the shoulders.

'Madam can 'ave eet shortened; I will call the tailoress.'

She came and crawled all round me on the floor with a mouthful of pins. Yes, it certainly looked better pinned up. As for the shoulders, I expected to mature one day and fill out; then they would fit. I had the hem turned up rather than cut; no one was going to take a cut out of my coat. And what if later I were to grow tall? I hadn't budgeted for the extra expense of alterations, but I knew it was worth it. The only alternative was to wait and see if I did grow taller. I handed over my three one pound notes with the air of a duchess.

And my thrift was rewarded: the coat never did wear out. The hem was eventually let down—whether because I grew or because of the dictates of fashion, I don't recall. I revelled in every moment of the coat's life and I always felt that the agonies of waitressing had been well worth it.

No salon in all my years of shopping has ever impressed me as that first one did. And no garment has ever given me as much joy and pride as that coat.

7. Relations

By now the school holiday had ended and my two sisters were back at school and my brother had returned to boarding school. Father had not yet relented. Grannie was still banished and braving it out at my aunt's.

I was alone in the house all day, except for luncheon when Father was home for less than an hour. I felt lonely and depressed. My life seemed an endless round of scrubbing, cleaning, polishing and washing, not to mention cooking. I lost my appetite and my spirits. My father still withheld his affection and showed no sign of recognising my existence apart from making sure that I attended to his creature comforts. I saw nothing before me but long years of domesticity. In those days it was the lot of the eldest daughter in a family where the father was bereaved to take over the responsibility of bringing up the younger brothers and sisters and to forego her own wishes for happiness.

I was doomed to be an Old Maid, the butt of music hall jokes, the 'rubbing rag' for all the family. It wasn't as if my mother was dead; she had deserted me. In that moment, crying into the roller towel hanging on the back door, I resented my mother; my love and adoration evaporated. Why couldn't she and my father make up their silly quarrel and my father have her home so that I could go out to work of some kind—teaching or secretarial work, which seemed to me to be the height of respectability? I was like Cinderella, among the sackcloth and ashes. I felt deprived, and I wallowed in my misery.

I missed Grannie; she would understand and comfort me—at least she would be there to talk to me. She could be trying, but if she would only come back I would forgive her little bullying ways; her annoyance when I failed to do some household task to her liking.

At last my father noticed my lack of appetite and lethargy.

'Eat your dinner,' he said. He could never understand anyone 'pingling', as he put it, over their food. 'Aren't you well? You must pull yourself together.' I began to weep forlornly. 'What is the matter with you?'

I didn't answer. 'Come, come, my dear,' he said, patting my head. 'It can't be as bad as all that.' At his touch and the first kind words I had had from him for months, my tears came like a flood.

'Oh Daddy,' I sobbed, all my pent-up emotions centred on one desire, 'I am so lonely in the house. When can we have Grannie back?'

My father looked startled. 'I had no idea you were

unhappy,' he said. 'I will give the matter my careful thought. How long has your Grandmother been gone?'

It seemed like an incredible question to me. Hadn't he missed her? I longed to shout, 'Years!' But instead I said meekly, 'I don't know for sure.'

I couldn't wait for my sisters to come home so that I could tell them the good news. They too had missed their Grannie, particularly my youngest sister, the baby of the family. She liked to sit on a little stool at Grannie's feet, contented just with her presence. Every night she had submitted to having her long dark hair brushed and screwed up into tortous paper twists so that the next morning she could have fat sausage curls. I could never do them right for her as Grannie could.

'Guess what!' I said as they entered the house and before they could answer, 'Grannie is coming back! Father promised me.'

I felt a wave of enthusiasm surge over me. I polished and cleaned so that everything would be spick and span. In spite of Grannie's cataracts she could see where I hadn't cleaned properly. In my estimation she was a hard taskmaster. I think her degree of blindness depended at times on how much she wanted to see; she was undoubtedly contrary.

I waited impatiently for my father to give me permission to fetch Grannie. I hoped he hadn't forgotten, but I did not dare risk his displeasure by suggesting such a lapse on his part. His word was his bond. So I had no choice but to wait.

Aunt Martha had now finished her seasonal job and she wasn't quite so busy as she had been cleaning and washing for other people. She was a little better off financially, too, because she no longer spent with abandon what she earned. Necessity is a good teacher. I went to bring her the good news.

'Grannie is coming back soon,' I told her.

'How soon?' she asked.

'I don't know. Father hasn't given a day, but he has promised.' And I told her how it all happened.

'I'm glad for you,' she said. 'You need someone for company. You should go out and make friends, Ann. You are alone far too much for a girl of your age.' She looked at me and sighed heavily.

'I would like to give Grannie a surprise,' I said. 'I would like to spring clean our bedroom.'

Over her rock cakes and cup of tea I questioned her about paper hanging, and she agreed to come and help me and show me how it was done. In my new-found interest in the house now Grannie was coming back, it seemed to me it was neglected and needed a face-lift. The only problem was financial—things were at a low ebb at this particular period after the War.

My aunt advised me to choose a small patterned paper in the interests of matching and of economy. She ran an expert eye over the room and assured me that the ceilings were all lofty in the big old house so it would take at least seven rolls to cover the bedroom, if we didn't have an accident or waste any.

A decorators' emporium across the river was well known for its cut-price wallpaper. 'Cheap and Cheerful' was its motto. Armed with the savings from a week or two's housekeeping, I walked the three miles to the ferry and crossed the river for a halfpenny fare. The shop, called Rudmans, was not far and I was soon rejoicing in selecting from the masses of patterns displayed for me by a very amiable young man. At last I made up my mind: a sweet red rosebud between lines of blue forget-me-nots with just the right amount of foliage was simple enough, I felt, not to present any problems.

'Can we send it for Madam?' asked the young assistant. 'And would Madam like the edges trimmed for another threepence the lot?' Madam would dearly have loved to answer 'Yes' but what an extravagance when all one needed were a pair of sharp scissors and a steady hand and a good eye—which I was not sure I had.

'No thank you,' I said. 'I will take it now. I want to use it tomorrow.'

I staggered out of the shop with a bundle of papers nearly as big as myself. The return journey was tiring, but I felt triumphant. The paper had cost me three-penny half pence a roll, plus one penny for my ferry fare to fetch it, I needed at least one pound of flour to make the paste, and I calculated two shillings would just about cover the total outlay to repaper Grannie's bed-room. My aunt said I had done well, but she suggested that the ceiling really ought to be whitewashed before I began the papering.

This entailed an unlooked-for expense of twopence for a block of whiting; I had to borrow the money from the fund set aside weekly to pay the baker. This put me in arrears with him, but the baker was understanding and somehow I managed to catch up the following week.

My sisters loved the paper and helped me trim the edges; they had great fun with the discarded trim-mings. I thought how much Grannie was going to love the paper too; she loved anything that reminded her of the country. I forgot the poor little darling was nearly blind.

The first step was to strip the old wallpaper which clung tenaciously to the wall as it had for years. 'Put plenty of water on the wall and the paper will peel off,' my aunt said. I threw buckets of ice cold water up on the walls. I soaked myself, the floor was swimming and even the bed did not escape. There must be an easier way, I thought; I gave up in despair and went to bed in a very damp room. But the next morning I found to my joy that the paper had absorbed the moisture and peeled off the wall as easily as if I were peeling an orange.

Next came the ceiling. I felt very insecure on top of the stepladder, a bucket of whitewash hooked over my bent arm; I had to stand on tiptoe and stretch my other arm to the limit to reach the ceiling. I was most uncomfortable and I discovered it was a race to slap the whitewash on the ceiling quickly enough so that it would not dry and lose the demarcation line. I had to go over a few places I had missed when I had taken a much-needed rest. The following day operations had to be suspended whilst I recovered from a stiff neck and a headache.

The room now looked much worse than before I had started. The whitewash had splattered over everything; I prayed the brass bed wasn't ruined. It took me a whole week to clean it and restore the room to its normal condition.

The test of success was to hang the paper without a fold or crease, with the edges matching all the way down, rosebud to rosebud and no gaps, not forgetting the forget-me-nots. I chased up and down the steps all the morning, trying to make the paper stay at the top whilst I manoeuvred it into position at the bottom; but all I had to show for this effort was a whole length parted into two in the middle. With determination bred of despair, I used one torn piece over the chimney breast and the other over the door lintel; I thought this was a clever and economical soution until Aunt Martha pointed out that it might not match up as we went round the room. Luckily Aunt came to help me all the next day. The paper seemed to hang on the wall just where she willed it. She was patient with me and allowed me to stick down one piece by the side of the window where the curtains would hide it. It was hard to believe that ordinary paper with a little paste brushed onto it could be so fragile.

Speed and as little handling as possible was the secret of successful paperhanging, I learned.

With the room redecorated, cleaned and refurbished, Aunt took the curtains and counterpane to wash for me. I was exhausted but triumphant and eagerly approached my father.

'Daddy,' I said, 'when can I fetch Grannie home?'

'You may fetch her next week. I will make the necessary arrangements with your aunt,' my father said. 'You can order the cab.'

'Been a long stay away the old lady has had this time,' said Mr Palmer suspiciously. I didn't answer. At the appointed hour on the appointed day I arrived to fetch Grannie home. She was waiting in the hall; the front door was open. Aunt Nancy had it all organised. Grannie's tin trunk was ready at her feet. As I got down from the cab and ran up the steps her little face puckered up and the ever-ready tears brimmed over.

'Oh Ann,' she cried, 'you have come at last. Thank God you have come!'

At the sound of my voice my aunt appeared in the hall.

'Now Mother,' she said, 'don't for goodness sake be so dramatic. You have been happy here with us, haven't you? I am sure we have all done what we thought best for you.'

But I secretly felt that I knew better than my aunt how to make Grannie happy.

'Good-bye, Nancy,' Grannie said. 'Give my love to Henry and say goodbye for me. And good-bye, Lizzie.' She pressed something into the little maid's hand as she helped Grannie climb, none too steadily, into the cab.

The little maid-of-all-work looked at Grannie with her big sad eyes full of affection. I wondered if she was like me and got a bit fed up doing chores in the house. She couldn't be much older than I was, I guessed. I think she was an orphan from a Home.

When Father came home Grannie was sitting in her chair next to the Grandfather clock. Oddly enough no one had sat in that chair all the while Grannie was away. It was a mute protest of her absence.

'Welcome back, Mother,' my father said. He went up to Grannie and kissed her. All was forgiven. My cup overflowed; Grannie, I vowed to myself, must never leave us again. When the two girls came home from school they would not leave her side. My little sister Laura, who was her pet, sat on her low stool at Grannie's feet. Grannie kept patting her head and calling her beautiful—which she was.

What a celebration tea we had! A tin of red salmon (no matter that it was bought 'on tick'), Grannie's favourite tea. I had made some cakes especially and there was black currant home-made jam and raspberry jelly— quite a feast. We were all so happy, we thought our happiness could never end again.

In bed that night I snuggled up to Grannie's warm little body. It had been cold, all alone in the enormous bed. I even welcomed Grannie's habit of piling up her voluminous petticoats over the counterpane for extra warmth. There was something homely and comforting about these familiar garments; I had missed them. What if she blocked up the chimney again and hoarded bottles of drops of this and that under the bed? She was back to comfort us all and give us the love which we had craved.

Gradually we gleaned little bits of information about life as it was lived across the water. Everything was done according to a routine. Grannie's breakfast was brought up to her on a tray by Lizzie every morning—a luxury she could have dispensed with, since she was not an expert tray handler and accidents were considered to be unpardonable. Then, among other things, my aunt was bent on improving Grannie's concept of personal cleanliness. Aunt was very proud of the new bathroom which had just been installed in the house, with hot and cold running water. At that time very few houses had bathrooms—especially older houses. Actually none but the really fastidious considered a bathroom a real necessity. Aunt Nancy decided that Grannie should enjoy this luxury in spite of the poor little thing's protests that she would catch her death of cold. Aunt more or less forced Grannie into the bathroom, undressed her and somehow got her into a bathful of hot water. The shock of all that water coming in contact with Grannie's body at once—not to mention the shock to her modesty—was disastrous. She was confined to her bed with shock and a cold for a week after the experiment. Aunt did not repeat it. As she told us about it, Grannie shuddered and trembled. To her it was a far more undignified experience than having any one of her twenty-one children, including the twins. Her daughter declared that Grannie was not really ill at all after the immersion—it was all her imagination.

Years later when I was living with my husband in a country village, I was reminded of Grannie. A farm labourer who had had an accident and was rushed to hospital told us that the nurses washed him all over with 'solid boiling water'. He never forgot that assault on his manhood.

Another small incident upset Grannie, who had always been a confirmed chapel goer. My aunt's two youngest daughters attended the convent high school and eventually became Roman Catholics. Aunt was expecting a visit from the priest and she told Grannie that when he came she was to address him not as 'Mister' but as 'Father'.

'Indeed I shall do nothing of the sort; he is not my

father—he's nothing to me. I am not a Catholic or a Roman!' the old lady said with spirit.

An angry argument ensued, but Grannie called the priest 'Mister' and I don't suppose he was at all bothered by it.

Then there was Grannie's nightcap. At an appointed time it was punctually measured out and poured from the cut glass decanter on the sideboard, diluted with hot water and one lump of sugar and—worst of all—drunk in front of everybody—nothing surreptitious about it at all. It definitely did not taste the same as a quiet nip from the bottle hidden under the bed, in the privacy of her own bedroom. In fact Grannie didn't think the grade of liquor was as good as the one from the pub across the way, and the measure was a mean one, and Aunt certainly spoiled it by diluting it with water. Even when Grannie suffered a mild heart attack she was allowed only a carefully measured teaspoonful which had no taste at all. She didn't hold with such meanness, especially when people had plenty of money.

Aunt Martha found these stories very amusing. She had brought Grannie six pennyworth of 'the hard stuff' to welcome her home—a thoughtful gift gratefully received.

When Aunt Nancy and Uncle Henry had company, Grannie said, wine was served at dinner. A watchful eye was kept on Grannie because a drop too much of wine made her very talkative or sometimes sad enough to weep. When she was talkative, she would regale the company with stories of her thirty years of 'setting' the market with the best pork sausages to be had anywhere in town. Aunt Nancy was not happy with these reminiscences. 'You know,' said Grannie, with a twinkle in her eye, 'they would make any excuse to bundle me off to bed as soon as the meal was over. Ashamed of their own flesh and blood they are!' There was no doubt that

Grannie could be difficult, but we were never ashamed of her; she belonged to us.

Time passed and soon winter was upon us. Grannie developed bronchitis. The doctor said she must be confined to bed, but he was rather taken aback when he discovered that there was no one but me to look after her. Aunt Martha came in to help whenever she had time to spare and relieve me of Grannie's washing. Aunt Nancy, when she heard of her mother's illness, came to visit her, cosily enveloped in musquash fur. She handed me a parcel and said, 'Now Ann, I want you to see that your Grannie eats all this; it is not for anyone else. Warm the broth and give Mother the chicken a little at a time, and make sure she eats all the breast.'

My father was not pleased when I told him what instructions Aunt had left.

Aunt Emily from the country did rather better. She came laden with fresh farm produce and stayed the whole day. Between us we blanket bathed Grannie. Aunt was quite professional and made the room spick and span. She even provided a vase of lovely country flowers to brighten the room. Aunt left with lots of good advice and promised to come the following week, which she did. She was an enormous woman, not so much height as width and puffed a good deal as she set about her work. My father rather unkindly likened her to an upholstered sofa, in her patterned velvet dress, and said that all that weight was bad for her, which proved correct. She died very suddenly without any warning, of a heart attack.

But my aunts sympathised with me; we all agreed that I, a mere young girl, should not have the sole responsibility of nursing an old lady of eighty. But neither was prepared to offer an alternative or any real help until my father forced the issue.

Grannie was wonderfully resilient and recovered as

the weather improved. Luckily coal was cheap and we always kept a good fire in the kitchen and the dining room, which was our living room. However the bedrooms were freezing; I remember undressing as a kind of feat of endurance.

My aunt from the country had suggested that it might do me good to spend Easter with her family, if Grannie was well enough to spare me by then. Alice was coming up to fourteen years old and could look after the house during her school holidays with Grannie's guidance. My brother was spending Easter with my father's parents; he was their favourite. They were not fond of me because I 'favoured' my mother too much—an expression which I found incomprehensible.

So with a change of clothes in a light Gladstone bag and with high hopes I set off for a week in the country. I had to take the tram car to the neighbouring town across the river, and walk a mile to the station. It was about a sixteen mile trip to my aunt's village and the train stopped at every little station, where there was much shouting and slamming of doors by passengers and porters alike. The engine had to whistle and chug, chug to get up steam to its maximum speed, only to give up with hissing and screeching of brakes as another little station hove shortly into view.

My jolly, hearty uncle was waiting at the station to meet me; he lifted me into the pony trap as if I were a little girl again and tossed my bag in after me as he took up the reins. The pony trotted easily along the country lanes to their house. It was a warm, balmy spring day. The trees were in their early fresh green leaf. We were surrounded by the wonders of nature's awakening in the countryside. We passed the bluebell wood I remembered so well from my childhood; its blue competed with the clear blue of the sky. I sensed the smell of the primroses and violets hidden in the hedgerows. My aunt's house came into sight, surrounded on every side by beds of daffodils, as it always was at Eastertime. The flowers seemed to bloom each year to be ready for the churches and chapels of the surrounding villages. Every year my aunt sent armfuls of golden daffodils to decorate the pulpits, the christening fonts and every ledge in the churches, be they High or Low.

My uncle was a fine sign painter, builder and decorator. Whether the daffodils had anything to do with it I don't know, but he had the contracts for keeping all the churches and chapels repaired and decorated. 'Cleanliness is next to Godliness' as the saying goes— Uncle earned his place!

The whole family were very keen chapel goers. There were now two boys (the eldest had been killed in the War), and two girls a little older than I. We all dressed in our best and filed to chapel on Easter Sunday morning. My uncle led the family procession. He was a fine handsome man, with dark curling hair, a merry eye and high cheekbones. He wore a light pin-striped suit and a grey bowler hat along with a spotless white shirt and black tie with a diamond tiepin. With his upright carriage he had a distinguished air. My aunt was large, as I said, and dressed flamboyantly. She loved enormous hats, flowing skirts, feather boas and frills, all of which enhanced her size. It seemed to me that her tight corsets hampered her breathing and gave her face its very high colour, which made her look healthier than she was.

I suspected the girls prayed more for good weather to protect their finery than for forgiveness of their sins, but in those days to be seen to be a Christian was to be thought a Christian. There was no one who was seen (and heard) more in church than my good uncle and so the 'holy' cheques rolled in to the decorator's exchequer.

The chapel service, with its lack of solemn conformity, was a revelation to me. We would all sit with bowed heads, some covering their eyes, but peering through their fingers, at their neighbours. We listened patiently while the preacher prayed that everyone renounce the Devil, and then called on a member of the congregation to speak. The chosen one would call loudly on the Almighty to forgive him his sins. If he were a skilled speaker, that is. If he were not, he could evoke a response from the audience by groaning and gesticulating like a creature in torment. The more tormented the repentance, the greater the reaction from the group. Many began to join in with shouts of 'Amen!', 'Alleluiah!' and 'Oh!' They were so ferocious that I trembled with fear.

The choir, which consisted of teen-aged girls and boys, would take advantage of their elders' preoccupation with the Devil to flirt, and surreptitiously pass notes of assignation from hand to hand right under the preacher's nose.

On the Easter Monday afternoon my cousin Irene said to me, 'Ann, we are going to the river today and have a picnic. Alf is taking one of Dad's boats out.' Alf was her boy friend, whom she saw with her mother's consent. Her older sister was actually engaged—a condition that I considered blissful, with all wordly worries solved. 'Such a nice boy,' my aunt said about Alf. I admit he was good-looking, but he never spoke to me. He and my cousin considered me gawkish and immature; they were quite open about their opinion that I was a nuisance who was in the way and cramped their style. It seemed to me that their courting consisted of a lot of 'slap and tickle' and I found it embarrassing.

But I liked the idea of going out in one of my uncle's boats; he had a boat house and a few boats that he hired out to townsfolk coming to The Broads for a few days fishing. I loved the water. 'That will be lovely,' I said.

'Yes,' Irene said. 'And we've found a boy friend for you, and you must mind and be nice to him—although

I don't know what anyone would ever see in you—' she sniggered '—else I'll box your ears for you!'

I was filled with apprehension, but I did not dare protest because I knew my cousin, who was twice my size, would keep her word, and probably pull my hair as well. She was fed up with me tagging along on her Easter holiday.

'Say hello to Fred,' she said, pushing him at me. That was her uncouth country way.

'Hello,' I said obediently and shyly.

'Steady on, Irene,' Fred said, I thought a little angrily.

He was a slim, athletic boy who was, I learned, head boy of his grammar school. He hoped to qualify for the university, a rare accomplishment in those days. His parents were the local butchers and had branch shops for miles around. They could afford to educate him; he was the only son. He was captain of his school cricket team and football team, a runner and a swimmer. He told me he had a new motor bike which he was very proud of, but much to our disappointment my aunt forbade me to go for a ride. As she rightly said, she was responsible for me and motor bikes were considered dangerous then.

Fred and I got on well and my cousin Irene and Alf were delighted. The four of us met and went for walks every evening for the rest of my holiday. Fred and I became engrossed in earnest conversations about his school life and his ambitions and I told him about my domestic life.

'I think it's wonderful,' he said, 'that you have virtually looked after your Grannie and sisters and brother and your father since you were thirteen, since your mother died.'

He was the first person I ever lied to about my mother. For years I could not bring myself to say that she had deserted us. What today is a commonplace was then shameful and a disgrace to the whole family. This attitude was fostered in me by both Grannie and my father, who wished, as they say, to sweep the whole thing under the rug.

The week passed all too quickly. My aunt fed me well. Every morning she let the ducks out of their pen; they quacked and waddled into a little stream that ran at the bottom of the garden. Every evening at sunset they waddled back to their pen, to lay dutifully their lovely greenish rich eggs, either at sunrise or before they were let out again. My aunt collected enormous baskets of eggs each morning; she supplied the countryside with them as she did with the daffodils. My aunt was an expert cook; her egg custards had to be tasted to be believed; her cheesecakes were a secret recipe and her cakes and buns were a dream. She baked all the bread, which, newly out of the oven, filled the kitchen with its aroma and drew us all in for hot rolls and fresh butter each morning.

'You don't look quite such a little scarecrow as when you arrived,' my uncle commented. 'Another week and I might admit to owning you!' I had gained a stone in weight.

'We shall have to see if that family of yours can spare you for another week,' my aunt said kindly.

'Oh Aunt, I should love to stay!' I said eagerly, thinking partly of the good life, and partly of Fred.

I don't know how it was arranged, but I did stay another week.

My two male cousins were still on holiday; although older than I, they were still at school. They were typical healthy, vigorous country boys, and not above having a little sport at my expense. They could ride the pony bareback and insisted I should learn to do it too. I was nervous of any animal, much less a pony.

'Come on, Ann!' They gave me a none-too-gentle hoist

into the saddle, where I clung to the pony's mane as if my life depended on it, which it may well have done.

They led the animal gently enough while we were in earshot of the house and in view of the village. But they started to run with it when we reached the narrow country lanes. I bobbed up and down and swayed from side to side as the pony trotted along. The hedgerows closed in on me, branches reached out and clutched at me and scratched my face. I lost my stirrups and the reins slipped from my frenzied grasp. Finally the pony had had enough of my cumbersome weight and, as my cousin gave her a resounding swipe with a stick on her rump, she started off at a smart gallop and deposited me on top of a hedge. I was lucky; it could have been the road, but as it was, no bones were broken. My cousins clambered up the hedge and rescued me while the pony stood pawing the ground triumphantly.

I was too bruised and shaken to walk home and my numerous scratches were bleeding. My cousins set me on the pony again and led me gently home. My aunt was shocked when she saw me, but she accepted the boys' explanation that the pony had been startled by a bird flying up in front of it. Of course I never told tales, no matter what indignity I suffered.

I was a Townie and Milk and Honey—that is, fair game—for my country cousins. On another morning they took me tree climbing. I had to do it to prove I wasn't a coward, or soft. Climbing up was not too bad with a helping hand here and a push there from one over-helpful cousin. Sitting high up in the fork of a huge elm tree, I surveyed the world spread out below and felt that I could stay up in that tree forever. The view was open over the undulating countryside: stretches of green pasture land, here and there orchards in fresh spring green leaf, the cornfields just beginning to show yellow—all stretching to the glistening waters' edge of the Norfolk Downs where it met the line of the blue sky.

'Come on, Ann, stop dreaming up there and come down. We're down here already,' the boys yelled up to me.

With sudden horror I realized that I was alone in my tree-top world with no one there to help me down.

'I can't get down!' I cried, hoping they could hear me in their world far below.

'Yes you can, silly. Just look for a fork in the branch near the trunk and climb down,' my cousin said. 'Don't look down. Then you won't feel dizzy.'

I started painfully and slowly to climb down, scratching my legs and arms plentifully in the process. All went slowly but well until my foot missed a branch and I was left hanging by my arms—suspended, it seemed, in limbo.

'Twist yourself back on the branch, pull your weight up!' my cousin shouted. Then seeing my frantic useless acrobatics he called, 'Hang on, I'll come and get you!'

Suddenly the branch, under my unaccustomed weight which was exacerbated by my wild movements, gave a sickening cracking noise and parted from its mother trunk. Clinging desperately to it, I sailed away just as my cousin was about to reach me. I landed with a thump in something squashy and soft. My teeth clicked together on the impact, my head thudded forward as if it had snapped from my shoulders. I felt sure my back must have cracked in two. I tried to move but only seemed to slip and slither in the soft, mushy substance which enveloped me. As my stunned senses returned, I noticed an unpleasant odor in my vicinity. At first I had thought I had fallen into a stagnant shallow pond; now I suddenly realized that cows were grazing on the meadow.

'Help me!' I pleaded to my two cousins who were standing by.

They dragged me out of the mess and tried their best to clean me up a bit with the long grass, which they pulled out in great handfuls.

'My goodness, Ann, you don't half stink!' said one of the boys. 'You *are* in a mess.'

'What are we going to tell Mother?' asked the other one fearfully. 'Don't tell her we forced you to climb that tree; say you wanted to do it. If Father thought it was our fault, we might get the strap.'

My aunt was horrified when she saw me. She said afterward that her bathroom stank for days and the stain never did come out of my cotton dress. However, I took my share of the blame and the boys didn't get the strap. My aunt accepted that it was an accident but my uncle scolded the boys and told them they should take better care of me.

My two cousins promised they would look after me on another outing. 'Ann,' they asked, 'would you like to come with us for a picnic on the lake? We are going to fish all day. You can come if you like.'

It was tempting. My cousin Irene had to stay at home to help her mother with the cooking. I felt I had had enough of cooking at home—after all, I was on holiday.

In high spirits we set out for the day with a packed rabbit pie, apple pie and fizzy lemonade.

'Now mind you look after Ann. None of your tricks!' my aunt said as we departed.

While the boys fished, I lay back on cushions like a princess. They were my two knights in armour. We drifted peacefully along the edge of the quiet waters. The yellow flags—irises—were in full bloom at the water's edge, the overhanging weeping willows dipped gently into the ripples we made in passing. Wild fowl were startled by the splash of our oars: a little black

moor hen skimmed across the surface with a disapproving flutter of her wings; behind her her brood tried
in vain to keep up with her. Bright colored mallards
drifted away from us on the calm water, and other birds
flew skywards. The whole setting was idyllic: a spring
day in the English countryside. I dreamed in peace.

Toward late afternoon, the boys had caught enough
fish for a good supper at home that night. They suggested I might like to learn to row. They assured me it
didn't require muscle as much as skill. It looked easy
enough when they did it; I was quite willing to be taught.

'Now take the oars loosely, one in each hand, so,' my
cousin said, helping me. 'Lift and plunge the oars in the
water, pull and bring your hands back across your chest.
And brace your body with your feet against the bottom
of the boat. And bend, and out, and plunge.' He counted
one and two and pulled as if he were coaching the Cambridge crew.

'No,' he said, 'dig your heels in!' My feet flew up and
I went over backwards from the force of the oars hitting
me under the chin.

'Try again!' they said, laughing, when I recovered and
sat upright once more. It was considered hilarious for
a boy to see a girl's underclothes. My aunt would have
considered that I had been very immodest.

'One and two and three.' I was going through the
motions but, as my cousin pointed out, we weren't
moving!

'Try and pull a little harder when you dip,' he said.

Anxious to please, I pulled with all my strength. It
was exhilarating. I drew great deep breaths of country
air into the furthermost depths of my lungs until they
felt as though they would burst.

I pulled extra hard too quickly and caught a crab.
The oar spun in my hand, I lost my grip on it and it
floated off into the water away from us.

'Grab it, Ann!' shouted one cousin whilst the other grabbed the second oar which was in grave danger of going after the lost one. I leaned over the side of the boat reaching for the oar at the same time as my cousin, a heavy lad, lurched across me. Too late, the oar evaded my grasp, the boat tipped and I, off balance, plunged head first into the water. My cousin was left clutching a remnant of my dress torn away in the debacle as he tried in vain to stop my total immersion. I resurfaced half drowned, screaming for help.

My cousins had really outdone themselves this time. It wasn't all their fault, but neither I nor they could convince my aunt of this. They took their punishment at my uncle's hands like men and never bore me a grudge. Even Fred, my hero, agreed that it was a little hard on them, but he was glad that I hadn't drowned.

I took leave of my kind aunt and uncle; I was half a stone heavier than when I had come, sun-tanned and light-hearted about my new-found friendship with my 'boy friend' who had promised to visit me. Of course that happy event would be subject to Father's approval, which I felt might be a little tricky to get. But never mind, there was always Grannie. She knew how to re-solve problems. I thought hopefully that she would find a way.

I had a grand homecoming. I brought a dozen new-laid eggs and a chicken for Grannie, fruit, and a huge homemade fruit cake for all of us and farm butter for Father who never took kindly to shop butter. And I had an armful of flowers from Aunt's lovely garden. My fa-ther loved flowers on his dinner table and sparkling sil-ver cutlery. I could hardly wait to get Grannie alone, to tell her about my hero Fred.

'So,' Grannie said, 'you are growing up at last.' She pursed her small mouth knowingly and her eyes gleamed.

'He's got a lovely new motor bike,' I said. 'And he wants to come and see me on Sunday afternoon. Oh Granny, do you think Daddy will let him?' I asked anxiously.

'Well, now, we will have to cross that bridge when we come to it. We will think of a way,' said Grannie encouragingly. That was always the way with Grannie; you never got a straight answer. But she loved scheming and romance added zest to her efforts.

Within the week I received a letter from Fred. He suggested I meet him on the cliffs the following Sunday afternoon. Grannie said she knew his parents: very respectable, was her verdict and she didn't think my father would object to him, but she thought we wouldn't let him into the big secret just yet. She didn't know exactly why, but she thought it would be better to wait a little while before breaking the good news that his daughter had a 'boy friend'. She urged me to trust her and be patient.

The weeks stretched into months. My father was predictable in his habits; he always spent Sunday afternoon reading and dozing in the lounge, which was the big front room on the first floor. We never disturbed him or he us. My two sisters spent the afternoon safely away at Sunday School, and were bribed into the conspiracy of silence with liquorice allsorts if they came home at an inopportune time. So Fred and I spent wet Sunday afternoons together on the horsehair sofa in the kitchen, whilst Grannie, forsaking her chair under the Grandfather clock in the dining room, took the rocking chair to keep me company in the interests of propriety.

This happy weekend routine went on for nearly a year. I was overjoyed to have a friend and a sympathetic ear in which I could pour, every Sunday, all the frustrations of the previous week. No doubt it was calf love. We talked in a very sensible way of getting married when Fred was established in a career. The years of waiting would go by easily and happily enough for me if I saw him just once a week and knew he would always be there for me. At least now there seemed to be a future for me at last. I was anxious about my father's welfare, but I thought Alice could take my place when the time came. There was, as Grannie said, no hurry to tell Father; he would know soon enough. And so the deception went on, month after month.

I don't think Fred realized that he was an unwelcome visitor in the house. We were completely engrossed in our own lives and in our feelings for each other. It was a pure boy-girl relationship. I suppose that compatibility, trust and affection could have developed into a happy life-long relationship.

We didn't hear the squeak of my father's slippers on the stairs one Sunday afternoon or the door opening.

'And who is this?' asked my father, fixing poor Fred with a withering glance. 'A friend of yours, my dear, have I met him?' the latter question with heavy sarcasm.

Grannie was about to intervene, but my father held up his hand. 'I was asking Ann for an explanation,' he said.

'Daddy,' I said, trembling, 'this is Fred. I met him at Aunt Emily's. He sometimes comes to see me.'

'So I see,' said my father. 'And now as it is our teatime, perhaps Mr Fred can take his departure. And you, my dear, can get the tea ready for your sisters and Grannie and me. I will discuss this matter with you later.'

Fred was only too ready to beat a hasty retreat in the face of my father's command of the situation.

That same evening my father dictated a letter for me to send to Fred. I wrote it in the midst of sobs and pleading, which had no effect. In my father's eyes the whole business was shoddy and underhanded. The young man in question, he said, had no moral fibre.

'Daddy, I did want to tell you,' I stammered, 'but Grannie thought it would be better to wait.'

'I have no doubt she did,' was my father's icy comment. He took the letter and posted it. There was never an answer. I did not see Fred again for years.

I went back to my miserable existence of doing joyless household chores and weeping into the roller towel on the back door. Once more I was in dire disgrace with my father and Grannie came in for her share too. I wasn't mature enough to keep the balance between Grannie's love and affection and my father's trust and love, which I longed for.

As the months passed and the seasons changed, the end of my romance became less painful to bear. Grannie tried to comfort me through the dreary time. 'There is as good fish in the sea as ever came out of it,' she said, coming up as usual with an adage for every occasion. Aunt Martha visited and she too tried to cheer me with bright forecasts from the tea leaves in my cup, but I was unhappy. During the summer I joined the local tennis club at my father's suggestion and made some acquaintances, amongst whom were a family of two boys and a girl about my age. The boys were a little older. They lived in a big house standing back from the High Street in its own grounds. My father approved of this friendship and was quite amiable to the young men when they called for me for tennis. The younger of the two fancied Alice, who was staying at school until she was sixteen. She was a little blue-eyed blonde and led him quite a dance. The elder brother liked me, but I had no eyes for any boy because of my hero Fred. Nevertheless the friendship between us all lasted for years.

That year the winter was hard and bitter. Grannie was approaching her eightieth year, and noticeably failing. One night she woke me, fighting for her breath. I fetched her some hot milk and put a drop of the hard stuff in it from the bottle kept under her bed, supposedly for emergencies. She spent the rest of the night propped up on pillows and seemed a little easier in the morning. The bedroom was icy cold, without any form of heating. As soon as my father left for work, I went to fetch my Aunt Martha.

When she saw Grannie she said immediately, 'You must have the doctor. You go for him, Ann. I'll stay with Grannie.'

In those days the doctor was a luxury which only the rich could afford. Grannie tried to protest, but I went for the doctor; while I was gone Aunt Martha, the kind soul, made Grannie comfortable, washed her and re-made the bed.

The doctor said Grannie had bronchitis; she was very poorly and must be kept warm and on a light diet. He gave her a prescription. Of course we had no antibiotics then; basically illnesses like bronchitis and pneumonia had to take their course. The doctor obviously looked askance at me as the sole nurse for Grannie. If only I could grow and look older, I thought. He said her relatives should be informed, which alarmed me.

'She isn't doing to die, is she, doctor?'

'Well, my dear,' he said, kindly, 'she is a great age. But I think if you take care of her and keep her warm we shall pull her through this time.'

As soon as the doctor was gone I unblocked the fireplace. I could have used some help, but Aunt Martha had had to leave as soon as the doctor arrived, so I set about the task alone of getting a fire in the bedroom to keep Grannie warm. I struggled upstairs with a bucket of coals and sticks. There would soon be a cheery fire; Grannie would be looked after like a queen.

I set a match to the paper. It blazed up and a great wave of smoke billowed out into the room. The chimney-breast was blocked! Hastily I dampened down the paper and sticks which were crackling. I could hardly see across the room. I took the pillows from under Grannie and covered her with a sheet to keep the smoke from her. I prayed she could breathe. I rushed to the window and threw it open; it couldn't be much colder in the room than it already was. While the smoke wafted out of the window, I sped downstairs for the flu brush that we used to clean the kitchen chimney every week. I pushed it up the bedroom chimney as far as it would go. Grannie was choking a little. The smoke had departed and cold air was coming in so I closed the window.

But the brush only went halfway up the chimney. 'What on earth is stopping it?' I asked furiously, wagging the long handle back and forth. Something moved. I gave a tremendous upward push with the brush, withdrew it and popped my head into the chimney to have a look. Something thumped me on the head. I repressed a scream and leapt back. A dead blackbird and a bushel of sooty dust lay on the hearth. Quickly I brushed it all up and rolled the lot—loose feathers, soot—into a newspaper. Grannie was still alive, I could hear her breathing. Soon the fire was burning merrily with the blockage removed, if not expertly cleared. I had the pillows propping Grannie and the dust sheet removed in no time.

'Oh it is nice to see a fire,' said Grannie. Propped up as she was, with the foot of the bed pointing to the fireplace, she could look directly at it. I took the mittens off her hands and she held toward the glow. Her little face broke into a wan smile for the first time in two days.

'Oh Grannie, we will soon have you better,' I cried, kneeling on the bed in spite of my sooty face and hands, and throwing my arms around her frail form.

'Yes, yes!' she croaked and tried to laugh. 'The old girl isn't done for yet. Tell the doctor.'

'Gran!' I said, shocked.

Luckily coal was cheap. I kept the fire burning night and day in the little black cast-iron grate with the pretty surround of cream tiles hand-painted with pansies and forget-me-nots. The china cat sitting on the mantlepiece seemed to be smiling appreciatively as the room went from freezing cold to cosy warmth. Soon Grannie was breathing more easily, and had a nip of whiskey to celebrate.

My father was very perturbed when he came home that day for his midday meal.

'Ann, you cannot nurse your Grandmother alone; this time she is too ill. I must let her daughters know. They have to do something.'

'Aunt Martha will help me,' I said. 'She promised.'

'Yes,' said my father, 'I have no doubt she will, but God knows *she* has enough problems of her own. No. Your aunts must be told.'

'Oh, Aunt Martha is good and kind,' I said.

'Umph,' my father said, 'I don't doubt it.'

Now the War had been over for years, it seemed to me, and I thought that surely whatever Aunt Martha had done then could be forgiven. I could not understand my father's attitude toward her.

The daughters were informed and they each visited their mother during that long cold winter; once while she was in bed and once when she was up and downstairs again. One aunt brought her a jar of calves foot jelly, impressing it on me to see that Mother didn't waste it, since it was as expensive as it was nourishing. Aunt Emily from the country did rather better, bringing me new-laid eggs, a chicken and fresh fruit. She stayed all day and helped me to wash and tidy Grannie.

'I'm sorry, Ann, it's a lot for you to do on your own,' she said. I felt like crying at these sympathetic words. I was getting very tired running up and down the stairs.

Both aunts were pleased that Aunt Martha came in

to help when she could. They assumed that Grannie was paying her out of the pension money of five shillings a week that Lloyd George had allowed her. Aunt Nancy generously left Aunt Martha two and sixpence. Conscience money, no doubt!

Every evening my father visited Grannie in her bedroom and sat with her for a little while. He read in his well-modulated voice whatever he thought would interest her from the daily paper. If the evening were light and the weather fine enough he would send me out for a short walk so that I could get some fresh air. He was concerned about my being shut up all winter with Grannie.

He told me to buy her any luxury she fancied, and he himself bought her a whole bottle of whisky and put it on the washstand in plain view. There it stood, shrinking nip by nip every day. It did Grannie a power of good morally, because my father had bought it, and medicinally because she knew best what was good for her. I thought my father must have come into some money unexpectedly, but on reflection I think it was his way of saying thank you to her for the love she had given his motherless children.

Aunt Martha told my mother that Grannie was ill. I know, because parcels of small luxuries and toiletries arrived from time to time. A large bottle of Grannie's beloved lavender water adorned the dressing table; a tablet of particularly expensive soap appeared; exotic dusting powder took the place of Grannie's weekly two pennyworth of Violet powder—and how she loved them all! I had to put pomade, a greasy substance, on her fine grey hair and brush it from time to time before plaiting it at night. It would then be combed out in the morning and gathered into a neat bun at the back. It was unusual in Grannie's day for an old lady of eighty to be this fastidious. Old ladies as a rule became neglectful of themselves and cleanliness then was not as easily achieved as it is today with all the modern conveniences.

Grannie got better and spent the rest of the year comfortably until winter began to approach again. She was very frail and needed help to get up and down the stairs and to dress and undress. It was not safe to leave her alone in the house with a fire. She would get the poker and stir up the fire when my back was turned, frequently tumbling the red hot coals out onto the hearthrug. Her intellect and wit were not impaired, though, and she became extremely cunning about getting her own way, often using my two sisters to oppose me.

My father did not doubt that she would have a recurrence of bronchitis in the winter; he was determined that this burden should not fall once again on my shoulders.

'Ann,' he said to me one day. 'I am making arrangements for your Grannie to go to your aunts this winter. I cannot have her ill here all the winter again.'

'Oh!' I cried, dismayed. 'You don't mean her to go away forever?'

'I am afraid so, my dear.' I was about to protest again; my father held up his hand to stop me.

'You must allow me to know best in this matter. I cannot have you overtaxed and end up with two sick women in the house. I will let you know when I shall want you to pack up your Grandmother's belongings. It will be soon. We must not wait until it is too cold for her to travel, must we? You will tell your Grandmother for me. She will take it better from you, poor dear!'

Grannie wept as usual when I told her. She said, 'Nobody wants a poor old woman when she is useless.' She didn't want to be any trouble to anyone; she would go into the Workhouse and end her days as a pauper! I cried and tried to comfort her.

'Grannie,' I said, 'I will get my work done early and come two or three times a week to see you, won't you like that?'

In the event it was settled that she went to Aunt Nancy for six months of the year, and to Aunt Emily in the country for six months. She had lived with us a long time. Now her life, I suspected, would never be as happy or as settled again.

Mr Palmer, the Cabbie, was engaged as usual to take her to Aunt Nancy's. He was cheery and greeted Grannie, saying, 'Going off on your holidays again, are you?' Quite the wrong thing to say. Grannie responded by allowing her feelings to overflow.

'No, Mr Palmer, they are sending me away for good this time, to my daughter.'

The Cabbie gave me a knowing wink as he helped Grannie up the three steps into the hansom cab; it was now nearly impossible for her to manage them. Her tin trunk followed, and then I climbed aboard and wrapped a travelling rug around Grannie's knees. The open top of the cab was closed for the winter, the window was pushed up shut and when the Cabbie slammed the door we were as warm as it was possible to be under the circumstances.

The cab lurched as the Cabbie heaved himself up into the driver's seat. With a 'Whoa up there!' and a crack of the whip, we were off. No waving and smiling this time; we were enclosed in the cab. The horses galloped eagerly in the sharp winter air; the Cabbie was anxious to get the journey over with. It didn't seem long before we were clanging Aunt's bell and Lizzie was there, all smiles at seeing Grannie again. She helped Grannie alight and negotiate the front steps. The tin trunk was deposited in the front hall. It was time to say good-bye to Grannie, knowing that this time there was not going to be an arrangement for collecting her and bringing her home. This time it would be for keeps. We clung to each other.

'Now Mother,' said my aunt, 'let the child go. You will be seeing her again next week.' And she none too gently disengaged me from Grannie's embrace. I left the old lady sitting in her coat and bonnet, a forlorn figure in an armchair much too big for her; her feet did not touch the ground.

'Goodbye, Ann,' said my aunt. 'Tell your father he need have no fear, your Granny will be properly looked after.' Was it my imagination, was the word 'properly' emphasised? What could she mean? No one could look after Grannie as we had, and no one could make her laugh as we did and have so much fun with her. The huge studded front door banged shut and with it my spirits sank. I felt Grannie was shut forever behind that impenetrable door and I was on the wrong side of it. It was like a prison! But how silly—all inside was comfortable, warm and luxurious.

I can hardly remember the journey home. The grey mare's hooves seemed to beat a refrain in my head: 'Grannie's gone forever. Grannie's gone forever. She's gone away, away, away.' That went on until the Cabbie pulled up at our house.

'Here you are, missy,' he said, gazing at my tear-stained face. 'Lor' missy, don't take on so. You will be a visiting the old lady, I'll be bound.'

'Thank you.' I murmured. 'Grannie said to give you this and thank you.' I pressed half a crown into his hand.

'God bless 'er.' he said, and climbed up once again into his seat and was off, driving out of my life as it seemed to me Grannie had just done.

8. Freedom

WITH Grannie gone I had much more free time at home. I lost myself in the wonders of *King Solomon's Mines* and the novels of Jane Austen, which carried me off to unfamiliar people and situations. I could indulge myself for hours, and no voice called me back to the realities of household chores.

I began to play tennis in the afternoons and evenings, my circle of friends enlarged and with it my zest for living a normal teenage life. All was well as far as my father was concerned, as long as meals were served on time and I didn't stay out late at night. My two sisters could now be left alone in the house for an evening. My new-found freedom was sweet, but I did miss Grannie.

Our tennis club was entered for the County tournaments and I was asked by a friend to partner him. It was an honour beyond my wildest dreams. I think on reflection that I was asked not so much because of my prowess as because of my submissiveness, but I was very flattered. 'All I ask of you, Ann,' he said, 'is your best service, which is good. Don't exploit your backhand whatever you do—it's weak. Leave the court to me, and stay out of my way!' Not a very flattering view of my play. But at the time I would have lain down on the court and let him trample all over me if he had wanted to.

'Ed,' I said, 'there are far better players than I. Why don't you ask one of them?'

'I want a partner, not a boss,' he said decisively.

How we practised! The tournament was to be held on the clifftop tennis courts, where you could be sure the strong breezes off the North Sea would compete with your best stroke. I was exhausted before the great day arrived. It was held at 'high season' to attract the summer visitors.

'You're doing well,' Ed said. 'You're like lightning on your feet. Keep it up!' I loved the praise. It made me feel like a marathon runner.

My father was pleased by this development in my life. He made a point of meeting me after evening practice to escort me home. I don't think my tennis partner had expected this. My father felt the responsibility of raising three motherless daughters weigh heavily on his shoulders. By the time my two sisters had reached the age of independence he had relaxed somewhat. I am afraid I was the guinea pig.

The great day came. I remember wearing a half-length white wool gabardine pleated skirt—considered very smart—one of my school white blouses, ankle socks and mercifully no stockings. A white band secured under my hair at the back kept it from blowing in my face. The men wore long white flannels, and a discreetly open-necked shirt.

The day was hot with a tempering cool breeze blowing off the sea. The hard courts glared red in the sun. The umpire sat in grand isolation at the top of his steps, master of all he surveyed. We won the toss and chose the side in the wind while we were fresh. I was careful not to 'foot fault' my service, when the player can charge from beyond the service line to smash the ball high in the air at his opponent's feet. My partner was like a Greek god: stretched to his full six feet, he brought his arm, with sleeves rolled up above his elbow, down to hit the ball full force with the racket. The ball skidded just over the net and evaded the opponent. My tactics derived no so much from force as from cunning. The ball would leave my racket to bounce just over the net and roll effortlessly and easily away before my opponent could reach it. The spectators Oh-ed and Ah-ed.

At half-time we were ahead. A hasty swig of lemonade and a rub-down with a towel and back we went. I obeyed my instructions and worked hard to keep from under my partner's feet. His stamina was terrific but mine was doubtful; I began to feel tired, a little wobbly at the knees. He was like a tornado and if I had not been fleet of foot I would have been trampled to death.

We won. As I approached the net for the traditional handshake, my arm suddenly went limp and my legs gave way. I did not walk off the court in triumph. I remember hearing a great murmur rumble through the spectators. It seemed to me the waves from the sea were closing over me; I was lying on the seashore, not the tennis court. I revived in the dressingroom and was well enough to claim my joint prize, if a little shakily.

I liked and admired Ed for years, but he never made

the grade with me as Fred had done. I envisaged him as a tennis partner, but never a partner for life.

This new phase in my life developed in another direction. I visited Grannie at my aunt's every week, and talked about tennis. Grannie liked to hear what we were all doing in her absence. I was growing up, and my cousin Maude, who was the youngest of my aunt's two daughters, became more friendly to me. She began to give me clothes she was tired of. I was good with my needle and, as they said, could make something out of nothing. She worked in her father's office and earned a good salary, which she kept to spend on herself. She was engaged to marry a bank clerk.

One day in the summer after the tennis tournament which she had heard all about, she asked me if I would like to make up a foursome with her, her fiancé Derek, and a friend. What an honour it was to be asked to meet and play tennis with my cousin's 'smart set'!

The friend's name was Kenneth. I judged he was about ten years older than I, a bachelor and, I gathered later, a very eligible one in the town. He, like my cousin, was a Roman Catholic, and I fancy he had been a boy friend of hers at one time. He was stocky and had a flat, round, pale face. But his hazel eyes were honest and direct and he had a ready laugh and most gentlemanly manners. He wore a battered old trilby hat set square on his head— for some reason the brim was permanently turned up in front, which made his face look even rounder and flatter. His charm and his attentions were old world; in fact, he was more like my own father than anyone I had ever met. He always raised his hat when we met and when he took leave of me; amused, I sometimes wondered whether I should curtsey.

Our friendship developed from the doubles to the singles, when he would cross the river to our town and meet me on the cliff tennis courts. At times he gallantly let me beat him. His game could not compare with Ed's: he was laborious where Ed was dynamic. And while Ed looked like a lean, handsome athlete, Ken looked portly and middle-aged.

On Sunday he went to church in the morning, to confession, and was busy for the rest of the day with his accounts. I would meet my friends on Sunday and it had not escaped their notice that I had a boy friend who was not one of our tennis set. 'Who is he, Ann? Where does he come from? Isn't he a bit old for you? Do you really like him?' They made fun of me in the end, but I didn't tell them anything.

My brother, too, was a little too perceptive for my liking.

'Ann, that fish merchant fancies you, doesn't he? How old is he—are you going to marry him?'

'Of course not, silly. We're just tennis partners.'

'Well, mind he doesn't make you a partner for life.' My brother laughed at me.

I found all this somewhat disturbing. It put ideas into my head that hadn't been there before.

Our tennis meetings graduated to theatre and cinema dates, dances and a race meeting. He opened up a completely new world to me and I felt like a princess. I knew the musical *No No Nanette* by heart. I only had to mention that I liked this or that and he would turn up with it for me. Only once I met him in the rain without an umbrella; the next time he had an umbrella for me. I had gloves, a handbag, silk stockings, jewellery—all in good taste. I believe a favourite sister shopped for him. But I never met her or any of his family. He bought me the best, most expensive chocolates and reserved tables at restaurants and seats at shows. I don't imagine he had ever stood in a queue in his life. It was such an easy way to live—like being on a magic carpet.

Aunt Nancy was delighted at this turn of events.

'It's a wonderful opportunity for you,' she said. I wondered why everyone was assuming that he would marry me.

'Aunt,' I said, 'I wish you wouldn't talk like that. Ken and I are very good friends.'

The Bankers Ball was imminent. Ken suggested that my cousin and her fiancé made a foursome with us. In dismay I went to my aunt. 'What can I wear?' I wailed. 'I haven't anything fit for an occasion like that.'

'We'll see,' said my aunt. 'You must go or Ken will take somebody else.'

'Oh, I wish he would!' I said. 'Anyway I can't go; Father won't let me stay out that late.'

'Now leave it to me,' my aunt said. She was a great schemer at the best of times.

I was groomed and dressed for that ball as never before. Aunt fixed all the details with my father and I stayed at her house for the night.

My cousin passed on to me a two-tiered beaded ball dress, a beautiful creation in blue, a color flattering to me. I managed to alter it and make it fit. I was to wear that dress time and time again until the beads dropped off from sheer overuse. It was like 'Alice Blue Gown' to me: 'it wore and wore 'til it went and it wasn't no more.'

I realised I had no shoes to go with the dress. 'Ken,' I said, 'I can't come with you. I have no shoes for dancing.'

'Poor Cinderella,' he said, 'let me be your Prince Charming.'

'Oh, I couldn't accept clothes from you,' I said, shocked. 'It wouldn't be right.'

'What an old-fashioned girl you are! Well, this time I insist. My evening is not going to be ruined because of a pair of shoes. We'll get them for you next week.' And we did.

I thought my aunt would be shocked, but she said

only, 'He is coming on,' in her mysterious manner. Grannie looked pleased and gave her usual advice: 'Don't tell your father!'

The hansom cab called for my cousin and me at my aunt's. Our beaux were waiting for us in the hotel foyer. They looked very smart in their dinner suits. I had never seen Ken dressed up like that before. I thought he looked distinguished and I felt a thrill of pride because I was his girl friend. I felt like a princess, in fact, until I went into the powder room where all the girls and smart ladies were putting the finishing touches to their toilettes. I couldn't think what they were doing, putting red powder on their cheeks and more red on their mouths, and black round their eyes. Cosmetics were not so subtle then so that, with their faces dusted with white powder—Swansdown I remember was the popular brand—they ended up looking like our six-penny wooden painted dolls, with white faces, two black eyes and vivid red patches on their cheeks. The intention was for every girl to have an English Rose pink and white complexion. The adventurous tried to improve on nature with what I thought were disastrous results.

I heard a few unflattering comments on my long curls which were held in place by a black bow. They had almost all lost their locks to the dictates of fashion and had 'bobs'. Then too my visible signs of womanhood were quite passé; they had all suppressed their natural curves to emulate the boyish figure of the heroine of the popular musical *The Boy Friend*.

'Did you notice that funny little creature in the Ladies with—my dear, can you believe it?—a black ribbon in her hair? I wonder who brought her?' I overheard one lady whisper to another.

I didn't realise it at the time, but I was with one of the most eligible bachelors in the town, one whom all the Mamas had their sights on, and I was Miss Nobody.

'Ken,' I said, 'do you think I should have my hair cut off?'

'Good heavens, no; what on earth for? Your hair is beautiful!'

'All the girls have a bob. It's the fashion.'

'I like you as you are. I wouldn't have you any different.' He looked at me fondly. I felt reassured and was happy dancing with him. I had never had a dancing lesson in my life, but Ken said I was light as a feather as he held me—a shade too closely, I thought—in his arms. I followed his steps and did the Charleston and twiddled my beads with abandon as I saw the other girls doing.

In the interval Ken suggested that I might like to freshen myself up. 'Oh, no,' I said hastily. 'I don't want to go in that place again. They all look at me so oddly!'

'Oh do they indeed. Well, there is not one of them worth half of you, nor one so pretty, in my estimation. They are a crowd of insincere painted dolls!'

We sat the interval out, cosily together on a red velvet plush sofa in one of the small withdrawing recesses dotted around the ballroom. Ken put his arm around me. I had been drinking champagne and was glad to rest my buzzing head on his shoulder. We spoke very little.

We danced the evening away. I was none too steady on my feet at one stage. I was not used to wine, let alone champagne, but Ken supported me and laughed at my embarrassment. I was happy dancing with him. The fairy tale evening ended. We found my cousin and her fiancé and we all went to my aunt's house together in a hansom cab. Ken gave me a long, lingering kiss on the doorstep.

The next morning my aunt allowed me the luxury of lying in bed an extra hour. I lay thinking of the evening, reliving it. A strong awareness of myself flowed over me. Ken had said I was pretty—that was not what my brother called me—and he had said I was worth more than all the other girls put together. What precisely did he mean? And that good-night kiss and the way he said my name was a little disturbing.

I went into Grannie's room to say good-bye to her before I left. She pulled me down to her as she lay propped up on her pillows. In a conspiratorial whisper she asked, 'Did he pop the question?'

'What question, Grannie?' I asked innocently.

'What a child it still is! But you wait, you will see, he will!' she said, and kissed me with affection. 'You are a good girl, Ann. God bless you!' Dear Grannie, how she loved her intrigues!

The winter passed. Ken still took me to the theatre, and we had tête-a-tête suppers at his house, and he was most attentive, but as far as I was concerned, the relationship was on a firmly friendly basis. I enjoyed the moment and the new world of entertainment which he opened up to me. One day he invited me to go to the races in a foursome with my cousin and Derek. I found all the places he took me exciting, so I looked forward to the races, although I was not too keen on horses after my experience with my country cousins.

My aunt was concerned that I should dress properly if I were to be seen at the races in company with her daughter. I owned nothing that approached their standard. It was easy to dress for tennis, but the races, where the whole town turned out, was another matter. Aunt said she wouldn't put it past me to wear a gym slip. They didn't seem to understand that I was mortified and miserable about not having any clothes, but there was nothing I could do about it. I wanted to look smart as much as my cousin did but all the money I had was sixpence a week pocket money from my father. My cousin declared she wouldn't be seen with me if I looked like a little tramp.

'Aunt,' I said, 'Ken would buy me a suit if I let him. Should I tell him I can't go unless he buys me a suitable rig-out?'

I thought my aunt would have an apoplectic fit. 'Ann!' she said. 'How can you suggest such a thing? Only kept women allow men to buy them clothes.' What she meant by 'kept women' I had no idea, but the tone of her voice indicated it was something distasteful. 'Well, what else can I do?' I asked.

'We must find you something,' my aunt said with determination. 'Unfortunately, there isn't much time.'

They had a dressmaker who was always willing to come when they sent for her. She was an Arab girl who had married an English R.A.F. pilot in Egypt, an action much disapproved of by the R.A.F. in those days. The rule was no fraternising. Fatima had been lucky; she had been educated in a convent and was clever. She must have been one of the first Arab immigrants. Her English was limited; she talked with her hands and her large dark eyes and much shaking of her head. With a mouth full of pins, she fitted my cousin's cast-off green two-piece to me—a pinch in there, a turned-up hem, new velvet collar and cuffs and tiny velvet-covered buttons. I managed to buy a straw hat for one shilling and elevenpence and my aunt trimmed it with a piece of the velvet left over from the dress.

'Leetle Miss look very nice. Miss very leetle, so!' said Fatima, spanning my waist with her hands. My aunt laughed. We all liked Fatima, she was always so cheerful.

I met Ken on the bridge.

'Why, Ann,' he said appreciatively, 'you do look smart!' He hailed a cab and we drove off to pick up my cousin and Derek at her house. We drove all along the sea front from my aunt's house. It was a beautiful spring day. The sea was lapping gently at the shore undisturbed by a soft wind. The racecourse was bounded by the sea on the one hand and wild open countryside on the other. It was reached by a road running across the sand dunes called The Deanes for about a mile out of town.

On this day the crowds were there in the thousands. We drove in style up to Tattersall's entrance, and the Guinea Ring: a guinea was, of course, a pound and a shilling. It seemed the height of wanton extravagance to me to pay over one pound in money for an entrance fee.

The crowd waiting outside were all in good spirits and cheered as the waggonette drew up with yet another load of people to swell their numbers. I thought, They can't possibly all get into the race course. It seemed to me that the turnstyles would only let a trickle through. The patient crowd showed no resentment of the privileged class who went through the expensive gateway without waiting. The waggonettes continued to arrive, loaded with passengers. The patient grey horses decked from mane to tail in gay ribbons, their leather harnesses polished and their horse brasses burnished to shine golden in the spring sunshine, stood quietly waiting to be rid of one load before being turned around to return to town for another. The waggonettes were long open carts which could seat eight to ten people on two sides of long, slatted wooden seats. For this festive occasion they were festooned with red and white bunting, vying with the bright colors of the women's dresses. The larger vehicles, which took four horses, needed skilful handling. The horses were mostly recruited for the occasion from the neighbouring farms where they spent their lives plowing and drawing loads of hay. I had heard that the Duke of Norfolk, who was in charge of ceremonial processions, often borrowed the splendid Greys from farmers for the day in London.

We wandered round the ring. I was conscious of Ken's

tight grip on my elbow as he ushered me through the crowds.

There were a number of races and Ken bet on all of them. It was a high-fashion scene; the women were be-frilled and feathered, wearing enormous hats that interfered with the view of the horses' progress. We watched the beautiful lithe creatures paraded before taking up their starting positions. Some were blinkered and seemed nervous because of the noise. Ken explained to me that they were highly-strung. They were treated like royalty; rubbed down at the slightest sign of sweat glistening on their shining hides. They pranced, picking their way delicately in front of the spectators. I liked the look of one called Henna Girl. I admired redheads, and I had never seen such a lovely spirited horse. She was practically uncontrollable.

'Oh!' I exclaimed, 'Isn't she lovely! Her coat is like a red velvet cape.'

'You fancy her,' said Ken. 'I'll put a bet on her for you, but don't be disappointed if she doesn't win; she's an outsider.'

He took me to the stand where a huge, red-faced perspiring man in a loud light brown, orange and white checked suit was shouting something about 'the Field' and taking people's money. Ken had to leave me to push his way through the crowd to place his bet. A cheeky-looking man leered at me as I stood alone.

' 'oo's taking you 'ome, sweetheart?' he said. I was saved answering when Ken made his way toward me. We pushed and elbowed our way back to the ring. I nearly parted with my one and elevenpenny hat.

'Oh Ken, you've never bet on that outsider for Ann,' my cousin said. Ken laughed his assent. 'How you spoil her,' she said with an arch look.

Henna Girl just held her own for three parts of the course. I felt anxious; I did not want Ken to lose his money. Then a number of horses seemed to tire and lag behind. Suddenly Henna Girl's jockey was up in the stirrups, bent nearly double, 'riding high', cracking his whip and giving the horse her head. I was pleased to see that the whip never seemed to touch her. 'Henna Girl! Henna Girl!' the crowd roared with one voice, mine included. My stomach lurched, my throat contracted, I was sure my heart and lungs would burst. With a tremendous spurt at the finish, Henna Girl just made a head in front of the horse she had been running neck and neck with.

'We've made it!' I gasped, clutching Ken's arm in my excitement.

'Well, I never knew you were such a gambler,' said Ken. 'Let's go and collect your winnings.'

'Oh, it's your money,' I said. 'I couldn't take it.'

However Ken appeased me by taking his stake money, and I had untold wealth in the winnings.

When we got back to my cousin, they were watching the brave winner being brought in. The proud owner was there to congratulate his jockey; the horse was covered in sweat and was restless and trembling. The steam rose off her like a heat haze. 'Do you think she has caught cold?' I asked anxiously.

Ken was amused at my concern. 'Don't you worry about that,' he said. 'The stable will know how to take care of her—she is worth a fortune now.'

That was my first race meeting: an unforgettable experience on an unforgettable day.

As time passed and we went out often Ken made it quite clear that he wanted to marry me. He said he would speak to my father. Of course I was flattered, but I was not at all sure that I wanted to give up my family and spend the rest of my life with Ken. And I did not want to become a Roman Catholic.

Eventually Ken made the decision easy for me. One

day, whilst trying to persuade me to accept his proposal, he said, 'I can give you everything you want, and take you away from that dreadful life you are living now.'

So! That was what he thought, was it? That my family meant nothing to me? And my life was to be completely changed?

I pulled myself away from him and jumped to my feet.

'I don't *want* to leave my father and sisters and brother! They all need me! We may be poor, and I know we don't have much, but we love each other and we're happy! Please go!'

The next day I told my father what had happened. He was sympathetic. He had not thought that Ken was suitable for me, but he had said nothing to me about it, preferring to let matters take their course.

After that I threw myself into vigorous spring cleaning. I began in the dining room; I opened the French doors wide and with my brother's help moved most of the furniture out onto the lawn. Father, much to his disgust, had to have his mid-day meal in the cosy old kitchen.

The Grandfather clock presented a problem. It was screwed in back to a board braced across the corner of the room where it had stood for years, keeping perfect time. I did not remember that it had ever been touched, much less moved, by anybody except Father who tended to it.

It must be filthy back there, I thought. I peered behind it: two screws held it to the board. I decided to remove them and do some thorough dusting. In a workmanlike manner, feeling rather clever, I oiled the screws and then with the biggest screwdriver I could find, I struggled and twisted and turned. My wrists felt as if they would break with the effort and then—success! One screw was out and the second was not so stubborn.

As soon as the second screw was released, Grandfather fell forward. The heavy lead weights hit me in the stomach at the same time as the domed case enclosing the face fell off onto my head. I was sent flying across the room. Now I understood why Grandfather was screwed to the wall.

At this juncture my brother came in.

'What on earth are you doing?' he said, surveying the scene. Grandfather lay face downwards in disgrace. 'Father will murder you.'

'I know, I know!' I wailed, holding my stomach in pain where the weights had hit me. 'Help me to get it together again before he comes home.'

Together we examined the near wreck I had wrought. Luckily, nothing was broken. The glass front had survived its nose dive. It took both of us to get Grandfather on his feet and screwed back in place. In protest he kept striking all the time. We discovered his lead insides had run down on their chains. The key for winding him was kept inside his case on a hook. It was missing. In my zeal for cleaning I had brushed it up with the dust and dirt. We retrieved it, but winding Grandfather wasn't easy, because the lead weights were very heavy. However, once he was upright the striking stopped—and so did the ticking! We adjusted his brass hands, we washed his ivory face, we swung his brass pendulum backward and forward. He coughed and ticked erratically; his hands moved with a jerk.

'I know what,' said my bright brother, 'he is off balance. Look at the floor. His feet should be on those exact dents in the linoleum. We must unscrew him again.'

'Please don't,' I cried in alarm. 'We shall never get him back again before Father comes home.'

'Silly, we won't unscrew him completely. Just enough so we can move his feet a little.'

I held Grandfather's frame whilst my brother released

the screws. We pushed gently until the feet moved into the dents and screwed the back up tight to the wall again. All was well. The pendulum swung in rhythm, the hands moved in time to the ticking. The glass-fronted dome sat once more on top. Not a scratch revealed the adventure. I bowed to Grandfather. 'I must say,' I said, 'your face looks better for a wash.'

'Come on,' my brother said. 'Stop playing about and get this room tidy before Father comes home if you don't want him to know what you've been up to.'

Father looked at his clock anxiously over the next week or two. The minute hand seemed to have been losing a little time. 'Odd,' he said, shaking his head.

I wasn't deterred by the clock experience from deciding to exchange wardrobes in the two best bedrooms. Our house had one and a half flights of stairs. The first flight ended in a small landing where a short hall led off to three back bedrooms. Another short flight of stairs directly opposite led to a much bigger landing off which were the big drawing room in the front of the house and my bedroom. The stairwell therefore had a solid wall on one side.

With my brother's help I got the small wardrobe easily on its end across the well between the rooms and the two stairways. It stood triumphantly on the top landing. The larger wardrobe, however, got firmly and truly stuck across the well. It was wedged on the step leading to the back bedrooms and across the hall to a stair on the half flight. It was hard up against the wall, and the other side was firm against the banister with the well of the stair gaping underneath it. My brother was imprisoned in one half of the house, I in the other.

'You and your moving! Now what are we going to do? I can't get out!' he shouted to me through the blocked doorway.

'Neither can I!' I shouted back. 'Push when I say three. One, two, three!'

We pushed together but it was no use; it just seemed to be wedged more tightly.

'If I could only get a screwdriver we might be able to do something,' my brother called. It was like calling to each other over Mount Everest. The wardrobe seemed just as immovable.

Presently my two young sisters came home.

'Where is everyone?' they called in unison.

'Up here,' I answered.

They thought it was funny at first, but not when they realised that my brother and I were definitely imprisoned.

'You two—make the fire up and get the tea ready,' I said. I was now beginning to wish my father would come home, but I dreaded his reaction.

'What is going on here?' he asked angrily; my sisters had told him about it as soon as he came in.

Poor Father. He crawled under the wardrobe in the well of the stairs where there was just room for him to move. He lay on his stomach and as we pushed, he lifted. I had to pull, my brother pushed and Father had to push upwards with his back and his hind quarters. Eventually the wardrobe moved and between us we got it into position, but not where I had planned to put it. It went back where it had been, where it belonged, and I was told in no uncertain terms to leave the furniture in the house where it already was.

My brother always said that Father had lifted the wardrobe bodily out of the stairwell on his back, but he never said it in Father's hearing. Tea was a trifle late that day.

I stopped moving furniture after that, but I did tackle the lounge with unfortunate results. The lounge, up the half flight of stairs leading off the top landing, was the biggest room in the house. I decided to clean it with my brother's casual help. At first everything went well. There was no time pressure, since the room was used only on Sundays. I could see that the heavy long curtains were going to present a problem. The mahogany curtain poles, one on each big window, were long, heavy and unwieldy. I climbed up pull-up steps and reached on tip-toe to get the curtains down. I had halfway un-hooked one curtain and had the weight of it on my arm when I reached to unhook a rusty, stubborn pin. I slipped and clutched frantically at the curtain pole; my weight pulled the bracket which held it out of the wall. The heavy pole swung loose knocking the steps over, and pole, steps and I and the curtains ended up together on the floor. It was a heavy fall. I felt as if my head had been knocked into my shoulders and my back broken. My arm had somehow gotten twisted under me with the curtains; I tried to raise it and screamed in agony as an excruciating pain ran from my fingertips to my shoulder. I fainted.

Fortunately my brother was at home. He took one look at my twisted arm as I moaned, coming to my senses, and said decisively, 'It's broken!' He called our neighbour, Mrs Piffen, the good soul, who hailed a hansom cab and came with me to the hospital whilst my brother went to tell Father at his Works. I remember the torture of that mile and a half ride to the hospital.

The doctor set the break with no anaesthetic. I opened my mouth to scream, but no sound came. I fainted again. When I came round, Sister had my arm between two heavy splints and a nurse was busy bandaging them in position. The pain was almost unbearable. I could only moan faintly. The doctor patted my head and said I would be easier in a day or two and left. Just as Mrs Piffen was wondering how to get me home again, my father appeared. He quickly got a cab, and I was soon at home tucked up in bed with a cup of tea and two aspirins.

My arm took three months to heal; I had to visit the doctor weekly for massage so that the wrist and elbow would not set in the position in which the sling held my arm. I had to move my wrist and fingers myself daily. I had a clever surgeon, but doctors in those days were tough, and patients had to be, too.

I became quite expert at keeping house with my left hand. That was a bad time for all of us. My brother had finished school; he had done well and should, according to his school report, have gone on to higher education, but there was no money. It was out of the question. My father took no interest in his son's career; it was his view that 'the boy' had had a good education and it was up to him to prove himself. My poor brother came down to earth with a bump and was in and out of a job. He was a butcher's boy for a while, getting up at six o'clock to cycle to the next town and not returning home until eight-thirty at night—a long day in all kinds of weather. Then he worked in a cycle shop; that didn't last long, and he ended up in hospital for a short spell with concussion, after the first floor ceiling of the shop collapsed, carrying him and a load of bicycles to the floor beneath. His next venture was work in a solicitor's office where he did well, and he enrolled in a commercial course at night school, paying for it out of his small earnings. When he was out of a job he was a tremendous help to me.

While I had been preoccupied with my own affairs, my sister Alice had left school without my father's permission and gotten a job as a cashier in a multiple store. She worked long hours, from eight in the morning to as late, often, as eight at night, with a half hour for lunch and, at four o'clock, a cup of tea by the grace of the manager's wife who lived on the premises. On Saturdays' late closing, it would be nine o'clock before the exhausted staff were released, to stagger home and recuperate on Sunday to be fresh for the new week Monday morning.

The managers of these stores were literally worked to death, often having to take stock and do other work on Sundays. It was not uncommon for managers to have complete breakdowns after a year or two. Such were the privileges of those in authority, with no one to appeal to except the owner, who decreed that if a man was 'broken at the wheel', he should be cast aside. My sister found some things about the job amusing. She told us about a poor old woman who came in for cracked eggs. If there were none that day, the sympathetic assistant would crack half a dozen for her, which she gladly had for half price.

But this sort of thing did not make up for the real discomforts of her work. The shop was located on a busy street which ran down to the sea front. Icy winds blew in from the North Sea through the open door and kept the commodities cool and the staff shivering. My sister endured this punishment all one winter and finally gave in to the long hours and wintry climate.

One morning she called to me. 'Ann, I can't get out of bed. My legs won't support me. They have been aching all night; so have my arms. I can't lift them.'

I looked at her flushed face and bright eyes. She was shivering and her lips were blue.

I called my father. 'Alice is not well. She can't get up,' I said as he came in the door. 'Her legs and arms ache.'

Father picked up her hand and raised her arm and when he let go it flopped down and she moaned. He turned down the bedclothes and took hold of her foot to raise her leg. She screamed.

'Daddy,' I said, 'she has got rheumatic fever.'

'Don't talk such nonsense,' my father said in alarm.

'What do you know about it?' In his anxiety he turned as if to strike me. He replaced the bedclothes carefully, his anger draining away. 'Get the doctor,' he said.

When the doctor came, he confirmed my suspicion. It had been sheer intuition on my part; I really knew nothing about it.

I bandaged my sister in cotton wool; she looked like an Egyptian mummy. I carried her somehow into my bedroom where a fire could be kept going night and day. Luckily there was no further trouble with the chimney as there had been when Grannie had bronchitis. I slept with her and tended her round the clock for six weeks while the fever lasted. The doctor left pills, which did little to relieve her pain. I cradled her in my arms and our tears mingled as I tried to soothe her.

After the fever abated, my father carried her downstairs and put her on the sofa. The firelight heightened the pallor of her wan little face in which her vivid blue eyes with dark circles under them looked enormous.

The rheumatic fever had left her with a weak heart which she had for the rest of her life. The doctor said she could never go back to that store, and she would have to rest for a year before she could even think about work.

9. Away from Home

MY sister gradually regained her strength. I took her for short walks along the sea front, and the colour gradually came back to her cheeks.

A cousin living in the country invited her for an indefinite stay. There were two small children there and my sister helped as she felt able, regaining her spirits and energy in their company. They sailed the Norfolk Broads and rode the pony trap—it was an ideal way to convalesce.

Alice had been away two or three months when I had an urgent message from my Aunt Nancy across the water. Her married daughter who lived in Huntingdon was threatened with a miscarriage and was not allowed out of bed. She needed someone to stay in the house all day with her, as a companion and to look after her little three-and-a-half-year-old daughter. Could I possibly go and help her for a week or two?

The idea appealed to me very much. I hadn't done much or been anywhere since Ken and I had parted. It had been a miserable period. I needed a change. Alice was a lot better, but she could not go back to work yet. I suggested she come home and relieve me so that I could take a working holiday with my cousin. She agreed: it would be only temporary, there would only be my father, my youngest sister and herself, since my brother was away at his paternal grandparents'. Aunt Martha agreed to do the laundry every week, so I knew my sister could cope.

I travelled the eighty miles from my aunt's house in the open back seat of her brand new Ford car. It was called 'the Dicky'. The Ford was known in those days as 'the Flying Bedstead' because it was built so high off the ground; the 'Dicky' seat was high and open and caught the wind. I was wedged in the seat between trunks, hat boxes, packages and parcels, as if my aunt were moving house, and not just visiting for a few days. My own belongings, of no consequence, were all contained in a string bag which I held on my lap.

My aunt had difficulty mounting into her black shining automobile. The step was high; there was only one door and she had to squeeze her ample figure and musquash coat past the front seat tipped forward, or climb over the seat. The latter was made impossible by a long, tight black skirt. Ladies' clothes were not designed for motoring. Both the car and the coat proclaimed my aunt's status in life and their acquisition had no doubt contributed to my uncle's present poor state of health. My aunt was an ambitious woman and had been the making of her husband and the driving force in the successful marriages of her three daughters. Her sons-in-law all stood in awe of her and all had removed their wives and themselves from the town where she lived, with indecent haste.

Uncle's health would not permit him to drive. For a small consideration a young apprentice from Uncle's engineering works would forsake his studies and act as chauffeur to my aunt. At times when she was between maids, he would do her housework. Aunt was very persuasive; no one could stand out against her. Philip, the apprentice, had at one time attempted to teach my aunt to drive, but was rather put off when she nearly drove him and herself into the river. On another occasion she drove under the outstretched arm of a traffic policeman, nearly knocking him off his beat.

'I thought you were waving me on, Officer,' she said politely to the speechless constable.

There was no ventilation in the Ford, no heat and no windscreen wipers. The window had to remain slightly open, because of the condensation deposited by the occupants' breathing under certain climatic conditions. This caused discomfort; rugs and hot water bottles fought a losing battle with the insidious cold.

Fog was lethal and brought most traffic to a standstill, the inside of the car being steamed up and the outside impenetrable. I remember on one outing buying candles at the local village store and holding a lighted one against the windscreen for miles to thaw the steam cloud on the glass in order to clear a patch for the driver to see through. On another occasion, I had to sit beside the driver and hold the door ajar with my head poking out to guide him past hedgerows and ditches and warn him of approaching bends in the road. We would both be freezing cold in the icy fog. Such were the joys of motoring.

There was little hazard, however, from other cars on the road. One seldom met traffic on country roads and pollution from petrol fumes was unthought of.

My aunt would backseat drive the whole way.

'Henry,' she would say to my uncle, 'tell Philip not to go so fast. I am sure he is doing forty,'; or 'Henry, Philip didn't slow down on that corner.' She swayed with the motion of the car or clutched her ridiculous large bedecked hat in alarm as she dramatised everything that happened. My long-suffering uncle ignored her and Philip got a certain satisfaction from her discomfort, as hens and chickens scattered on the road, dogs barked and people stopped to stare at our stately progress.

I stayed with my cousin until her son was born and after that, for the sum of seven and sixpence a week and my keep, I remained happily with her for over a year, since my sister seemed to be managing very well at home without me. When the maternity 'living-in' nurse who ruled the household with her routine rod of iron mercifully left, we became a happy family on our own.

The little girl, Polly, was so delighted with her baby brother that her attentions were in grave danger of ending his life. I had to rescue him often, and to keep an eye on her. We lived in a large flat in the High Street over a gentlemen's outfitters. There were six big rooms with huge windows overlooking the street. My cousin, Vera, a delicate Dresden China blonde, and her husband Albert were an 'arty' couple and their home, with its grand piano and Chinese carpets, was a revelation to me. They delighted in music, and had records, piano recitals and musical evenings. I learned much about the great composers while I was with them. Sometimes I was even asked to sing during one of their musical evenings; to my surprise the audience seemed to enjoy it.

I read and learned at their flat. Albert seemed to me to be a fountain of knowledge and he patiently answered all my naïve questions. He was vastly amused when I asked him who had knocked the arm off the statue of Venus de Milo. Albert had a small car, an Austin Seven. It was 'coach built' and was like a small box on wheels. It had no 'Dicky' as my aunt's Ford had, but it had two seats in the back. There was very little space between the back seats and the front but somehow Polly and I and the baby in a 'carry cot' managed to squeeze in. We drove for miles exploring the countryside. I discovered the beauty and grandeur of Oxford and Cambridge—the wonder of cathedrals, old churches and university buildings was opened up to me. It was a whole new world.

Bedford was only a few miles away. We visited there often to listen to the brass band on summer Sunday evenings. The band played on an island in the river, until one Sunday the island sank with all hands on board. Luckily there were no casualties. On another occasion when we were travelling in traffic on the main road, Albert was trying to overtake a lorry; just as he began to pull even, a hand repeatedly appeared and waved him back. Finally we passed the lorry, to discover that the 'hand' was a pig's trotter, which slipped out of the side of the vehicle everytime it gave a lurch. The pigs, poor things, were on their way to a slaughterhouse.

I saved my pocket money carefully and used it to extend my wardrobe. My cousin was skilful with her needle and she taught me how to cut and sew patterns. I began to feel and look like a different person and my cousin began to concern herself about my loveless life, although somehow my enthusiasm for the male sex had diminished. She did her best to introduce young eligible bachelors to me, although I was completely unaware of most of them and of their intentions. I sang 'Pale Hands I Loved', from the *Indian Love Lyrics,* with feeling, along with many other songs, to my cousin's piano accompaniment and the discomfort of an assortment of young men. However I did eventually become friendly with a smart young man who managed the gentlemen's outfitters shop downstairs. My cousin invited him for morning coffee and enjoyed what she imagined to be a romance flourishing before her eyes.

The town was built on either side of the river. We had a small rowing boat and often had picnics on the river banks or on small islands in the river. Every year the town held a regatta. The river would be crowded with people out in small craft for a day's holiday. During this particular regatta the young man from the outfitters shop had been invited to join us. Since it was a public holiday both he and Albert, who was a cashier in the bank, were free. We took our picnic and moored at one of the leafy, shady islands. It was a lovely summer day. There was an overall air of festivity and everything went well. The baby was safely landed and was sleeping in his carry cot. Polly was dancing about with excitement.

'Come and make me a daisy chain,' she demanded, darting about, sometimes perilously near the water's edge. Her copper hair shimmered like gold in the sunlight and her green eyes danced with mischief. She was a high-spirited child who needed a watchful eye. 'Catch,' she shouted, and threw a ball at no one in particular. It landed among the picnic, causing chaos, and her mother scolded her roundly. Crestfallen for the moment, Polly soon recovered to go on to higher adventure and keep me on the alert.

The competing craft passed by lazily, waiting for events to take place. They created a swell on the water which rocked our boat and made us feel insecure. I had passed most things from the boat to the shore; the boat bobbing up and down as the ripples spread from the passing craft to the bank where we had moored. I was stepping across from the bank to the boat when the swell suddenly lifted our boat away, causing me to misjudge the distance.

I stepped into the water and went down like a stone. I shall never forget that feeling of nothing under my feet as I was drawn into the river by my saturated clothing, and the water closed over my head. A reassuring voice said, 'Don't struggle; put your arms around my neck.' I did and two hands grabbed me and we started floating together, my head now above the water. My arms and legs felt as though they were being dragged out of their sockets, my lungs were bursting; I couldn't breathe. I was dragged out of the water by willing hands and laid on the grass, gasping like a fish. Faces floated in the atmosphere around me. A weight left my chest and a voice said, 'She'll be all right now.' The pressure on my lungs was relieved. I felt better.

But I was humiliated beyond words at the spectacle I presented. My thin white cotton dress was clinging to me, revealing all. I felt as if I was standing naked in front of everyone. All I wanted to do was go home and crawl into bed. I felt worn out and disheveled. The outfitters' young man made no progress with me at all after that. I avoided him almost as if my calamity had been his fault. I felt embarrassed every time I saw him. A beautiful romance was thus nipped in the bud.

The river, which was such a great attraction in the summer, was a menace in the winter and spring when heavy rains caused it to swell and overflow its banks. While I was there a flood warning was given. The river was in a low-lying part of the town, and people walked down to the bridge and looked apprehensively at the water lapping over the bank. It was dark green and ominous-looking. Many of the older residents shook their heads and muttered amongst themselves.

'It's still rising,' one said.

'Aye, she don't seem to be going down at all,' said another gloomily.

'The morrow will tell; it's a full moon tonight. Tide will swell and she'll be flooded all over the town for sure,' said a third.

Albert overheard them. 'I think he may well be right,' he said. The old men judged the tides by the moon and the weather by their rheumatism. We went home disturbed, wondering what the 'morrow' would bring.

Downstairs the outfitters' young man was frantically putting all his stock onto the shelves. Nothing was left on the floor. Chairs were stacked on the counter along with removable fixtures; he was taking no chances. The window was empty, as were the windows of all the other shops on the street. People were taking what they could to upstairs rooms—all but a few who thought it couldn't happen to them, and elderly people who couldn't manage and had no one to help them. I heard about one poor old soul who cried and implored neighbours to move her precious piano upstairs; not one of its keys had been struck for years, but she kept all her family portraits on top of it. I don't suppose the piano ever sounded again; that street was flooded to the window sills.

We were lucky: because we lived in an upstairs flat, the flood did not reach us. Only the hall stand in the downstairs front entrance never stood quite straight again, and Albert's cap was found floating in the dirty water, which lapped onto the third stair. The carpet never regained its pristine beauty. But ours were minor casualties. Albert waded through the water in the High Street in his Wellingtons, with his shoes, tied together, hanging round his neck.

My cousin and I had a grandstand view from the front windows. People in Wellingtons and people with no shoes on at all were paddling about, trying to do last minute shopping at the few shops which had opened their doors and were salvaging and storing what they could on shelves. The water was creeping insidiously higher; a stray cabbage, a lost shoe, floated lazily by. By noon that day the water had reached the level of the window sills and letter boxes and the ground floors were flooded.

By mid-afternoon Vera was growing anxious about Albert. Then we saw him staggering and floundering in the water on his way home. The water was up over his knees.

The following morning small rowing boats were out in the Street delivering bread and other odds and ends. People leaned out of their windows and the bread was passed to them on a spiked pole. The scene was reminiscent of Venice, but not nearly so picturesque. The true agony came as the water began to subside. People's homes were ruined. Furniture was broken and waterlogged; decorations were destroyed, carpets were saturated and indescribably filthy. Pets had been drowned, as were farmers' chickens. I remember passing a small farm where the wife looked at me with unseeing eyes as she tried vainly to clean a carpet which she had slung over a hedge. A barrow full of dead chickens stood in the farmyard, their long necks dangling as if they had been stretched, their feathers matted with mud.

The sludgy water left a trail of misery and chaos long remembered by the townsfolk, who received a doubtful notoriety in the nation's press. The flood was not the only newsworthy event in the town while I was there. A very smart couple came to live there and took an enormous Georgian house which they turned into a boys' preparatory school. Albert thought this was an excellent idea, and promptly enrolled his son, and in addition became firm friends with the principal, who had a string of letters after his name and appeared to be a learned man, after Albert's own heart.

At the same time Albert had certain reservations about the man. His degrees, for one thing, were American and did not measure up to Albert's Oxford standard. 'He seems a gentleman and a nice fellow, but there is something there that I don't quite trust,' he said.

The school flourished, but there was gossip in the town nevertheless. For one thing, rumour had it that 'they' weren't married. That would have been a shocking state of affairs then, guaranteed to contaminate the young pupils. Here and there a dissatisfied parent spoke up. Finally one of the parents lodged a complaint to the police and the school was investigated. The gentlemanly principal vanished overnight and the school was closed down. It turned out that the principal had invented all his degrees and was a phony. It caused quite a sensation in the small market town.

I had now been living with my cousin for over a year. She had recovered her health and energy; Polly was going to kindergarten and becoming more obedient and settled. My cousin felt she could cope alone with her little family and it was time for me to leave them; they had been very kind to me, but I was excited at the prospect of seeing my family again. I wrote home to say that I would be coming back.

My father wrote back promptly to say that although my sister's health was much improved, she was not well enough to hold a regular job. She managed the house very well and he felt would like to continue to stay at home. Since he could not afford to keep and clothe two big girls at home, it was up to me to find a suitable situation and to support myself. Of course I would be welcome home for a short visit but I could not stay there permanently.

I read and re-read my letter through a mist of tears. I felt rejected. What was I to do? I was untrained for any work, and I was being thrown out into the world to fend for myself. It was a time of serious unemployment. The precarious state of the economy had escaped me in the happy existence with my cousins. Up to now my life had been sheltered in domesticity. I was ill-equipped for the wicked world.

I did not know that my father was having a difficult time. The Works he managed were practically closed down because of crippling tax demands left over, supposedly, from the War years. Father was receiving only half pay and working with a skeleton staff. My youngest sister Laura was at that time finishing her matriculation course at school and hoping to get a Bursarship for teachers' training college. A Bursarship was a local government grant which the young teacher would repay when she was qualified. My father had a lot of worries, but, being my father, he wrote to me without adding any touch of warmth or gentleness.

I was completely shattered. It had never crossed my mind that I might not be able to go home and take up where I had left off. I saw nothing for it but domestic service. I would be another Lizzie like my aunt's maid in a print dress, apron and cap. 'Come here, Lizzie, go there Lizzie . . . Don't do that, you stupid girl . . . Fetch me this, fetch me that . . .' Oh, I wailed to myself, I couldn't stand it.

I had had such dreams . . . singing to an audience, standing beside a beautiful, shining ebony grand piano . . . vanished into thin air. My cousins had given me a taste of a different, broader life. I liked what they had taught me. I now had a decent wardrobe, mostly made by my cousin's skilful little hands. Never again would I travel with my belongings in a string bag. I would have a suitcase like a lady!

But what was I to do? Where was I to go? Should I write to my aunt Nancy and go and live with her and kind Uncle Henry? No, no—that would be imprisonment and servitude. I would be at her beck and call from early morning until late at night. She couldn't keep a maid for a month. I couldn't stand it, I said to myself, what am I to do?

Albert read my letter and looked grave.

'Well, Ann,' he said, 'we shall have to think very seriously what to do about this. Have you ever thought of becoming a governess? Teach and care for children, live in a family. You have handled Polly very well and taught her to read and count. I could give you a good reference. It shouldn't be too difficult.'

I was captivated by the idea. 'Oh,' I said, 'do you think I could?'

I answered advertisements in the daily press and, with a glowing reference from Albert, I was engaged by a family in Nottinghamshire. They were farmers and landowners in a big way. I was to be paid ten shillings a week salary all found. I would have status living with the family as I had done with my cousin. I was even going to teach music, which I feared might tax me a little, and French—not my best subject. But there were always textbooks. I hoped that *French Without Tears* would live up to its name. We had found it a very helpful book at school.

Armed with my brand new suitcase, a chequebook and modest bank account and lots of good advice I set out all on my own for my first real job—out into the competitive world of which I was ignorant.

I sat in the compartment of the train watching the fields and the beautiful countryside flash by. There was something majestic in the bare trees foreshadowing the coming winter. I wondered what sort of life I was going to. There were four children in the household, a bit of a handful, I suspected. I re-read the letter which had come from home that morning. There was no expression of disappointment at not seeing me; I could not be buoyed by good wishes. Was I forgotten by my family so soon? I had a dreadful feeling of belonging nowhere. My spirits sank; I wiped away a tear of self-pity.

The train raced on and took me to my destination.

Sitting beside Mr Roberts, my employer, in his beautiful Daimler automobile, I became more depressed as miles of fields and hedgerows went by, with never a sign of human habitation. The earth, lying fallow for the winter, stretched endlessly to the horizon.

'The Old Roman Fosse Way,' said Mr Roberts, indicating the road ahead; we were traveling in grand isolation. An eternity of straight road, I thought, stretching into the beyond!

Eventually we took a turning into a narrow lane; the hedgerows nearly met, and there was barely enough room for the big car to pass. We came to a village of forty or fifty houses dotted along the lane and around a village green. The farmhands' cottages, Mr Roberts explained. At the end of the village he swung into the gravel drive leading to the entrance of a great stone farmhouse, around which sprawled outhouses and stables in apparent disarray; some looked old and broken-down, some more recently built. I learned later that it was mostly a sheep farm and my employer kept hunters. He followed the hunt and had kennels of hounds. I never came to terms with these animals—I was too timid. They sensed it and took advantage of me.

A beautiful, pleasant lady waited for us at the entrance to the house. She extended her hand and smiled. 'I'm glad to meet you. I hope you're not tired out from your journey?'

Mrs Roberts was a beautiful woman with raven black hair drawn into a bun on the nape of her neck, olive skin and wide-spaced violet eyes. She introduced me to the children: David, the eldest, was fair and blue-eyed like his father; then came Barbara who had her mother's long black hair, and two little girls, the youngest still a baby in a high chair. It was an attractive family, and they seemed friendly. 'We hope you will be happy with us,' Mr Roberts said. 'We are not as bad as we look.'

The maid of all work was summoned to take me to my room. She was a cheerful, friendly girl named Janet. 'I 'ope you stay longer than the other one, Miss,' she said. It's Miss Babs—she plays up something cruel, no one will put up with 'er. I'll fetch you some 'ot water, Miss, for your wash.'

My room had a country freshness: it was large, and papered with tiny rosebuds; the armchair, curtains and bedspread were covered in matching chintz. There was a small table next to the elegant shining brass bedstead. The window opened out to a view of miles of grazing land; I could just discern the sheep in the gathering dusk. There seemed to my untrained eye to be hundreds of them. They were amazingly tough; I learned that they withstood all kinds of weather. They had their lambs with the first snowfall.

My room had a carpeted floor, a dressing table with a chintz petticoat, a marble-topped washstand with a china ewer and basin and a closet where I could hang my clothes. I was delighted with it, and with having it all to myself. I had shared the bedroom at my cousins' with Polly. But here the night nursery was across the landing, and I had privacy. I must be happy here, I told myself. I just must be. Janet came back with a water can of hot water.

' 'ot water is in the kitchen,' she said. 'Fetch it in your can when you want it during the day. The nursery maid will bring it in the morning and knock you up. Oh— and staff use the back stairs and so do the children when they come in from walks.'

I washed and combed my hair and hesitated about which stairs to use to go down for tea. I finally decided to use the front stairs, because that was the way I came up.

At seven-thirty the next morning there was a knock on my door and a heavy, solid-looking girl entered.

'I've brought you your 'ot water, Miss,' she said. 'I'm the nursery maid, my name is Gladys. I light the nursery fire at seven o'clock and clear it, then I helps Missus to get the two little ones dressed and down for breakfast. You 'as to see to the other two and have them to breakfast at eight o'clock sharp. Master don't like latecomers.'

She gave me a bright smile as she crossed the room to draw the curtains. Her father, I learned later, was the head shepherd on the farm; a responsible position.

Breakfast was a feast: huge joints of boiled ham, bacon, eggs, mushrooms, tomatoes, preceded by porridge laced with thick cream, and followed by toast, home-churned dairy butter and home-made marmalade. The coffee was a dream, freshly ground and topped with cream. I was to gain a stone in weight in a month to the approval of Mrs Roberts; I was too thin before, she said.

Breakfast and tea were family meals, but Gladys had to see to lunch for the two little ones and put them to bed for a midday rest.

As Janet had said, Barbara was the difficult one. She loved chasing across the fields with the dogs, which she would let off the lead. They jumped at her and often knocked her down in the mud; it didn't bother her but it did me, because I had to help clean her up. I was terrified of these big animals. They would leap up on me and put their paws on my shoulders, panting into my face with their tongues lolling out of their wide mouths. Barbara could bawl at them like a man and bring them to heel. She rode the horses fearlessly: she had been given her own as a birthday present, a young, spirited animal.

She hated her lessons and the rest period after luncheon, when I read to her and David. 'Do you *have* to read that dreary old story?' she would ask. 'Isn't the rest hour up yet? I'm sure it's two hours now, not one. I want to take Rover across the fields this afternoon.'

I would tell her that she could do whatever she wished when the hour was over. As a treat when she was good I would read her *Black Beauty* or some other animal story. She would have loved television and my job would have been a lot easier if we had had it then.

David was a quiet boy who suffered from asthma and numerous allergies. His father did not understand and would not forgive the boy for being, as he put it, 'a bit soft'. He tried to toughen him; his attempts usually brought on one of David's attacks and left Mr Roberts frustrated. His mother, who was all concern, coddled him, according to his father. It was pathetic to see David's look of mute pleading whenever his father started one of his toughening-up sessions. But the boy had pluck; he said nothing and went like a lamb to the slaughter.

David was a romantic boy, a dreamer, and he read voraciously. He would listen to me read all day if I had time. We became fast friends.

One day he had been roaming the fields and dreaming as usual whilst I had been occupied with Barbara and the horses. I never learned to ride which was a mistake, really, but I was too timid.

'Dad,' David said at luncheon, 'there's a big fire at the Red Lion on the Fosse Way. The fire engines from town are there, and all the farmers are helping.'

'What!' His father jumped up from the table. 'Why didn't you tell us about this before? I must take some of the farmhands to help. Come!' he said to David, who followed him out of the room. A few minutes later

Mr Roberts came back. 'Where is David?' he asked. 'I shall have to go without him; that boy is always missing when he is wanted.'

David was missing all the afternoon. His father came back in a foul temper. 'Where is that boy?' he shouted. 'I'll teach him to make a fool of me. He lied and deceived us—there is no fire. Look for him and bring him to my study the minute you find him.'

David was found hiding in the barn behind some farm machinery. He said he had been thinking about a fire and had actually convinced himself that he really saw one. His mother pleaded for him but Mr Roberts would not accept any excuse. He thrashed the boy and stalked out of the study to disappear until supper time.

Mrs Roberts' tears mingled with David's. She bathed his bruises and undressed him and put him to bed with hot milk and aspirin. But still he had an attack of asthma; he was in bed for a week. The doctor was not called because of David's bruises, which might have caused some unwanted gossip. Mr Roberts insisted that he had dealt properly with the disgraceful episode. He wasn't going to bring his boy up to be a liar, he said.

I read to David and spent a lot of time in his room that week. Barbara was out riding with her father who seemed to take extra pleasure in her prowess during this time. 'I really did see that fire,' David said to me. 'And the fire engines. I heard their bells clanging and people crying for help. I really did! I don't know why Father got so upset.'

I tried to explain to him that he should try and keep fact and imagination in their proper places, and that he must not retell his dreams as truths. His father, I said, considered he had been lied to and did not understand and could not forgive.

Christmas came before I had been with them very long. I was too far away to travel home for the day and

I had not yet earned a holiday. I had only a half-day off a month, and I did not know what to do with it in that isolated spot. I was able to buy some Christmas presents and cards during the week on market day when the family took me along. Mr Roberts would visit the cattle market and the children liked the old castle ruins in the town. My relaxation was to go shopping with Mrs Roberts.

I knew the family were going to relatives for Christmas Day, and I expected to accompany them. But Mr Roberts said that he did not expect me to go along, because everyone there would be a stranger to me. He said he thought I would enjoy a whole day to myself; the kitchen staff would all be away too.

I was shattered. I was going to be all alone in the house on Christmas Day. I felt like taking the next train home. I received a few Christmas cards, but I felt mocked by them and by the holly and mistletoe. I couldn't join wholeheartedly in the children's excited anticipation.

'We shall not be home late, Miss Wood,' Mrs Roberts said. 'I wonder if I might ask you to keep the kitchen fire going so that the children's bathwater will be hot?'

'Certainly, I will attend to it,' I said, feeling miserable.

'I have left a meal for you on the kitchen table. It will need warming up,' Mrs Roberts said.

I watched the excited children pile into the Daimler. They shouted at me to have a merry Christmas. David had said that he wished I was going too, when I helped him with the presents he was taking with him.

I stood and watched the car turn out of the driveway until the cold wind forced me inside. My footsteps echoed through the stone passage and up the uncarpeted back staircase which I used from force of habit. The nursery was eerily silent. I sank into the old armchair by the fire and gave way to forlorn feelings. A tear trickled down my cheek as I thought of my father and brother and sisters. I wondered if they would miss me at all. 'All our love and best wishes for a Happy Xmas,' their card said. Would they think about me, alone in the big house, forsaken on Christmas Day? I pictured them sitting round the table, Father sharpening his knife expertly on his 'steel' before attacking the turkey; the plum pudding with the sprig of holly on top and the Ohs and Ahs as Father put a match to the brandy poured over it and flames engulfed it and died away in blue smoke. And there was the excitement over the threepenny pieces and charms. 'You're going to be an old maid,' my brother had teased me once when I bit on the silver thimble.

I tortured myself by envisaging them all laughing and joking without me, wearing their ridiculous paper hats and crowns.

Mrs Roberts had given me a leather-bound edition of Dickens' *A Christmas Carol;* it was inscribed to me from the family. I still have it. I opened it in a blur of tears and started to read. I lost myself and my misery in the excitement of happiness of the Cratchit family with their enormous turkey.

The Grandfather clock boomed one o'clock, resounding from the hall over the empty house. Force of habit took me to the kitchen for my Christmas dinner. I lifted the enormous metal cover off the dish on the table. Jugged hare met my gaze. If you have ever smelt the strong aroma of jugged hare, you will understand why I had no Christmas dinner that year. I learned later that it is an acquired taste; perhaps my abrupt introduction on Christmas Day prejudiced me against it. Possibly if it had been served while I sat with fellow sufferers wearing paper hats and with a welcome gift beside each plate it would have had some appeal, but as it was it was an abomination, as unwelcome as I apparently was at the family feast to which my charges had gone. 'You would not feel at home,' my mistress had said. But what could make her think I would feel at home in a deserted house with a jugged hare?

I stayed with the Robertses a year and a half. It was a lonely life. I belonged nowhere; I was not one of the family, although they were kind to me and occasionally invited me to meet their friends and play cards. And I could not become friendly with the maid and the nurse-maid, who were nearer my own age.

The maid Janet was lonely too; she was a few miles from home. She often crept up the backstairs to my room for a gossip. I learned a lot about the Master and the Mistress from her. Janet worked from six o'clock in the morning when she got up and lit all the necessary fires in the house, until after supper was cleared and the dishes washed up, when it would be nine o'clock and time for bed. Many times when I went down to fetch my can of hot water before supper I found her stretched out like a dog fast asleep on the piece mat in front of the kitchen fire.

'Don't tell the Missus,' she would plead if I woke her. 'I'll be sent packing if I'm caught asleep.'

Her faith in the future rested on the hope of a great romance entering her life and the five shillings a week which was her pay.

One market day, when master and mistress had gone to town with the children, Janet and I were alone in the house. A motor bike roared through the village and back again. The second time Janet was at the gate.

' 'ere, wait for me,' she called to the dashing driver. 'Keep a lookout for me,' she cried to me as I popped my head out of the nursery window. She was on the pillion roaring round and round the village and waved delightedly to me every time she passed the house.

The sound of the motor bike ceased without return-ing to the house and I concluded that Janet had gone for a ramble in the nearby woods with her new-found friend. And in half an hour Janet had lost her heart, if nothing more vital, and planned more excursions. ''aven't you ever been in love, Miss?' she asked me dreamily. 'You don't know what you're missing. It makes you feel good all over.'

As it happened, the good feelings were fleeting. 'Miss Wood,' my mistress asked me some months later, 'have you noticed anything unusual about Janet? Or is it my imagination? She seems to be putting on weight and has slowed down.'

I said I hadn't noticed but in time the sad truth was only too obvious. Janet had been making love ardently while the Mistress and Master and I were having supper. She had half an hour in the evening when she could be sure not to be disturbed once she had set the cold meal.

'My mother will starve if you give me the sack, Missus,' Janet cried. 'She needs me wages every week to 'elp with the little ones. I'm strong, really I am, I can keep going up to the last minute and me Mum will take the babe when it comes. She ain't never got over our little Annie what drowned in the mill stream last summer. It'll be a comfort to her.'

Her mother was a widow with a young family to support. She took in washing from morning to night every day of the week. I was appalled at this helpless, casual attitude to the whole affair. Janet was worried only about losing her job. Bringing a baby into an impoverished household did not upset her. Poor baby, I thought, no father, no future. I felt dreadfully guilty when my mistress said, 'I wish I had known of this affair so that I could have stopped it before it went so far. I do feel a little responsible for the girl.'

I was upset but I wisely said nothing. Janet went home for two weeks and had her baby. She didn't lose her job, but came back well and bright and unchastened.

Since I went so infrequently to town, I kept my wages

in a tin box in my drawer. Gladys the nursery maid cleaned my room. When I discovered a few pounds missing, I suspected Janet, who had no occasion to enter my room. I got a home safe from the bank to keep my money in and after Janet returned from her confinement, I asked her about it.

'Janet, I'm missing some money from my room. Do you know anything about it?'

'No, Miss, I 'aven't touched your money. Gladys cleans your room, not me.'

'Then how did this come to be on the floor near my chest of drawers?' I showed her a blue uniform button, matching those on her morning dress. 'Gladys wears pink,' I said.

'I don't know that, Miss, but God's truth I wouldn't touch nothing of yours.'

'Well, I shall have to go to the Mistress and she will call the police.'

'Oh!' she said, and burst into tears. 'Don't do that, Miss; I didn't think you would notice it, not having anyone to want it. Me mum wasn't well and got be'ind with the washing. I give it to 'er to feed the kids, as true as I stand here. You don't know what it is to 'ave nothing. You 'aven't got brothers and sisters with no father and no shoes on their feet.'

'Oh, Janet, stop crying,' I said, nearly in tears myself. 'It is wrong to steal; promise me you will never do that again ever in your life and I will forget all about it. You should have asked me.'

'I didn't think you would understand, Miss, about being poor. You should see me mum; she's all worn out with work and worry.'

I didn't tell Janet but I thought I understood more than she realized. My sister had written that my father was still on half pay. The Works were almost shut down. Many of my father's workmen were begging for his old clothes. I had already sent money home. I prayed we never got as poor as Janet. The Janets of this world, I thought, knew how to survive and fend for themselves.

Not long after these shattering events I came down with flu and although everyone was kind and thoughtful, I got depressed and homesick. The Robertses suggested I take my two weeks vacation and go home to my family.

I knew, I had a feeling that when I left that house I would never return. I had not been unhappy, I had learned a lot, but I was lonely there; I needed company. I had a dreadful vision of growing old in their service. They would have all my youth as my family had had all my adolescence. I was beginning to feel that life was not offering me much.

But I was happy to be home. The excitement of being with my own family made me put off telling them my decision, and the longer I put it off the harder it became. I had money now to pay for my board. My father, although officially on half time, stayed all day at the Works from force of habit. Little economies were evident, but there was no real hardship.

But here I was, back at the beginning. I had no prospects, but I did have a little experience of the outside world and a little money in the bank, which gave me a certain amount of confidence.

I finally told my sister I was not going back to the farm.

'But what will you do, Ann?' she asked, worried. 'Father won't let you stay here much longer.'

'I don't know,' I said, 'but I shall watch all the papers in the library every day and see what jobs are advertised. There must be something I can do.'

The meagre number of jobs available were mostly for skilled workers, and there was not much at all for women except domestic work, which I hated to think about. I wouldn't be a Janet or a Lizzie for anything on earth.

I was beginning to understand why so many girls married young. The obvious escape was 'Mr Right', of whom Grannie spoke so fondly. Well, I was too independent to try to make any man 'Mr Right'.

An advertisement in *The Times* caught my eye. 'Lady companion cum secretary. No typing or shorthand. To help partially blind man with his correspondence etc. Good wages, all found.'

I answered it, giving my experience as governess, and was accepted.

'I don't know how you dare,' said Alice. 'Going into some remote country district! He might be mad and lock you up or something horrible.'

'Don't be silly,' I said. 'He's nearly blind, poor man; he needs someone to read to him and write his letters.'

'But why doesn't his wife do it?'

'Maybe he's not married. He might be young and handsome and very rich and marry me. You never know.'

'Ann, you are a stupid romancer. I don't like you going off on your own like this. Please promise to come home at once if it looks at all suspicious, won't you?'

'Oh, I promise, if it makes you any happier,' I said. 'But really the world isn't full of wolves waiting to devour unsuspecting girls, you know.'

I arrived at the nearest station and asked the porter cum station master for directions and a cab.

'There ain't no cab,' he said, 'unless the butcher or the baker is going to the big house and would take you. I would take your luggage on my bike myself, but I'm expecting another train through this afternoon. It's about two and a half miles along the road.' He pointed to the dusty road leading out of the village to 'No Man's Land'.

I murmured my thanks and picked up my suitcase which, luckily, was not too heavy. I had a very small wardrobe.

It seemed a long two-and-a-half miles. I remembered how I had walked the three miles to the ferry at home to cross the river for a halfpenny when I hadn't two-pence for the tramcar. In those days the three miles seemed nothing. I thought I must be out of condition. But it was a lovely sunny afternoon. I took my time, stopping to gather violets in the hedgerows. The trees looked fragile in their spring green. I saw no one and no vehicles on the road, which narrowed about a mile and a half from the village. Eventually it became all but impassable, the hedges nearly met on either side and were about ten or twelve feet high.

Presently, a footpath wide enough for a small vehicle veered sharply off the lane; it led to a long grey stone wall about six feet high. Through the hedges and trees I could glimpse what appeared to be a large grey stone house. The wall seemed to encircle a large garden with acres of fields on either side.

I walked up to a heavy brown oak studded door, grabbed the wrought iron ring hanging by a heavy rope near the door frame and pulled. A loud clanging rent the air, followed by the fierce barking of what I took to be more than one dog. A grille opened in the door and a human eye, nose and mouth were visible. A voice said, 'Yes?' as the mouth moved.

'Is this the Manor House?' I enquired.

'Yes,' said the voice again.

'May I see Mr Horseberry? I am the new secretary.'

The grille snapped shut and there was the sound of bolts being drawn and a key turned in the lock. The door opened cautiously, just wide enough for me and my suitcase to pass through.

'Come,' said the voice. I followed the thinnest figure I had ever seen in my life, enveloped in a faded blue dress; a none-too-clean white apron was tied round a waist my one hand would comfortably have spanned.

The dogs I had heard followed us, quiet now and obedient to her command.

She carried what looked to me like the trumpet from an old gramophone. But it was actually her ear trumpet; she was deaf. I found that to hold any conversation with her, I had to put my mouth close to the trumpet and shout down it while she pressed the small end to her ear. It was exhausting to me and at first embarrassing. Her name was Nan. She had greasy sparse grey hair scraped into a small bun, expressionless eyes set close together, a long pointed nose and taut flesh over high cheekbones. Her thin blue lips covered a few black teeth. I had never seen anyone so thin and wraith-like. She seemed ageless, and I thought she would frighten any child out of its wits.

She hadn't caught my name. I had to lean forward and shout down the horn.

'Yes, I'm expected,' I yelled. 'Miss Wood. I would like to see Mr Horseberry.'

'Oh aye, I daresay you would,' she muttered. 'Another one of them. I hope you'll be better than the last. Follow me.'

She hobbled down the path leading to what I took to be the front door; we passed one door leading into the house which I found out later was the kitchen door. The house was long and narrow, backing into the road, set against the high wall. As I followed Nan from the gate, I could not help feeling that this place was like a prison, with bolts and bars and keys. Nan had a bunch of keys jingling under her apron, suspended from a string around her waist.

We went in the front door, and down a passage into a room dominated by a huge round table being set for a meal by a round-faced woman with dark frizzy hair which looked as though it had just been released from curling irons. She was dressed in black and wore a white frilly apron.

'She's the parlour maid,' Nan said, pointing to her. 'She's deaf too.'

I noticed then that she was wearing a cumbersome-looking box on her ear; a cord ran from it under her apron, where I detected another cumbersome box.

'She's got one of those new-fangled hearing aids,' Nan said. 'But she only hears when she wants to hear.'

I got the impression that Nan and the parlourmaid were not on the best of terms.

'Who's that?' asked the maid, pointing ungraciously to me.

'She's the new one, come to help the boss,' Nan replied, jerking her head toward me. I felt like an exhibit at a deaf and dumb show.

'Better go tell the master she's here.' Nan shuffled out.

The parlourmaid continued with her duties, ignoring me. Suddenly she said, 'Don't take any notice of her. She's only the old housekeeper. She interferes and takes things on herself.'

Nan came back, jerked her head at me and crooked her finger. I followed her. We passed from the dining room through a door opposite the one we had entered, across a passage into another room: Mr Horseberry's study.

He was an old man—I guessed in his seventies—and came to greet me with outstretched hand. He was almost blind.

'You have to watch him, Miss, all the time. He knocks himself about something terrible, he does,' Nan whispered to me.

'That will be all, Nan, thank you,' he said.

She left us, muttering to herself and he and I shook hands. 'How do you do,' I said.

'Ah,' he said. 'You have a pleasant voice, a change from the last one. Now I am sure you would like to refresh yourself before tea. At tea you will meet my wife, who is in very poor health. Yes. Very poor health,' he repeated, more to himself than to me.

He rang a bell which sat on his writing desk. 'Sarah,' he said to the parlourmaid who answered, 'show Miss Wood where to wash her hands and get the gardener's boy to take the suitcase over to the cottage and bring Miss Wood into the drawing room for tea when she is ready.'

I followed Sarah out and was grateful to find I was able to wash and freshen myself for tea. I was enchanted with the tiny closet at the end of the passage with a minute porcelain washstand, ewer and basin decorated with pink rosebuds. Sarah brought us a gleaming copper can of hot water from the kitchen, I presumed. There was a barbola mirror in white, with rosebuds, hanging over the washstand, and a comb and brush for guests, decorated to match. A tiny lattice window let in the fading sunlight. The curtains matched the basin. The closet was the only cheering thing I had seen in the house.

How mobile was Mrs Horseberry, I wondered, and who looked after her? What would my sister say about this house full of deaf and sick people? What kind of life would I have here? Only time would tell.

As I entered the sitting room Sarah was helping her mistress to sit in an armchair. The mistress was frail and had the pink and white fresh skin of a much younger person. She had sharp features and a small pointed chin. Her china blue eyes were innocent and childlike. She was not, mercifully, blind or deaf, but she had some obscure disease which had made an invalid of her for all her married life. I learned later that apart from a walk round the beautiful garden and grounds of the manor house, she spent her days on the sofa. In those days it was common to find many semi-invalids, especially among women.

Her chair was moved to the table and she presided over the tea things as her husband entered and sat down.

'Did you have a nice sleep?' he asked her. 'And is your headache better?' I soon learned that he adored her and hung on her every whim and fancy.

'Better than it was dear, thank you,' she said. She had a high-pitched voice and her words seemed to jerk out of her in a staccato manner. She handed him a weak cup of tea in a dainty almost transparent china cup.

The meal was frugal in the extreme. A penny currant bun was buttered and sliced to serve three people; it was followed by three small pieces of homemade cake. I was starving and could easily have eaten all three portions. After tea and some polite conversation, the gardener's 'boy' was summoned to show me to my accommodations, a small cottage in the grounds.

The 'boy' was about fifty years old, barely articulate and answered every question with a chuckle and a 'Yes' or 'No'. He had an enormous head which wobbled from side to side on his skinny neck, large vague protruding eyes and a mouthful of uneven rotting teeth. He dribbled a bit when he spoke. His body was too big and cumbersome for his short legs and his long arms hung disproportionately at his sides.

'Here,' said the boy as we came to the cottage, and he proceeded to unlock the door. I entered. A coal fire was burning in the grate. In the middle of the room stood a kitchen table covered with a plush cloth with a paraffin lamp on it; a wooden rocking chair was near the fireplace and on the wall opposite the fireplace stood a kitchen dresser with shelves filled with willow-patterned crockery and various storage jars. There were two windows with chintz curtains. Next to the fireplace a door with an old-fashioned latch led to the bedroom staircase. The bedroom, I found, had a closet for my clothes, a chest of drawers and an iron bedstead. A chair stood on one side of the bed and a small cabinet with a candle in a candlestick and some matches on it stood on the other side near the head of the bed. The floor was covered with linoleum as it was downstairs; here a worn rug lay next to the bed; downstairs a piece mat was on the 'lino' in front of the fire.

This then was to be my home. The only ornament in the house was a china cat on the kitchen mantlepiece which watched me with an enigmatic grin. Eventually I found myself talking to it. It was less trouble than a live cat, but its green eyes followed my every move, or so it seemed to me.

'How do I get out of this place?' I asked the boy, whose name was Lennie. 'Is the gate in the wall always kept locked?'

'Yes,' he nodded his insecure head. 'Nan, she have key. Only Nan.'

The next morning I asked Nan about it.

'No one has a key, Miss; only me. You have to ask me if you want to go out and ring the bell when you come back. Nan'll let you in again,' she said, with some relish.

A prison indeed, I thought. As far as I could see, I was the only healthy, normal person on the premises. I felt I was trapped in a madhouse. I wondered if I should give my notice straightaway. My sister was right: it was foolish to rush into jobs in places you knew nothing about. I decided with some misgivings to give it a trial.

After a week I felt more than ever like running away. I had luncheon with my employers every day. The table was beautifully set and appointed with china and silver. A leg of lamb was roast on Saturday, and served in transparently thin slices to the household for the rest of the week, with meagre portions of vegetables from the manor garden varying daily. This was followed by roughly two dessertspoonfuls of milk pudding, rice, tapioca or semolina, depending upon the day of the week. I had never seen so little served so beautifully and with such regularity. Other meals I had to get for myself. The staff, I gathered, had porridge only every morning for breakfast, with salt, no sugar or milk. There was bread and butter for tea and jam only as a treat on Sundays!

My duties included reading *The Financial Times* to Mr Horseberry every morning. He dictated letters to me daily and I had to read his letters to him. I discovered he was a man of considerable wealth and had far-reaching investments in India. His business affairs were kept in strict order and I had to maintain the standard. He was patient with me and I learnt quickly.

I felt that his wife could have coped with everything that I did for him, apart from his daily walk to the village and back which was no hardship for me; I was used to walking. He liked to post his own letters and buy his own Mint Humbugs which he rationed for himself: two every day after luncheon.

Boys and men in the village touched their caps to him and women sometimes curtsied and, if the sun was shining, said, 'Good morning, Sir, nice morning.' He recognized people by their voices and enquired after the well-being of a pig or cow, or asked whether a mare had foaled yet or how crops were doing this year.

Mrs Horseberry languished at home on her sofa. She embroidered a little and read a little and dozed a little between meals. Sarah the parlourmaid was devoted to her and acted really as a lady's maid. She carried huge cans of hot water laboriously up the stairs every day for her mistress's bath in her room. The bath was a white-painted tin affair with a high back and ledge to sit on, almost like stepping into a bowl and sitting on a stool. After the bath the water had to be carried downstairs again and emptied away. This operation, which included dressing the lady and installing her comfortably on her sofa, took a good slice of the morning. Sarah then did her parlourmaid duties until evening, when her mistress needed assistance again to get to bed. That was Sarah's life.

After luncheon both master and mistress had a rest. Then I had to help in the garden. I was supposed to weed the flower beds. The gardener in charge was a bent old man who should have retired long ago but was forced to earn his living still. The old age pension of seven and sixpence a week provided bare subsistence for the majority of old people. The gardener was a surly old man who seldom spoke, but grunted in response to most questions. His face was wrinkled and weatherbeaten and reflected the arthritic pain he bore stoically.

'Now, Miss,' he would scold, 'them's not weeds, them's my little plants to come up next year. Can't you see the difference in weeds and seedlings? No, no! It's the shoot wants cutting down and dead wood taking out.'

Well, it all looked dead to me, and most certainly would be if I was not watched. Even Lennie, the so-called idiot, was a better gardener than I. I never learned the names of plants and when to sow and when to pull up. However I had to do it every day. How I hated the feeling of the cold wind when I bent over—women did not wear slacks then—and getting my hands dirty, in spite of gloves. I collected scratches and bruises from the shrubs and stings from the nettles. I had never realised how vicious the innocent-looking rose could be if one dared to prune it. The dogs sniffing round me added to my misery. I definitely was not a country girl.

Not having a key, I felt imprisoned. I decided something must be done about my freedom to come and go.

I eyed the window opening into the lane; the sill was low. I tugged and wrenched at it: it was screwed shut.

'Lennie,' I said, 'will you do something for me? I want a screwdriver to unfasten my kitchen window.'

I had got used to this odd 'boy' by this time and found him affectionate and willing.

'Lor', Miss,' he said, 'Master wouldn't like that. He fastens everything.'

'Well, then, he won't know if we don't tell him, will he?' I said.

When Lennie came to light my fire for me the following morning, he brought a screwdriver and together we unfastened my locked window. I threw it open wide and noted that it would be easy to climb in and out onto the road—no drop. Lennie viewed it suspiciously but I felt it wise to say only, 'You won't tell anyone, will you, Lennie? It'll be just our little secret.' And I gave him a bag of sweets.

'Not tell,' said Lennie, the sweets being the deciding factor. I had to put my trust in this dubious object of bribery.

I now had my freedom and I went for long country walks in the summer evenings. I walked into the village and chatted occasionally with people there. I learned there were seven little villages, beginning with Burham and that Lord Nelson was born in one of them. I visited the church where he had worshipped and tried to capture his presence. I gathered that the village people all thought the people at The Manor were mad.

'No place for a young woman like you, Miss,' one villager said to me. 'You must be as mad as they if you stay too long.' One young woman they had there, I heard, had been taken away in a van screaming her head off—'proper crazy she went,' they said. I learned later that the 'young woman' was an elderly spinster who found solace in the bottle and having overdone it she departed inebriated and in disgrace.

Beyond the fields was an expanse of land, called the salt marshes, which extended to the coast. It was pleasant when the tide was in to swim or fish. The neighbourhood abounded in wildlife; in season shooting parties roamed the marshes. I found many a wild duck shot and made a delicious meal together with fresh-gathered mushrooms. It was a lovely sight to see a V-shaped formation of geese flying high in the sky above the marshes. I acquired a taste for a leafy green substance, half fishy and half vegetable, called sea kale; it was not unlike cabbage and was cooked the same way. During the spring and summer months a few visitors came for sailing and fishing, bringing a little life to the place.

My sister Laura came to stay with me in the summer and we explored the marshes together. We walked, paddled and waded across dry patches and swamp patches, nearly to the coast line. One day we failed to notice that the tide was coming in and realised with horror that the level of the water was creeping higher and higher, faster than we could move.

'We shall be cut off,' I said fearfully. 'How far can you swim?'

'I'm not very good,' said Laura.

'Nor I,' I answered.

We plodded on, occasionally floundering as we struck a pot hole in the uncertain ground beneath our feet. Suddenly I spotted what looked like a rowing boat on the horizon.

'Look!' I said. 'If we can get to that boat, I can row us to safety.'

By the time we made the tiny boat, the water was up to our waists. I scrambled aboard and pulled my sister in after me. I rowed for the shore with all my ebbing strength as the water rose higher. We never discovered who owned the boat. It had broken away from its moorings and had been washed out seawards. When we saw it, it was on its way landward again. We overtook it, and it saved our lives.

'I shall never tramp over these marshes with you again,' said my sister. 'They are treacherous.'

I didn't know that the tides had seasons and were governed by the moon: high tide with a full moon, and so on. I should have had to be born and bred there to appreciate the finer points of the landscape and the hazards.

After Laura departed, I continued my walks in the country lanes in the pleasant late summer and autumn evenings. Sometimes a small Austin car passed me in the lane, driven by a very pleasant-looking young man. He smiled at me, but being respectably brought up, I ignored this friendly gesture.

One evening I was caught during my stroll in a heavy rain shower. A car splashed by. I had to dodge into the hedge to avoid being plastered in slush.

The car pulled up a little ahead of me and stopped.

'I say, I am so sorry.' The driver was my friendly young man. 'I must have absolutely drenched you.' He looked at me. 'My goodness, you are very wet. Can I give you a lift?' He bent forward and opened the door. 'Hop in,' he said without ceremony.

I was only too happy to hop in. I directed him to stop at the cottage.

'Never mind about stopping at the door.' I said. 'I have to use the window.' I got out of the car and pushed the bottom window open.

'You live here at the crazy Manor House?' he asked. 'I have often wondered where you came from.'

I explained that the window was my only means of exit and entrance; apart from the huge door in the wall, there was no other way out. It was lucky for me this one window overlooked the lane.

'Very clever of you,' he said.

'Come in and have a cup of tea,' I said.

He was so free and easy, I felt I had known him a long time. The disarming smile I had hitherto ignored sent my pulses racing as he swung one long leg over the sill and landed in the room without effort. My laboured scramble was graceless compared to his.

'Kevin Smith is the name,' he said.

'Ann Wood,' I replied and we shook hands.

'So you live here all alone?' he asked, looking round the room. The fire was burning cheerily in the grate; the kettle singing merrily. The lamp burned low in the centre of the table; I turned it up.

'Cosy,' said Kevin. 'May I sit down?'

'Do please,' I said. He threw himself into the rocking chair. I felt a mess and asked to be excused while I went upstairs to towel my wet hair and tidy myself. 'Don't be too long,' he said. 'Else I shall fall asleep in this rocking chair.'

'I'm glad you find it comfortable,' I said.

I soon returned and shut the window and drew the curtain. Kevin sprang to his feet when I entered the room. 'Don't get up for me,' I said. I went to the dresser for cups and saucers and the coffee. Then I pulled up a hard wood kitchen chair and sat decorously at the table.

'I've wanted to get to know you,' Kevin admitted. 'But you didn't respond.'

'My father always told me not to speak to strange men,' I said.

'Unless you were caught in the rain?'

He said that the village liked to gossip about the Manor House and they all wondered how long I would remain normal if I stayed there. 'What made you come to such an out-of-the-way place?' he asked.

'I had to earn my own living,' I said.

'But your mother? Wasn't she worried about you?'

'I have no mother.'

'I am sorry,' he said hastily. 'Forgive me, I didn't mean to pry. So what do you do with yourself, apart from your job?'

'Well, I do a lot of reading; I knit; I sew. And I talk to myself or my china cat.'

'There you are, you see, the first signs of mental disturbance; the cracks are showing already. Bad. Very bad.' He shook his head and we laughed together. Then he looked at his watch. 'My goodness,' he said, 'It's getting late. The time passes so quickly in good company. I am intruding on you. I must be off. Madam, will you show me to the door?'

I drew the curtains and opened the window. He was about to throw his leg over the sill, a gesture I was to learn to love, when he paused and looked at me.

'Ann, would you like to go to the village hop on Saturday? It's not smart but it's pleasant. The local band is quite good. I play the drums myself sometimes.'

'I'd love to come,' I said, without hesitation.

'Right then. See you at your window at eight o'clock. Evening dress optional.' That was a joke; I could tell by his expression.

This stranger had swept me off my feet. The way he laughed at the peculiarities of my situation, the genuine concern he showed for my welfare. Yes, he was handsome and charming. How gallant he looked standing hatless in the pouring rain by the window, leaning slightly into the room to say goodnight. I wanted him to kiss me goodnight but oh! he was too much of a gentleman to take advantage of me. He said my name differently from anyone else. He didn't have to be told to go, which showed he was a gentleman. He would never take advantage of an innocent girl in a lonely cottage. How many men would behave as well as he had, not even trying to kiss me? But I wished he had. No! I would have been outraged—well, not outraged exactly—disappointed, rather, in his behaviour. I sat in the rocking chair by the dying fire, rocking back and forth, reliving the magic of my evening.

Yes, my girl, you are alone too much, I told myself. One young man looks at you and you are undone. But oh! what a young man!

My job seemed especially tedious for the rest of the week. The *Times* financial supplement didn't mean a thing to me. What could all those figures and percentages mean to my employer? Was he enormously rich, I wondered. He certainly didn't spend much on living. The maids weren't exactly living in luxury, with their porridge and their candles to light them to bed. He behaved like a masochist, the way he punished himself. I wondered if he had ever enjoyed himself, even when he was young. He seemed to enjoy his wife being an invalid, as if it gave him a chance to be heroic and long-suffering.

Nan gratefully took her porridge; it never seemed to occur to her that she deserved better. She had been in service all her life, with no thought of moving on. She would take her ear trumpet to a pauper's grave. The parlourmaid too was getting on, and had no thought for another life, or for the future. How hopeless it all seemed. The old gardener was a childless widower. He said he supposed he would be found by someone when his time came and put in a hole in the ground, it didn't matter where. 'When you was gone,' he said, 'you was gone.' I was shocked, but I couldn't think of anything to say.

And what about me? Where did I fit in this menagerie? What had the young man said?—'the first signs of a disturbed mind'. Would I, this time next year be running around the lawn barefoot like the March Hare in *Alice in Wonderland?* Or would I go into a decline? On reflection, I had certainly fled from one form of seclusion to another. At least as governess I had young children and normal people to talk to. I had an open front door and I did not have to scramble in and out of a window.

I heard the car draw up; we had decided he should not hoot the horn since someone might hear. The dance in the village hall was very friendly; it was a relief to be surrounded by laughing young people. Kevin introduced me to one or two friends, but claimed every dance himself. Our steps fitted perfectly; I could have danced with him all night. The music had never sounded so romantic. Kevin held me tighter and closer than anyone ever had before. I floated in his arms. Did he feel transported, as I did, to another world?

'Hi, come back,' a voice said. 'I've been asking you if you're enjoying yourself. You haven't heard a word.'

'Oh yes, yes, I am. It's wonderful,' I stammered, blushing like a schoolgirl, hoping he could not read my thoughts.

'You are as light as a feather, Ann, and your eyes shine like stars,' he said, looking at me seriously.

'Do you mean it?' I said. 'I am enjoying every minute of it. Do I dance well enough for you? You're an expert.'

'You dance divinely,' he said, whirling me into a quickstep. 'We're perfect partners.'

Oh! I thought, I wish we were for life.

There was no need for further conversation; the intervals between dances were a waste of time. We were up and I was gliding and floating in a magic world in his arms at the first note of music. I hoped people could see how happy I was—I wanted them all to know as we circled the floor all by ourselves for the first few bars. 'Your love belongs to me,' the band played. It does, it does, my heart echoed. I floated in space; my feet didn't touch the floor. My heart was bursting.

The last waltz. I circled the floor in a trance in Kevin's arms. The music stopped and we stood to attention as the band played 'God Save the King'. It was over; my ecstatic night had nearly ended. Kevin folded my wrap about me and whispered tenderly in my ear, 'It's been a lovely evening, Ann, thank you.'

We drove home to the cottage in silence, with me leaning against him as he drove. I couldn't bear to break the physical contact. He helped me over the windowsill in my long dress. 'Goodnight, Ann,' he said, in the tone of voice that set my pulses racing, and was gone.

Why, oh why, hadn't he kissed me goodnight just to make the evening perfect? He was too much of a gentleman, I told myself. His kisses would mean something; they wouldn't be given lightly or flirtatiously. I must be patient and wait. But oh! he surely cared; he wouldn't have danced so intimately with me if he hadn't.

Our friendship progressed; I was more in love with him than ever. I would no longer even consider leaving my job. Laura wrote to me and advised me to leave before the winter really set in. I wrote back that I now felt more settled and had no immediate plans to leave. I couldn't envisage a day spent without seeing or hearing from Kevin. The gardener's boy was our go-between; he took and delivered notes, bribed by a packet of sweets, and as far as I know never told a soul about the window or about Kevin.

My mistress asked me what I did with my evenings. I told her I read a lot and did my little household chores. 'You must come and see us if you get lonely,' she said. 'I play a game of Patience. . . . Do you like cards, Miss Wood?' she asked kindly.

'Yes, sometimes. I would like to join you.' I hoped fervently that she would not ask me to come.

Here I am, I thought to myself, in a Grannie's kind of situation. 'Don't tell anyone. Don't tell your father,' I could hear her saying. Oh, why did I get involved in these compromising situations? I wasn't really a deceitful girl, yet somehow I was always put in the wrong.

Perhaps I should be brave and say to Mr Horseberry, 'Look here, I am not going to stay here like a nun locked up in a convent. I want my freedom. I want a key to come and go as I please or I leave at the end of the month.'

But my resolution failed me whenever I met his steely blue-eyed gaze or saw his gaunt form. I was a coward. I let things drift and lived in my fool's paradise.

Grannie would have thrived on my latest intrigue and she would have loved Kevin. He took me to the cinema in the nearest town. Often it was midnight before we got back. He treated me always with the greatest respect. We had picnics at weekends in the pleasant countryside and explored old churches and museums. He took me on a shopping spree for the whole day to the cathedral city of Norwich. We had days at the salt marshes in his little boat when I could get a day off ostensibly to go shopping. We went to neighbouring villages and towns to dance, often coming home in the small hours. I saw no harm in this deception. As Kevin said, my private life was my own.

The first time Kevin kissed me after one of the episodes, I was in heaven. He put his arm around me as the car stopped and somehow our eyes met and our lips melted together in a long, lingering kiss.

'I'm sorry, Ann,' he said. 'I shouldn't have done that.'

'I wanted you to,' I whispered. 'It's all right. Please don't spoil it by saying you're sorry.'

After that he made a habit of putting his arm around

me and kissing me. He spoke to me with affection but he never said the words I was longing to hear: 'Ann, I love you.' I must wait, I thought. Grannie said actions speak louder than words. His actions were gentle and loving, and I trusted him.

We would sit in the car now, when we arrived back at the cottage, as if we could not break the magic spell that bound us together. I, with my head on his shoulder, he with his arm around me. We had no need to speak. The silence was pregnant with love and understanding. No girl ever had such a considerate lover.

Sometimes Kevin came to the cottage for an evening meal which I delighted in preparing. 'My word, Ann,' he would say, 'you are a good cook, where did you learn?'

It occurred to me that we never talked about our respective backgrounds. I knew he lived in the village, but he never suggested that I meet his parents. But I really thought nothing of it. I told him about my up-bringing and Mother and Grannie.

'My word,' he said, 'you *have* led a sheltered life. And then to be turned out into the wicked world! No wonder you ended up here. What do you think you'll eventually do?'

'Marry you,' I longed to say, but suddenly I felt cold and apprehensive as if Kevin had shut me out of his life.

'I don't know,' I said forlornly.

'Well, it will have to be thought about,' he said. He did not seem to notice the stricken look on my face. 'Good gracious, it's eleven o'clock. I must be off.'

He kissed me and went out through the window.

The blissful weeks went by, month by month. I was even happy in my work. Kevin lent enchantment to my life. He never declared his intentions or said that he loved me. I didn't say anything, because in those days girls did not take the initiative. The male set the pace.

I knew that my father would not have approved of my relationship with Kevin, innocent as it was. I had no one to turn to for advice. Once when Kevin mentioned his mother I did say that I would like to meet her, but he didn't take up my suggestion.

One evening Kevin had been at the cottage for a meal. He rocked gently in the rocking chair while we sipped our after-dinner coffee. Suddenly he said, 'Ann, I shall not be able to see you for a week or two after tonight.'

'Why?' I asked. 'Are you going away again?'

He had been to London recently for short visits to relatives. He was the local baker's only son and helped in the business and seemed to be able to take time off whenever he wished. 'Nice to get away from the village for a week or so,' he would say, and I would agree with him, although the week would seem endless to me.

'No,' he said. 'My parents are having company and I shall be expected to chauffeur them around.'

'Well, they surely won't make claims on all your time. What shall I do without you?'

He stood up and bent forward and kissed me on the forehead. 'Ann,' he said in a strained voice without a trace of his usual bantering tone, 'I hope you won't be too upset when I tell you that one of the guests is my fiancée.'

My world fell apart and I burst into tears. 'Please go,' I said, sobbing uncontrollably. I simply couldn't believe it could be true.

I left the crockery on the table and rushed upstairs to throw myself on the bed. I hardly slept a wink that night, and the next morning I felt very ill. The noise of the gardener's boy lighting the fire downstairs brought me back to reality. I called from the top of the stairs that I was unwell and would he tell Mr Horseberry that I wouldn't be able to work that day.

The next thing I knew Nan was at the door, insisting

that her mistress had sent her with strict instructions to see me. I put on a wrap and walked shakily down the stairs.

'You do look poorly, Miss,' Nan said. 'Is it the flu you've caught?'

'Yes,' I said, 'I think I've caught a chill; I shall stay at home for a day or two. If Lennie can come and light the fire for me and fetch the coal, I'm sure I shall be all right.'

Nan left but soon returned with a basin of her revolting porridge, which I had to force down with the aid of sweetened condensed milk. The kind old soul made me a cup of tea and from the kettle boiling on the fire Lennie had kindled, filled a hot water bottle she had brought from the house.

'I'll bring you some soup at luncheon,' she said. Poorly as I was, I wondered what she would find in that spartan household to make it from. Actually, it turned out to be leek soup, and it was very good. I stayed in the cottage for a week and saw only Lennie and Nan once or twice a day.

As I lay nursing my broken heart, I knew I could not stay there. The giving of a month's notice, a most unpleasant task, loomed before me. I decided to write to my sister Laura and ask her to come and stay with me. She would be having her summer holiday from college in a week or two. The prospect of having someone close to talk to sustained me over the next few weeks until Laura arrived.

My sister was taken aback at the Horseberry household when she was introduced to it, and she was scoldingly sympathetic about my blighted romance. 'Ann,' she said, 'you really are not fit to be left in this world alone. Couldn't you see this young man wasn't behaving properly toward you? Weren't you ever suspicious of him? Why didn't he ever invite you to his home—he knew what a lonely life you led.'

'I thought he was just being cautious,' I said miserably. 'I thought he wouldn't commit himself until he was quite sure.'

'You're well rid of him, Ann,' Laura said firmly. 'Now come on and stop fretting and crying. You must get out of this dismal place and live among normal sane people. The Horseberrys have plenty of money. Why do they want to keep this circus going?'

For the first time I saw the rather comic side of the household.

'Now that's better,' Laura said. 'Now sit down and put your month's notice in writing and I will take it to the house for you. And,' she went on, 'I am going to tell Father that you are coming home. I shall tell him you are living all alone in a damp cottage and that you look half-starved and that the only company you have are old, blind, deaf, lunatic people. We'll leave the romance out of it. Make a fresh start, Ann, and you'll soon be yourself again. And for heaven's sake don't take any more lonely jobs in the country again. Something will turn up.'

When I was on the train for home I felt like a fugitive from captivity, and that I should never have escaped without Laura's support.

10. Training

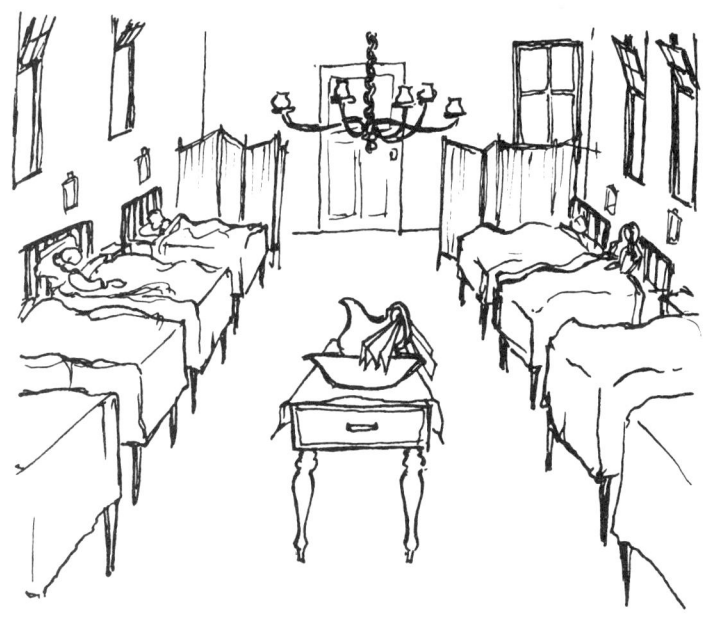

'WELL, my dear,' my father said, 'what are you going to do with yourself now?'

'I don't know, Daddy,' I said miserably. 'I keep looking through the papers but all the jobs seem to need experience or training—except domestic work and I don't want that.'

I had been home now for two weeks. It was lovely, we three girls being together again. My brother was away on some lord's estate where he had a job as secretary. Alice was firmly established as housekeeper and was engaged to a young man whom she had met in the country whilst staying with my cousin. They were saving to get married, but she had only her pocket money at home, and he was poorly paid. It was to take them six years to save enough to get married; they hadn't had many treats. Their honeymoon was their first holiday together or apart.

One morning when I had been at home for five weeks, I was poring over the paper in the local library when I saw an advertisement for nurses to the District Council to be trained free in London in return for services at a reduced salary for three years.

This really sounded as though it were for me. I would be a trained worker, I would have a profession, and I would be training with people my age. I would never have to take a job without qualifications again. The only drawback was the 'qualifying guarantee'—I assumed if I did not pass, I would not have a job. But surely, I thought, I had the intelligence to pass nursing examinations. True, it was a bit daunting to have to promise to work for three years at £105 per annum to repay the generous Council, but they would make me a useful member of society. My unfortunate experiences with the opposite sex had convinced me that I would never marry and I would have to support myself for the rest of my life. If I did not find a career I would end up in domestic service as the despised 'skivvy' at everyone's beck and call.

My Aunt Nancy said that she did not believe my health would stand up to the strain. She asked me to come and live with her, a suggestion my sisters had made to me also. But my aunt had had a succession of maids; none had ever stayed in that house for long. 'My own girls are all married,' my aunt said. 'You would be like a daughter to us.' Honeyed words indeed, but I knew my aunt.

I went for an interview. A severe, rather masculine woman looked me over critically. She said my education appeared to be all right, but I didn't look very strong. I assured her I had had no operations and no major illnesses and my health was good. I passed a medical examination, and was declared fit.

Then there came the excitement of having uniforms made: six cotton dresses with high-buttoned necks and nipped-in waists and voluminous calf-length skirts. A dozen white bibbed aprons, frilled caps, stiff cuffs and collars and black cotton stockings—silk were not allowed—and flat-heeled black shoes completed the wardrobe.

My sisters thought I looked very impressive when I was dressed in uniform but I felt as though I were trapped from head to foot in a stiff cardboard box; nothing yielded to my figure or my movements. The stiff stand-up collar which was secured by a stud just like Father's, cut my chin and chafed my neck. It took me and my sisters about twenty minutes to get me into the entire outfit.

'I shall never be ready for roll-call at six-thirty in the morning,' I wailed. I began to doubt for the first time that nursing was the career for me.

London in those days seemed to me to mean gaiety, theatres, wealth and excitement—the land of plenty. Arriving at Liverpool Street station for the first time in my life, I was in grave danger of being lost forever in the crowds and hustle and bustle. There were so many platforms that no one had ever heard of the one I wanted: East 13. I should have asked for Plaistow, it developed.

At last I found it and settled again in the train which whistled and clanged past miles and miles of backs of houses with tiny backyards and lines of dreary off-white washing hanging motionless in the sultry air. Not a tree or any hint of green anywhere; hot dusty air wafted in through the open window. My allergies started up; I hoped I wasn't going to meet Matron with a red nose and watery eyes.

'Johnny, come away from the lady and sit quietly here beside me,' said an anxious mother. She gave me an unfriendly look as I sneezed unrestrainedly into my soaked handkerchief.

Plaistow Station seemed like the end of the world—scruffy, seething and unwashed humanity, reeking abominably from an adjoining 'bone factory'. I found a porter who hailed me a taxi and stood looking at the shilling I pressed into his palm as if it were manna from heaven. I didn't know that the usual tip was a three-penny piece which in those days was pure silver coinage. A shilling would keep that porter in beer for a week.

The taxi bowled along the never-ending streets with their rows of tiny houses, their front doors opening directly onto the pavement. They were so closely packed and the streets were so narrow that the sky seemed blocked out and the air was stale and still. There was nothing to break the monotony of the small unwashed windows with net or cotton curtains drawn to exclude any hint of sunshine or fresh air which might struggle through. We went down a street with unpainted shop fronts, the display windows very little larger than the house windows. Women stood gossiping on doorsteps or scrubbing the steps or leaning on mops; they all stopped to stare as the taxi went by.

Were these to be my patients? I wondered. Should I have to bathe them and wash their nitty hair? It was the Depression: money and cleanliness were both scarce. The country was still rich, but no one had given much thought to spreading money around, or to equality. Very few women worked then outside the drudgery of the home. They produced the annual child, preferably a boy who could fight to keep Britain great. In the course of my training I was to see many of these men, casualties of the 1914-1918 War, limbless or with wounds that would not heal and had to be dressed daily by the District Nurse. They were tied to wheel chairs, their lives broken, with no hope for the future; their wives and families living on pensions from a grateful country that were barely enough to keep body and soul together. I learnt about all this in the first few heartbreaking weeks of my training in the richest city in the world.

The taxi driver carried my suitcase up the steps of the Nursing Home and rang the bell. By the time a maid answered the door, I had tipped and dismissed him. My cousin Vera had taught me always to tip people who fetched and carried for me. I gave my name to the maid and she ushered me into a waiting room where there were a number of other girls around my age. It was a bare room with highly polished brown linoleum, and hard wooden chairs pressed up against the walls. Large windows looked out onto the first bit of green I had seen since I got off the train. The ceiling was lofty, the room light and airy.

A girl smiled at me and asked me in a Scottish accent where I was from.

'Norfolk,' I said.

'Scotland, me,' she said. She offered me her hand. 'Jenny Tulloch.'

'Ann Wood.'

'Bit quiet in here,' she said. 'Been waiting here for half an hour. We're all to see Matron. I wonder how long the old dragon will be.'

At that moment the door opened and a Sister, looking very smart in a navy blue uniform without an apron, came into the room.

'Nurse Smith,' she called. A girl rose and the Sister said, 'Follow me please.' The girl disappeared with the Sister, whom I learned was the Home Sister, and her job was to look after the nurses' welfare. She was always very kind to us.

'We're off,' said my new-found friend. 'Let's you and I stick together if we can, try and share, shall we?'

Of course I was delighted and readily agreed.

'Nurse Wood.' The Home Sister was back and looking enquiringly round the room. I hesitated and Jenny gave me a nudge. 'Isn't that you?' Somewhat confused, I followed Sister down corridors to a door marked 'Matron'.

Sister knocked and waited.

'Come,' said a voice. Matron was sitting at a table with papers and files in front of her. She was not a dragon, really, but a rather large woman in her fifties with short greying black hair.

'Nurse Wood,' Sister announced.

'Ah, yes, you are from Norfolk, I believe, Nurse,' Matron said, glancing at the paper in front of her. 'If you are anything like my previous girls from Norfolk you will be a good worker. Splendid girls, Norfolk girls. You look a bit pale and not too robust. Still, no serious illnesses I see, mother and father in good health.' She looked me over as if I was a horse. 'No disabilities. Well, I hope you stay the course.'

I was dismissed with the feeling that I wasn't altogether a success.

I was taken to another room where the girls who had seen Matron before me were waiting. As soon as the last girl had seen Matron and joined us, we were taken to our dormitory. Two rows of six beds faced each other, nearly touching at the sides and the feet. We would be living—or at least sleeping—in close proximity.

'Let's keep together,' Jenny whispered. She managed to get the bed in the corner near the wall, and I was allocated the one next it. We shared a tiny locker at the foot of the beds. A room leading off the dormitory was equipped with a cupboard locker for each girl. Here we were to unpack and stow our belongings and change into uniform. Each locker had a key, and each girl was responsible for her own possessions. We were advised to keep our cupboards locked. Like being in prison, I thought.

'Report to Sister-in-Charge in a quarter of an hour, in uniform,' we were told.

I was glad I had had a trial run with my sisters to help me with my uniform as I struggled with collar studs and elusive buckles. There were cries of 'How does it go?' and 'Can you fasten this for me?'; one girl was already in tears as she lost the tape to draw up the cap which at the moment resembled a pancake. Someone else was on all fours searching for an elusive collar stud.

'Leave out the one at the back of your neck and use it in your cuff for now,' Jenny said. This ruse did not, however, escape Sister's sharp eye.

'Nurse, your collar is not on properly. It should be anchored to your neckband at the back with a stud. Say "yes, Sister" when you answer me, please. Always address me as Sister; I have a title.'

I felt my collar stud resting on the vertebrae of my neck and had difficulty holding my head straight, whilst the front stud was trying to push itself through my neck to my throat. We soon learned to ignore these minor discomforts. Nevertheless the first thing we always did when we went off duty was unfasten our collars. They were pure starched torture.

The girl who had the bed on the other side of me from Jenny's was named Jane. She was a beautiful girl with masses of black wavy hair framing a perfect oval face with large wide-set hazel eyes. She had a full, generous mouth and a cheeky little upturned nose. She was everybody's favourite. She and I often carried on long conversations after lights out—at ten o'clock sharp—and Jane told me she had a good education and had no financial need to work but she felt she wanted to do something worthwhile with her life.

Eventually we found our way to the dining room for the evening meal at 8 o'clock. It was beetroot, bread and butter and cheese. This menu turned up regularly twice a week. At four o'clock every day except Sunday we had a cup of tea and bread and butter; on Sundays each girl was allowed a slice of Madeira cake. A girl who was overheard complaining about the food was told tartly by Sister that it was frugal but wholesome; she reminded us that we were living in a nurses' hostel and not in the Ritz—as if we needed reminding.

Three trestle tables ran the length of the dining room. Matron presided at the head table, Sister at the lesser table. We nurses had to assemble and stand by our places awaiting Matron and her retinue. Matron said grace and, with a scraping of chairs on the bare wooden floor, we sat down. Food was passed from hand to hand from the head of the table, each portion equal regardless of the size of one's appetite. All this, and the meal itself, passed in strict silence. Only Matron and her cronies conversed in a restrained manner.

When Matron was finished, we were all finished and stood while she made her dignified exit. Then we all filed out of the dining hall in an orderly way, never daring to put a foot out of place. This was the routine life considered fitting for trainee nurses in most hospitals.

At breakfast on the first morning my herring seemed to take a long time reaching me on its precarious trip down the length of the table, tossed from hand to hand as it had surely not tossed on the ocean waves. When it did reach me I did not think it looked very appetising and I wasn't hungry anyway, so I left it untouched on my plate.

I reported for my first morning's duty.

'Nurse Wood, Matron would like to see you in the office,' Sister said.

'Good old Woodie, getting special attention already,' a nurse joked.

Apprehensively, I knocked on Matron's door.

'Come,' the dreaded summons sounded.

'Nurse,' Matron said as I entered, 'I believe you left your herring untouched this morning. Can you explain why?'

'I wasn't hungry, Matron.'

'No nurse is allowed to leave or waste food in this establishment. How can you expect to face your duties on a busy District with no breakfast? In future, nurse, you will eat all your meals as served to you. You may go. Close the door on your way out, please.'

I felt humiliated and near to tears.

'It doesn't matter,' Jenny said. 'We will find a way to get round all that old nonsense. I for one shan't eat all they serve up here.' And she didn't. Happily, Jenny could take care of both herself and me. 'No, Matron; yes, Matron,' she would mimic with a curtsy and make us all laugh.

The first three months were to be spent with a Staff Nurse—one who had passed exams—so that we could be trained in District work in general.

Was I just unlucky or did I imagine I had drawn the bitchiest Staff Nurse in the bunch? I was her lackey. I fetched and carried. I did all the dirty jobs. She made me look small in front of patients. If I hurried, I was not thorough; if I was careful I was too slow. She reduced me to shreds and near-hysteria. I was clumsy, I was ignorant, I was useless. I felt I would never learn anything with her.

'If I am useless, perhaps I should resign,' I said.

'That was insolence and insubordination and shall be put in my report,' she said.

We would walk the long, dreary streets from one end to the other, each carrying a black Gladstone bag with first aid equipment and minor instruments of which I had to learn the names and uses. Often the numbers of the houses ran to four or five hundred and we would be at the wrong end. My feet ached and blistered in the stout unyielding walking shoes and my ankles swelled. I saw some girls sitting with their feet in enamel bowls of hot water to ease them, tears running down their faces. Soap, methylated spirit and borax and starch powder intended for patients' sore bottoms often found their way to nurses' sore, blistered feet.

We 'did' the District from eight in the morning until twelve-thirty, when we returned for luncheon. I never got used to the smell of methylated spirit lingering on my hands and mingling with the aroma of hot pot which I forced down to allay the pangs of hunger and escape Matron's disapproval. Even today carbolic soap and methylated spirit conjure up a vision to me of backsides to be massaged and of, I must admit, the patient's gratitude for a brief respite from pain.

Life became a little more bearable when I graduated from General Attention to Minor Dressings and got to know a probe from a pair of scissors. I found surgical work interesting. We had to improvise in the houses we visited, using any old saucepan to sterilize our instruments. In our bags we carried only one or two small bowls for dressings. My Staff Nurse, in spite of her objectionable manner, proved to be an excellent nurse and since I learned easily, she taught me well. One thing I discovered early in my course was that East Enders were allergic to soap and hot water. Their attitude to cleanliness was appalling; their knowledge of hygiene nonexistent. On occasion we had to overcome strong opposition to the minimum demands of cleanliness. But my Staff Nurse was equal to anyone.

There was great competition among the nurses to get the best jobs. Restaurants and pie-and-eel and fish-and-chip shops were much sought after: the nurses' gentle ministrations could be rewarded with a delicious supper and tea and cakes. I never tried the eels although they did look fascinating, swimming around in their tanks before meeting their fate in a pie. Fortunately or un-fortunately—depending on your viewpoint—people in these places were accident-prone. We never complained about an emergency call at a place that served food.

Our street, nicknamed Rag and Bone Street, was in a rough part of town. Here on a market day the street was filled end to end with stalls selling goods at cut prices. We had to go about the neighbourhood and on our visits in pairs. Jenny and I often contrived, as we became responsible trained nurses, to pair up on cases. The most popular assignments were the evening visits from five 'till eight o'clock, since under the cover of darkness it was easier to visit forbidden territory. At that time the stalls and the shops stayed open until nine or ten at night. A few pence bought pounds of fruit—bunches of grapes or bananas, three or four oranges for a penny. There was an abundance of underwear at a few pence a garment.

There were a lot of rogues among the stallholders, who were no doubt selling stolen goods. The police con-stantly patrolled the street, and it was amusing to see a salesman vanish before your eyes with his goods and your money—if you weren't sharp—at the approach of the cops. One man, who danced around in vivid pink ladies' bloomers, was doing a roaring trade until one unfortunate customer discovered that her drawers had only one leg. There were suitcases that didn't lock, coats with two left-hand sleeves, stockings with no feet, men's socks with no opening, gloves with four fingers and no thumb, and even one-sided bodices for lop-sided ladies.

And there were quack doctors and quack vendors for every kind of healing and potion that could be thought of.

I remember one of them extolling the virtues of his lotion for curing arthritis. 'Stiffness and pain gorn overnight, there you are, Ma, yours for sixpence, guaranteed or money back. I was a poor cripple myself until I discovered Jim's Instant Relief.' Here he caught my disbelieving eye and added, 'Well, that's my bloody yarn and I'm sticking to it.'

Another, selling stockings, shouted, 'Fully fashioned, semi-fashioned.' As Jenny and I passed in our black cotton stockings he added, 'Old fashioned.' We really had to laugh.

The East Enders were a light-hearted, quick-witted fraternity.

Our District was a squalid slum: the narrow houses usually had six rooms, three up and three down and a separate family lived in each room, except the kitchen, which, shared by the household, had, as a rule, a stone sink and cold water tap and a rickety old gas cooker with perhaps a small oilcloth-covered table and an enamel bowl in the sink which everyone used for bathing, washing up, cleaning vegetables or whatever. Rubbish accumulated in the corner until it became uncontrollable; then some public-spirited occupant would tip it out into the street for the dogs and cats to enjoy and eventually be removed by the scavenger men. The living conditions were so appalling it is amazing that anyone recovered from an illness or that mothers and babies survived. The mortality rate from influenza and pneumonia every winter was disastrous. Few if any ever recovered from pneumonia with its false crisis and real crisis; there were no drugs to combat it. We nursed pneumonia hopelessly day and night in rooms where the wallpaper hung off the wall in damp sheets. Some-

times the only light was candlelight. I think that, mercifully, these slums are no more.

Twice a week the *Daily Mirror* soup kitchens came
round the streets and I am sure that was the only decent
food those poor souls had, week in, week out. I received
food parcels from home supposedly to encourage my
appetite; Jenny did too. We enjoyed watching those
starving children devour our cakes and pies. 'God bless
you, Nurse'—the gratitude of those deprived people
rings in my ears until this day. I had thought we were
poor, but what my father had given me to keep house
for us would have kept a family in the East End for six
weeks. At first I fretted over what I saw and could not
sleep, but eventually I got used to it, although I never
accepted it.

The two sisters who had originally started our nursing
home were spinsters and had come to London to nurse
some few years before my time. They were so upset by
the poverty and squalor they encountered that they gave
up their incomes and their lives to these poor people
and created the home. We nurses now lived in their
house and hospital, and a new hospital had been built
adjacent to the old one. It was a maternity hospital only.
Our Nursing Home ran the General District Branch
and kept up a number of branch homes in the neighbourhood. There was always an emergency pack of baby
clothes and bedding ready for needy cases; any such
cases we reported received immediate help since the
Home was well endowed and generous. And the Home
and the nurses were greatly respected and welcomed.
Although as I have said, we went out in our district in
pairs as a precaution—mostly through fear of drunks—
I never remember hearing of a nurse being molested
or abused.

We did six months maternity training at the Maternity
Hospital with a view to specialising in Maternity. The

routine was to do twenty 'watch' cases—that is, watching the delivery of the baby without taking part—and then deliver ourselves, under supervision. This procedure usually took six months, and we worked on the wards during this time too, looking after lying-in 'mums' and bathing and nursing the babies during their ten-day stay in the Hospital, after which the poor little things had to go home and face their squalid world.

Every expectant mother was encouraged to come into the Hospital for delivery. At first some were apprehensive, but after the first time they looked on their visit as an annual holiday. The mortality rate among these babies was very high; it was a state of affairs which would not be tolerated today.

The Hospital was always over-booked. It was not unusual for a baby to be born quite comfortably on a board improvised as a delivery couch over the bath in the bathroom. Emergency beds were rigged up in the wards until there was barely room to move between the beds. As soon as one mother went home, another took her place. From a training standpoint, this was wonderful. We learnt as much in that Hospital in a month as we would have learnt in a smart clinic in six months. We worked long hours and got little sleep, but the work was rewarding and we encouraged one another. When lectures were missed, there was always someone to lend her written papers and explain fine points.

The weeks flew by and Christmas was upon us. A traditional concert was organised: the Sister Tutor and the Staff Nurses all joined in to produce a mock pantomine and even Matron danced with the Senior Lecturer after the show. I was prevailed upon to sing 'Why Am I Only the Bridesmaid, Never the Blushing Bride?'—an appropriate song for my state of mind at that time. We had a huge turkey carved by Matron and the general atmosphere, with the help of holly and mistletoe, was relaxed—but why mistletoe in our manless state, I will never know. Our dear old lecturer was seventy if he was a day. The male medical students all came from other hospitals; there were no men on our staff. The students did not attend our lectures but patrolled our wards and came to deliveries for the experience. Some of our nurses used to say that they would like to give the medical students some real experience, but I was too busy with my work and my studies to think about men.

After the relaxation of Christmas we all had to get down to work in the wards again. 'Come on now, High Flyer,' Sister would say to me. 'You get that extra mother and babe washed up for me.' I was called High Flyer because I did two cases to the other nurses' one. Or Sister would call out to me, 'Nurse, get the screens round Mrs So-and-So and get started on her treatment until I can get to help you.' She was nice to me and often left me a boiled egg or a dish of milky porridge from the patients' kitchen as a reward for extra work. I was Sister's favourite until an unfortunate incident occurred.

Sister used to keep the soap on the top shelf of the airing cupboard to hide it from the night staff whom she felt were wasteful. Once when she climbed up to get it, I was helping her by holding the steps; on the top rung her cap became entangled in some obstruction. It came off and her hair with it. She never forgave me for knowing that she wore a wig.

The cry we all listened for was 'Watch case!' when all nurses who needed another case to make up their quota of twenty left everything to dash to the delivery room. The delivery ward was usually unbearably hot; the air was heavy with sweat, carbolic and ether or chloroform. Grouped round the bed watching the patient in her agony would be student doctors and nurses, all intent on only one thing: seeing the miracle of birth. No one spoke except the Nurse in Charge who gave instructions or the doctor in attendance if it was a difficult delivery. Sometimes a female student, or a male one, would be overcome with emotion or with the atmosphere and faint, to be dragged unceremoniously out of the room.

My first case was such a revelation to me that I almost swooned. To come from a sheltered country life to the horrors of a delivery chamber, to see a woman writhing in agony and being anaesthetised and watch the actual birth in the mixed company of thirty or forty strangers was rather like being thrown in at the deep end. Then and there I decided that I would never get married and never, never go through the ordeal of having a baby.

But one can get accustomed to anything. By the end of my twenty 'watch' cases I had decided that it was worth it all to see the joy on the mother's face when she was holding her new-born baby. The sordid details were quickly forgotten.

After we had learned the mechanics of delivery and hygiene at the Hospital, we moved to a branch house where we worked and practised our midwifery in the district, under adverse conditions. Jenny and I were not separated. I don't know how she managed it, but we kept together.

The railway train ran close to the back of our nurses' home and trains rattled past day and night. There were ten of us trainees and two Staff Nurses and a Sister in Charge, an enormous woman whose sole job was administrative; she did no actual nursing. She appeared to have a grudge against young nurses and later against me in particular. The old house was looked after by one little maid of all work who also did the cooking. We had to take a share of the cleaning as well as the demanding routine of nursing and studying. We ate in the dining room where Sister, who presided over the meal and served at the head of the table, kept an array of enamel plates on the floor at her feet for her dogs. She served the dogs and then the nurses. All during the meals the dogs yapped round us. We had our tea and bread and butter in peace by ourselves but the evening meal we shared with the dogs under Sister's watchful eye. In fact our whole lives were lived under Sister's watchful eye.

'Nurse,' she said to me, poking her finger at my eye, 'nurses do not wear eye shadow or makeup. You are a nurse, not an actress.' In fact, my eyes were dark-circled from lack of sleep and not from makeup.

'The Old Bitch has a grudge against us because we are young and she isn't,' said Jenny. 'I don't think she was ever young. She picks on you because you don't look strong. Don't take any notice of her. We won't be here forever. I'd love to kick one of those beastly dogs.' Jenny was a great comfort to me in those days.

All the branch home domestic staff, like the domestic staff at the Maternity Hospital and the Nursing Home, were unmarried mothers who worked day and night for a pittance. In return for this, their illegitimate babies were delivered free at the hospital and kept in a nursery until they were school age. Because of this trainee nurses got a thorough grounding in infant welfare right on the premises. It was an excellent arrangement for the poor little children, who were well cared for until they were five years old, and it gave the mothers a chance to get on their feet. I suspect that when the children were old enough to leave, the mothers were helped to find new situations.

We slept in a tiny room where four beds took up nearly all the floor space. The foot of my bed was under the open window; one night I awoke screaming when Sister's big ginger cat suddenly leaped onto my chest. I woke the whole household.

Since there was only one bathroom in the house, bathing was by rota. You took your turn on your appointed day at the appointed time; otherwise you washed in cold water in a china washbasin in the cramped bedroom. Privacy was a luxury.

In addition to delivering the district's babies, we ran clinics from our home; a room on the ground floor was set aside for this purpose. We had to keep our brown linoleum highly polished. One day a nurse named Skinner was swinging the heavy polisher back and forth with gay abandon across the floor; she had worked up a wonderful rhythm when the handle slid out of her hand and the polisher shot straight through the French windows. The crash brought Sister storming in. She stood aghast. Skinner, however, was resourceful.

'I really couldn't help it, Sister,' she said coolly. She appealed to those of us who had been in the room. 'You saw it, didn't you? Sister, your ginger cat leapt in front of the polisher. I had to avoid it; it would have been killed. Your beautiful cat. It would have been cut to pieces.'

'Spare me the details, Skinner,' said Sister, 'and clear this mess up.'

We all admired Skinner's quick thinking and felt that the ginger cat had been well used for once; we felt sure that it got all the cream off our milk.

Part of our training involved visiting the homes of expectant mothers who couldn't or wouldn't come into the hospital. There were still a number who regarded the hospital with suspicion, as a place of no return. We advised them and helped them prepare for the birth as much as we could under the appalling conditions.

I remember one unexpected incident. I went to visit one of our pregnant outpatients. No one answered when I knocked on the door. Usually women stood gossiping on the doorsteps and children played hop-scotch in the street, but today it was deserted. I opened the street door and entered the communal passage. I knocked on the downstairs front room door. A weak voice called, 'Come in.' The woman lay on the bed in the room writhing and moaning.

'Thank God you've come, Nurse,' she said.

I stood terrified, surveying the scene. The rickety iron bedstead with its lumpy mattress and filthy bedding took up most of the floor space. In the far corner was a cot with a crying baby about eighteen months old. Against all training and better judgment I picked up the baby's dummy and stuck it in its mouth; immediately the howling stopped and a contented sucking took its place. At the same moment the woman's pains subsided and she relaxed and sighed with relief.

'We ain't got much time, Nurse,' she said.

'I will fetch help,' I said, trying to keep calm.

'Don't leave me, Nurse.'

'*Never* leave a woman in the last stages of labour,' Sister Tutor had said. 'It is against the Midwifery Rules. You could be struck off The Register for such conduct.'

Well, I'm not on The Register yet, I said to myself. And here I was faced by this dilemma. Why did these things always happen to me?

I found sheets of newspaper and put them on top of the dirty chest of drawers so I could put my Gladstone bag on it. I opened the top drawer hoping to find something I could use for the confinement. What I found there was a half loaf of bread, sugar in a soiled, screwed-up bag, an opened tin of sweetened condensed milk and the remains of a packet of margarine. It was the pitiful larder. The next drawer held a few chipped crocks and a dirty frying-pan. And in the next were two dreary torn sheets, a nightgown and a scruffy-looking towel.

'Only me sheets and nightie, Nurse. Sister always brings for the baby and what she needs.'

I waited while another spasm of pain came and went, and I tried to reassure her. As I bent over the bed my foot kicked something hard under it. It was half a sack of coal—the only place she had to store it out of the way. At least I could try to light a fire, I thought. It was chilly.

I went out to the passage and shouted, 'Is anyone in the house?'

A door creaked open upstairs. An old crone appeared on the landing, leaning heavily on a stick. 'What yer want a hollering the place down?' she asked.

'Mrs Brown is in labour. Can you help me?'

'Well, I can't get down the stairs. I ain't been down for three years. It's my 'ips won't go at all.'

I went outside and looked again up and down the street. Only a stray dog was to be seen. I ran down the street looking for a telephone. Finally I found a little general store and made a frantic phone call. I was hysterical now and breathless from running, which had broken another rule. Nurses don't run. 'Sister,' I said, 'please come at once to Mrs Brown. She is in the last stage of labour.'

'Nurse, get back to her at once. I will be there immediately. Do what you can.'

I flew back in a frenzy. The poor little soul in the cot had lost its dummy and was howling again. The mother was moaning and tossing on the bed. I told her help was on the way: Sister had a Morris Minor and I knew she would be quick.

I spread newspaper around over the scruffy floor and set the kettle to boil on the rickety old gas stove in the kitchen which I thought served the whole house. I found a large pan which I filled from the one cold water tap and put it to boil as I took the kettle off. The gas ran out. I took two coppers from my purse and searched for the meter so I could insert them. Luckily it was easily accessible under the stairs. I found two old enamel bowls in the kitchen and a dredge of Vim in a tin to clean them. I ran back into the front room. Thank God nothing had happened yet.

'Don't force yourself,' I said, as she heaved and pushed. 'We don't want the baby born before Sister gets here.'

'I bloody well want to get it over with,' she said. 'Ow long will she be?'

'Not long. She's on her way. Try to relax between the pains.'

'You bloody well want to try it,' she said. Her swearing rather shocked me. I wasn't used yet to the everyday vernacular of the East End.

I undressed her and using the kettle of hot water, mixed with cold, washed her from head to toe. The water running down her legs left clean rivulets. I combed her hair, which was full of lice. I couldn't do anything about that then, of course; it had to be left until later.

Sister arrived just as I had kindled a fire in the grate. She took the situation in at a glance. 'Well done, Nurse,' she said. There was a cry from the bed on which I had managed to put the clean sheets and another little baby had entered the slum world.

A step sounded in the passage, and a man looked in, pushing open the door. 'When was she took then?' he enquired. 'She was all right when I went out this morning.'

He had been to collect his dole money. He was a victim of gas in the 1914-1918 War and was almost unemployable. The baby was still crying for its dummy. There would be two babies crying now.

Our six months on the District maternity nursing was finished a week or two before Christmas and we returned to the main Nursing Home. I was detailed for three months night nursing in the nursery where the babies of the unmarried mothers lived. The nursery was on the grounds of the Hospital. I was very nervous being all alone in the big building all night. Jenny used to come to say good-night to me before she went to bed in the main building. Night work did not suit me very well. I could not sleep during the day; the cleaners kept me awake banging and clattering their buckets as they scrubbed the corridors on their hands and knees with strong carbolic disinfectant which lingered in every crack and which we thought we tasted in every cup. Lack of sleep made me tired and depressed.

I had to bottle feed and change about twenty infants from eight o'clock in the evening to eight o'clock in the morning. Apart from an inspection round by Sister at eleven p.m. I was solely in charge of these scraps of humanity. The older toddlers were in dormitories and I had to patrol these between chores and also wash the babies' nappies.

I had a meal, work permitting, in grand isolation about three o'clock in the morning. Often, if I wasn't busy, I would doze while keeping an eye on the pan of nappies boiling on a gas ring on the hearth of the fireplace in the nurses' small sitting room.

One evening I must have dozed off and perhaps caught the handle or kicked the pan as I was waking up. I remember the agonising scalding sensation of the boiling water splashing up the front of my leg; somehow a napkin, saturated with boiling water, had wrapped itself about my foot and ankle. I pulled it frantically away and with trembling fingers rolled down my black cotton stocking. The blistered skin came with it. My ankle and leg were visibly swelling; enormous blisters hung off them. I felt sick and dizzy; the room turned upside down and spun round. I sank to the floor.

When I recovered and sat up, still dazed, I saw that the pan lay on its side and the floor was swimming in soapy steaming water and strewn with nappies. The gas ring was out and gas was escaping. My instep was one huge blister and another extended halfway up my shin. I hobbled to the first aid kit and applied a cool gauze dressing, bandaging it to keep off the air. I shall never be able to bear it till eight o'clock, I thought. It was extremely painful and putting any weight on the leg was agonising. I looked in the tiny mirror. 'My God,' I said aloud, 'you look green!' I had to clutch the back of a chair to keep myself from fainting again.

Somehow I got the water mopped up and the general mess cleared away. I struggled through my duties. It didn't occur to me to phone the main building for help. The telephone, I thought, was only for emergencies, and I couldn't call a nurse in the middle of the night just because something had happened to me!

When the day staff came on I explained to them that I had had an accident. Since I had carried on gamely and my leg was bandaged, no one realised how badly scalded it was. 'Report your accident to Matron when you take her your night report,' said Sister in Charge.

I stood in the queue awaiting my turn. A few nurses asked what had happened, and when I told them they were sympathetic.

'Come,' Matron said through the door.

I hobbled through the door to stand in my place in front of her desk. 'Excuse, Matron,' I said. 'I have had an accident.' I handed her the night report book, and slipped into oblivion.

I woke on a stretcher in the nurses' casualty ward. The nice kind Sister was at my side. 'What happened?' she enquired.

I told her about it. There seemed to be a lot of activity. A nurse had removed the dressing and bandage I had applied. Everyone was aghast at the extent and degree of the burn.

'You poor child,' Sister said. 'Why didn't you get help?'

'I couldn't, Sister,' I said. 'I was alone. On night nursery. I couldn't leave the babies.'

'Nurse, there is a telephone to the main building for emergencies.'

'I didn't think I was an emergency.'

My foot went septic. The treatment was cruel: hot fomentations every three hours night and day, and complete rest in bed. But eventually it healed. It was six weeks before I was allowed to put my foot on the ground.

Everyone was kind and sympathetic, except Matron. She looked at me with contempt and said in the presence of all her entourage during one of her routine daily rounds in the sick nurses' ward, 'Ugh! Nurse, you are about as much good as a red herring where you come from.' She was referring, evidently, to the herring fishery port where I was born.

I fancied the young doctor winked at me, which took some of the sting out of the remark.

In any case, that was the end of my night nursing.

When I returned to duty Matron, for some reason, decided I could be trusted at least to come in at a respectable hour at night and put me in one of the many dreadful lodging houses she rented in the road to ease crowding in the Home, where there were then two hundred trainee nurses. This meant much more freedom, since we trustworthy nurses had our own key. Ten o'clock was the latest we were allowed to come in from off-duty. It was a status symbol to be considered trustworthy and much sought after. Jenny was granted the same privilege and we soon managed to share the same room in a lodging house. Jenny had found herself a boy friend, one of the student doctors, and she had many a narrow escape coming in after hours. We never knew who might be spying on us. Unfortunately there are tale bearers in all walks of life.

I must say the privilege of sleeping out could also

have been called sleeping rough. The small bedroom contained four iron bedsteads with incredibly bumpy flock mattresses and one lumpy flock pillow which felt as if it was filled with rocks. The only light upstairs was from candles, which were rationed. We bought our own to enjoy surreptitious reading or late studying. I had to do a lot of studying by candlelight and to copy lecture notes because I had missed six weeks while I was in sick quarters. Being away from Sister's eagle eye on lights-out patrol had its advantages.

Now it was back to the district for Jenny and me, to finish our training there before taking exams in about three months' time. We were both considered experienced enough to be sent out without a staff nurse now and we often managed to work together. We arranged to get back early so that we could give our report and then miss supper so that we could slip back to our lodgings, change our clothes and go to the Flea Pit, the nickname of the local cinema, which was out of bounds to nurses and therefore particularly attractive. Since we didn't have to report to the Nursing Home, we had many entertaining evenings when we should have been in bounds. We were trusted, you see.

Jenny spent her free evening every week with her boy friend—the free evening depended on the demand of work, of course. Consequently I was alone on these evenings and occasionally I went out, keeping my uniform on for reasons of security. One evening, having missed supper, I went into a Lyons to order for myself, a rare luxury. I was almost finished eating when a man a few years older than I came and sat down at the table with me. I pretended to take no notice of him, but I was acutely aware of his presence. He was a big, tall man; I judged he weighed about sixteen stone. He had well-defined features with high cheekbones and a heavy jaw, a fresh complexion and bright blue eyes.

'Nice evening,' he said politely.

I didn't answer; I didn't want to be picked up. I finished my pudding and got up hastily to leave, knocking over my cup of coffee which was still half-full. It ran all over the table and into the stranger's lap before he could jump up.

'Oh,' I said, 'I am so dreadfully sorry!'

'No consequence,' he said. He brought out his handkerchief and mopped his trousers; the waitress came and wiped the table. He asked her to bring two coffees. 'Please,' he said to me. 'I seem to have had most of the first cup in my lap.'

I had to be polite and sit down again.

'You know,' he said, 'I've seen you around this neighbourhood quite a lot.' He said he had been born and bred in the District and remembered the two sisters who gave all their money to the Nursing Home. He was a mechanic at the sugar factory. His name was Bill. When I got up to leave, he followed me. 'I'm going your way,' he said. 'Mind if I walk with you?'

I couldn't say no; it was months and months since I had had a male escort. It was a lovely evening for a walk. But what if I ran into one of the Sisters? He asked me my name, and when he could see me again.

'I don't know,' I said, with downcast eyes.

'Shall we say the evening after tomorrow at eight-thirty on this corner? Give or take a few minutes. I know nurses are often delayed. Duty and all that.'

I had to laugh at his boldness. I agreed.

Jenny wasn't too impressed with my encounter. 'Do be careful, Woodie,' she said. 'I can't let you off on your own for one evening, can I?'

She was much more sophisticated than I. I wished she could meet Bill and give me her opinion. I wasn't sure of myself. 'You're such a little mouse,' she said, looking at me kindly. 'Have fun, but don't get hurt.'

I knew I wasn't a flirt and I decided this man wasn't going to play with me; I had already had fun and gotten hurt. I was more sensible now, and he was too old for me anyway, quite thirty-five, I thought. Odd that he wasn't married, but married men didn't pick up girls in restaurants.

Bill was standing under the gas lamp, lighting his pipe. How big and masculine he looked! He advanced to meet me, raising his checked cap; he always wore a checked cap and a navy blue Melton overcoat. 'Nice to see you,' he said, looking into my eyes so that I had to look away. He suggested we hop on a bus and take a ride into the countryside. He said he knew a nice quiet little spot where I wouldn't have to worry about meeting any nurses.

We sat on top of the bus, which wound away from the busy noisy streets out through a veritable forest. I inhaled deeply, filling my lungs with the fresh sweet air. I longed to clutch at the green branches as the bus passed them.

'I never saw anyone enjoy a bus ride so much,' Bill said. 'We must do it again.' I thought that 'we' sounded a little too familiar, as if he and I were well-established friends. But I wanted to enjoy myself; I didn't want to be critical.

The quiet little place turned out to be a pub with a beer garden. I hesitated on the threshold, but Bill took my arm, and gently propelled me to a table. I smelt the beer; I was suddenly reminded of Grannie and my excursions to the Bottle and Jug on her behalf. A great lump came into my throat. What was I doing here? Was I no better than the tipsy, leering women in the pub at home? I imagined my father's incredulous look if he should walk in and see me sitting in a pub with a strange man whom I knew only as Bill; I didn't even know his last name. I leapt up from the table and rushed out of the room. Bill was at the bar ordering; he came after me and caught up with me in the garden.

'I couldn't ever go into a pub to drink,' I said. 'My father would never forgive me.'

'Let's sit down outside here then,' Bill said. He asked me if I had ever had an intoxicating drink. Oh yes, I told him, at parties or at a dance or at home at Christmas, but never more than one.

'Well,' Bill said quietly, 'tell me, what is the difference between a drink at a dance or a party and a drink in a pub with me?'

'I don't know,' I said. 'But Grannie would call it disgraceful for a woman to drink in a pub with men.'

'Oh, would she now, Miss Prim? Well, would she call it disgraceful to have one drink with me in this lovely garden on this lovely evening? Because I think a drink would do you a world of good.'

Well, it was a pretty garden with spring flowers and little round wrought iron tables and chairs, and the moon was rising. I don't think Grannie would have condemned me out of hand. It wasn't noisy or raucous. There were one or two couples at the tables, talking quietly and behaving with decorum. I broke my rule and had two drinks. Bill had several beers, but his manner and his speech did not reflect it. I had heard my father say that some men could carry their beer. The expression had always mystified me. Now I saw what he meant.

The delightful ride home on top of the bus with Bill's arm around the back of my seat dispelled my qualms about sitting in the pub garden. 'Enjoyed yourself?' Bill asked when we alighted at the bus stop. 'Oh, yes, thank you,' I said honestly.

The next day I felt relaxed, as though I were still breathing clean country air. That night I asked Jenny, from the discomfort of my lumpy mattress, whether she would go into a pub with a man.

'I would go anywhere with a man if I liked him enough,' Jenny said.

'No, seriously. Bill took me to a pub to have a drink. I felt depraved, cheap, common, vulgar. I hated myself,' I said passionately.

'Well, there are pubs and pubs. You can be selective. If you don't like the atmosphere you don't have to stay. Some pubs are more like hotels, but there is nothing wrong with a girl having a drink with her fella, if he wants. Don't worry so much, Ann. You'll learn.'

After that I saw Bill two or three nights a week. Jenny and I worked our district very well together and, unless we were on call, that last three months were the easiest time we had. We could usually slip off from our digs between eight-thirty and nine o'clock in the evening. Since we had to be at roll-call at seven in the morning, it was rather a long day.

Bill and I usually took bus rides into the country; he knew endless haunts. Sometimes he insisted I have a good meal. And he took me around London on the buses and showed me points of interest I would never have seen otherwise. He always had me back by eleven o'clock because he had an early shift at the factory, and we never met on the weekends. He said he was always on duty or on call in case of a breakdown. I accepted this and I was glad to catch up with my studies and lectures at weekends.

'Woodie,' Jenny said, 'I hope you're not getting too fond of that hulking great brute of a man, are you? Remember we shall soon be leaving London and you may never see him again.'

'No, of course not, silly. It's nothing like that. Of course he kisses me goodnight, but that's only being good friends.'

'Well, just don't get too involved, my love,' Jenny said.

I found myself thinking of Ken and the lovely balls he had taken me to. No pubs for Ken; only the best was good enough. I still wasn't sure it was right to go into a pub to drink where there were a lot of men. And Ken had danced divinely. Bill had said that he didn't dance so he couldn't ever take me into a dance hall for a drink. 'I drink beer, a man's drink, in a man's world,' he said. Oh, yes, Bill was a man's man all right. Jenny had called him a hulking creature. I could imagine him dancing with Matron at our Christmas party. They would have been two towering figures together. I laughed out loud at the thought.

'What's funny, Woodie?' one of the girls asked.

'Oh nothing really,' I said. 'I just had a picture of Matron dancing with a friend of mine.'

'Not that Tarzan we've seen waiting for you at the bottom of the road?' another girl said.

They all laughed. My word, I thought, I should have to be more careful. I didn't want it to get around all over the place.

We were now all getting exam fever. We scurried about borrowing notes from one another, copying lectures, explaining obscure points to each other. Jenny and I shared a candle and studied in bed. We gave each other mock exams and alternately despaired or felt sure of success. Jenny had a photographic memory while I really had to swot, but I had a flair for remembering the abnormalities, the chance in a thousand cases. The senior lecturer, who must have been at least eighty, with a face wrinkled and screwed up like a monkey's, so stressed these cases that they got 'curiouser and curiouser', and I never forgot them.

The great day dawned. We were taken to Central London to do our written exam. We entered an enormous, forbidding stone building. A wide flight of stone stairs led to the upper room where there were desks, each with a nurse's name on it. They were spaced well apart to avoid any cheating or whispering. We were given strict instructions about silence. I lost the pit of my stomach on entering and could not have uttered a word to save my life.

I glanced at the enormous folder with the questions and the blank sheet of paper which I, in my wisdom, would strive to fill.

'Eyes down.' We were off.

Writing was easy for me and I answered most questions. The problem was had I, in my enthusiasm, given the right answers? I felt reasonably confident. Finally the ordeal was over. Out in the corridors everyone was asking everyone else, 'What did you put for so and so?' And then in surprise at the answer, 'You didn't, did you? Well, you could be right. What about abnormalities? Woodie, tell me what you put for Evisceration? Oh, you clever girl. I couldn't spell it.'

So it went until Sister Tutor rounded us up to return to the nurses' home.

Next came the oral exam. This I dreaded and I had nightmares about it: some old lecturer was chasing me all over London shouting questions at me. I awoke in a fright just as he was about to catch me and shake the answers out of me.

'Woodie,' Jenny said, 'you need a sedative.' But I was afraid to take anything in case it should make me dopey.

The day before the exam Sister Tutor tried to calm us down.

'Now girls, you all know the answers to any questions the examiners may ask you, I'm sure. Keep your heads, think, and don't panic. You should all pass. Good luck.'

With these encouraging words ringing in our ears, we queued up outside the doors, waiting for our name to be called to face the august body. Because my name was

Wood, and it was alphabetical, I was one of the last to be called. I was beginning to feel weak as each nurse came out of the room looking stricken. I felt sure my questions would bear on my weakest points and they did. 'I can't be lucky in anything,' I thought, 'I must always strive for what I have; nothing will ever come my way easily.'

As I came out of the examination room, through the huge double doors, I ran straight into Sister Tutor. Immediately I burst into a flood of tears.

'Now, now,' Sister said. 'It can't be as bad as all that.'

'Oh Sister,' I wailed, 'he asked me what I would do if a new-born baby was losing weight. And I just said, "Test feed it!" '

'Well, what's wrong with that? I would say that was the answer he was looking for.'

'You don't think he wanted fluid ounces and grams and milligrams?'

'Not unless he specifically asked,' said Sister.

Suddenly my world was put to rights. To celebrate the end of the ordeal we went to the London Coliseum to see the musical *The White Horse Inn.* It was a splendid spectacular, with a revolving stage. I was transported to another world. I thought that if I failed as a nurse, I would be a chorus girl.

We had to wait weeks for our exam results; it was agonising.

Finally the day came, and the results were pinned up on the notice board in the communal nurses room, for everyone to see. My name was nearly last on the alphabetical list and Jenny's name was there too.

We hugged and kissed each other and cried a little. Jenny had a bottle of wine hidden in the lodgings and we drank to success and to ourselves.

I was a professional at last. All the hard work and privation had been rewarded. I could hardly believe my good fortune. I even had letters after my name. No more scouring the paper for insecure jobs or seeking references from reluctant employers. I was somebody in my own right at last. I vowed that I would frame my certificate: it said it all. I walked six foot tall and sent a wire home with the good news. My father, I thought, would be pleased and relieved.

The time came to leave smoky, foggy, dirty East End London. There was of course no Clean Air Act, and chimneys belched forth black smoke into the damp air which hung low in dense black fog enshrouding the whole neighbourhood. I would never forget London, the good and the bad.

I took leave of Bill. He was delighted I had passed, and called me his 'clever little sweetheart'. I was a bit taken aback; I had never agreed to be his sweetheart. He would write to me, he said, and he would come and spend a few days and meet my family. He gave me an ebony hairbrush with a silver 'A' on the back. 'Brush your hair every night and think of me,' he said. 'I love your silky hair and I'll think of you sitting before your mirror thinking of me with your hair on your shoulders. Will you do that just for me?'

I was touched and near to tears as he put the hairbrush in my hands. 'Oh it's beautiful, Bill,' I said. 'I will use it every night. I'll never forget.' We parted sorrowfully. I was vaguely disturbed by the intensity of his parting kiss. It seemed to draw my heart out of my body and stop my breathing. Through my tears, I watched him stride away down the street but I wasn't really unhappy. In fact, I left London in a haze of happiness. I was going home to my family—this time a success.

11. The Professional

I WAS at home this time on a real holiday, actually being paid by the Authority which had sent me to London to be trained. After the two weeks' holiday I was to take up an appointment as District Nurse in a country village. I didn't know yet which one it was to be. But it was to be all my own responsibility, no Matron, no Sister. I would make all the decisions. And I vowed I would be a good nurse. I would save people's lives by my care and attention. All on my own I could bring relief to suffering humanity. I would be totally dedicated.

My family rejoiced with me. I think my father was relieved that one of us had at last done something toward being self-supporting. His only sister, my Aunt Ellen, was a nurse in Australia. She had always been a mystically heroic figure to me, in a far-off land.

My pleasure was dampened when my Aunt Nancy told me that Grannie was very ill.

'I didn't know,' I said in alarm. 'Nobody told me. I must go and see her. Maybe I can stay a day or two and look after her.'

'You mustn't upset yourself. Grannie is very old now, you know. We cannot expect her to live forever. She has had a good life,' said my aunt.

I wondered how my aunt could talk that way about Grannie—as if it didn't matter that she might be dying. I didn't see how life could be the same without the thought of Grannie living somewhere within reach.

I gathered that Grannie had lived in the country for the past two years. I had been so busy with my own affairs that it had never occurred to me that Grannie might possibly have been neglected. Apparently she had been ill with her usual chest complaint—bronchitis— the first winter she went to stay with her daugher, my aunt, in the country. The aunts got together and de- cided to pay a woman a small sum to take Grannie into her little cottage and look after her. There, it seemed, their obligation ended. Grannie knew the woman she went to live with; the woman's family had been farm- hands on Grannie's farm in her more prosperous days, when Grandad was alive. At first Grannie was moder- ately comfortable in the cottage, talking about old times, children, the horses, Grandfather and setting the mar- ket. But when Grannie's health deteriorated and she was not mobile, it was a different story.

My aunt and I set out on the train to see Grannie. Aunt kept telling me she didn't want me to be upset; she sounded upset herself. I wondered why she was so nervous. I decided that I would cheer Grannie up; I would show Aunt how to wash her and make her comfortable in a professional way. I would stay for the rest of my holiday and nurse Grannie back to health. I would be careful not to tire her, but I knew she would be pleased to see me and we would have a good chat. I knew how to make chicken broth just the way she liked it. And I was no longer a pauper, I thought proudly; I could go to the local and buy the little drop of 'medicinal spirit' she enjoyed so much. I knew she would purse her mouth in disapproval of some of the things I had done, but her eyes would sparkle.

My aunt and I walked from the station through the pleasant village and down the lanes to the cottage. We went round the garden path to the back door and walked straight into the low-ceilinged kitchen. A scruffy woman sat peeling potatoes at an oilcloth-covered kitchen table pushed up against the wall near the fireplace where an unwilling fire was struggling to take the cold and damp from the room. The cold brick floor, with only a piece mat at the hearth, was dirty; I knew from experience that it had to be scrubbed with hot soda water. A huge whitewood chest of drawers stood under the tiny kitchen window on which a soiled net curtain kept out light and air. A cupboard on one side of the fireplace I guessed was the larder; on the other side was a door opening onto the staircase leading to the two rooms above. Opposite the fireplace was a closed door which I thought led to the front room.

The woman rose, wiping her hands on her dirty apron.

'How is she today, Emily?' my aunt enquired.

'She won't last much longer,' the woman said. 'She's sinking fast.' She looked at me for the first time.

'My niece,' my aunt said by way of introduction.

A horrible fear took hold of me. What was my Grannie doing in this poverty-stricken cottage with only this old woman to look after her?

I swallowed. 'Where is Grannie?' I asked, finding my voice.

The woman crossed the room and opened the door facing the fireplace. My aunt and I followed to enter a murky room; almost no light penetrated the tatty cotton curtains. I saw now why we had gone round to the back door. A cast-iron bedstead was pushed right across the front door which opened directly into the road. The door was ill-fitting; light showed all round it. The draught from it must be blowing directly onto the little shrunken figure on the bed. It was Grannie lying there, covered with lumpy bedding topped by a man's old overcoat, no doubt to ease the effect of the draught from the door.

Someone was standing at the foot of the bed in the dimly lit room busy with leaves and a few wintry flowers. I realised with horror that she was making a wreath before the dying patient's eyes. I looked closely at the woman. It was my mother!

With a strangled sob, I threw myself on Grannie's bed. 'Speak to me, darling,' I said. I stroked her hair; I took my handkerchief and wiped her dear little face. She was feverish. I cried as she opened her eyes and began to cry on recognising me. She tried to speak my name, but she was too weak.

'Grannie, Grannie!' I cried. 'What have they done to you!' I slipped my arm under her frail shoulder and lifted her toward me as she struggled to breathe.

'She shouldn't be lying flat; she should be propped up on pillows to help her breathing,' I cried angrily, looking around the room. I now became aware of two more people in the shadows. They were an aunt and uncle whom I vaguely knew. Someone gave me an old cushion from the rickety armchair in the room and I managed to prop Grannie up; her breathing was harsh and difficult, but the cushion seemed to ease her efforts to breathe.

'Why isn't there a fire in this room?' I asked. I went to the door and called the woman in from the kitchen. 'Please light a fire in this room immediately,' I demanded. The woman looked startled and answered triumphantly, 'She ain't got no coal left. We didn't think it worth getting any, her being so near the end, like.'

'Use some of yours and light a fire at once,' I said. I gave her two shillings and sixpence for compensation. 'I am a nurse,' I told the room in general, 'and I shall take charge of nursing Grannie now. I want a bowl of hot water to wash her as soon as the fire is lit and the room warms up. No wonder an old coat had to be put on the bed,' I added with disgust.

I moved the bed away from the draughty door, with the help of the shamefaced relatives. I drew the curtains and let in the wintry sun, and gave Grannie general attention as I had been taught to do. One of my aunts helped willingly, taking my instructions. I took some of the flowers intended for another purpose and arranged them in a jar on the mantlepiece. Propped up on two pillows fetched from upstairs, with clean sheets and a bedspread in place of the coat, the fire burning brightly, Grannie looked as comfortable as it was possible to make her.

We left in the late afternoon. I gave the woman instructions that the fire was to be kept up all night and five shillings to ensure that she carried out my wishes. I told her that we would be back again tomorrow.

I never saw Grannie alive again. She died during the night. The death certificate said 'Bronchitis'. I could have added my own diagnosis to that.

In my grief and preoccupation with Grannie, I had almost forgotten that I had told my sister about Bill, and my father had agreed that he could come and spend the night with us in order to meet everyone. The day before he was to arrive a letter came from him explaining that his shift had been changed and he could not get away after all. I was used to Bill's irregular working hours, but my father took a dim view of the situation and I couldn't convince him that it was unavoidable. I was disappointed and I felt obscurely that my family was against me.

I tried to explain. 'Bill would lose his job if he protested, Daddy,' I said. 'He is a maintenance mechanic and if the machinery breaks down he has to put it right; superintend it. He must be there.'

My father was not swayed. 'I must say, my dear, that I have charge of men who service machinery, and they know well in advance what their commitments will be, week by week. I think you would be well advised to challenge your young man on his excuse.'

I thought my father was very hard; he never made excuses for anyone or anything. He was trying, I thought, to put doubt in my mind. I was very upset that Bill was not coming. I picked up the ebony hairbrush with the A in silver on the back and a tear, always near the surface with me, splashed down onto my hand. He had said he loved my hair. It hadn't been a happy holiday—Grannie dying, and now Bill not coming. Never mind, I thought, Bill had said I should not be too disappointed; he would come and see me when I got settled in my district.

I felt I could not wait to get away and start my new life. I will be in full control of everything when I start my nursing, I told myself.

The secretary of the village Nursing Association met me at the station. She was a young woman married to the head gardener on the nearby estate of a wealthy farmer. It was a lovely day in early spring; aconites and snowdrops were showing in the grass. I was to lodge with a Methodist lay preacher and his wife in a house in a hollow in the centre of the village. The preacher was a preacher only on weekends and evenings when necessary; he was a blacksmith by trade. His smithy was a barn-like structure on one side of the house. On the other side was a small outhouse, which I was to use as my surgery. My landlord was a huge muscular man, as one would expect a smith to be. He had a big head with a shock of black tousled hair, a fleshy face, bushy eyebrows meeting over dark brown eyes and a loose, full sensuous mouth. He preached away from home every Sunday, saving souls and collecting a good hot luncheon from zealous chapel goers.

He fitted up shelves and a cupboard for me in the outhouse, which I whitewashed and scrubbed and cleaned. I planned to spend all my free time there; I loved the peace and quiet of it and the privacy and importance of having my own place. I had a slate to hang on the door when I was out, so I could be found if there was an emergency. A District Nurse is on call twenty-four hours a day. Sunday was my day off, if nothing cropped up, and I had one half-day a week.

I took my meals with the blacksmith and his wife, son and mother. The wife was a wiry little woman with a thin, lined face and sharp, bird-like eyes. She told all and sundry how 'Our Father', which was what she called her husband, relished his food. And he did indeed: his lips smacked together when he ate and sussed when he drank. Since I sat opposite him at mealtimes, my enjoyment of the food was somewhat restricted. 'Our Father' always said grace before and after meals; I received many a disapproving look for sitting down too soon. He was very forceful about the ravages of sin, especially the temptations of drink and women. He drank surreptitiously himself every evening after his meal, sitting with his glass and bottle boldly on the table, but ready to conceal them hastily under the table if anyone came into the room. A huge bobble-edged chenille cloth covered the table and reached the floor where it would hide the incriminating evidence if necessary. At first he was careful with me, but after I had once surprised him, he didn't bother to try to cover up. He even confided to me in one of his convivial moods that his wife was frigid. It is amazing what magic powers people attribute to a nurse.

The son, Albert, also lived at home. He spent his spare time chasing the village girls. He obviously tolerated his father because he had no choice. My landlady's mother shut herself in a world of woe. She was waiting for The Call and frightened to put a foot wrong.

One of my first calls out started with a young boy knocking loudly on the door on a cold wet night, about seven o'clock.

'Can you come, Nurse? Me mum is took,' he said.

I recognised the boy; it was a delivery I had been expecting any day at a farm cottage a couple of miles from the village.

'You get back as quickly as you can,' I said to him. 'Tell your father to have a fire lit in the room and plenty of hot water for me. I'll follow you immediately.'

It was hard going uphill through the village on my bicycle against a head wind. Leaving the road I walked across two fields, half-leaning on my bicycle and keeping well into the hedge for shelter. The headlamp on the bicycle saved me from falling on the rough plowed land where the rain collected in great puddles.

The light streamed from the open cottage door across the field like a beacon.

'She's bad, Nurse. Been struggling all afternoon she

has, and no further on.' Her husband was anxiously waiting at the door for me.

I scolded him. 'Why didn't you send for me before?' It was a well-known fact that the ignorant country folk delayed sending for the nurse until the last moment. They didn't see the necessity for all the washing and preparation and fuss over having a baby. To them it was a simple, straightforward, once-a-year-occurrence that you just got on with. When things went wrong and the local Gamp, a woman who 'did' for everyone, couldn't cope, the doctor would be called in too late to perform a miracle.

Hot water was scarce and the necessity for it was viewed with suspicion. Personal hygiene was unknown. As a new District Nurse with fussy modern ideas I had a lot of ground to cover.

'We didn't want to trouble you too soon,' the man said apologetically.

The woman was lying on the bed downstairs in the front room. Beside a washstand with an enamel jug and basin and one chair, the bed was the only furniture in the room. No cot for the baby—it could sleep in the bed with its mother. In those days babies frequently got 'laid over' by their mothers and suffocated. It was quite common for nurses to make an improvised cot from one of the drawers from a chest, if the mother could be persuaded to allow it. The floor was covered in linoleum, with no rug to take the chill off one's feet. No curtains; they were not considered necessary for a farm cottage with no neighbours, miles from anywhere. A feeble fire in the grate did nothing to alleviate the cold or cheer the atmosphere.

I quickly spread newspapers, which I had previously told the woman to save for me, about the room as I had been trained to do, and set up my equipment. A drop of carbolic in hot water gave the room at least a profes-

sional smell. The patient was half undressed and unwashed, writhing helplessly on the bed. After a wash
and brush up, in a clean nightdress, with the bed tidied
and with a clean sheet, she looked more comfortable.
But I was not happy with her progress and I thought
I would have to summon the doctor.

'Don't you send for the doctor, Nurse,' she said. 'I
have had seven without a doctor and I don't want him.
I'll be all right—you'll see—if we just bide our time.
This one is a bit stubborn but it'll come just like all the
others.'

'Well, Mrs Smith,' I said, 'you must leave that to my
judgment. I can't let you go on in labour all night without one sign of progress.'

'I'll be all right, Nurse, I tell you. Ain't never had no
doctor yet.'

Mercifully, the children were all in bed upstairs. The
husband did his best. He brought in fuel for the fire
and numerous cups of strong tea to help keep us awake.
He was out of his depth: if it had been a cow or a pig
or a mare, he would have known what to do, but this
poor suffering creature bewildered him.

'She ain't never been like this afore,' he said. 'Wonder
what's stopping it?'

So did I, but I didn't say anything. Only doctors had
instruments or mechanical aids; nurses had largely to
rely on nature. I listened for the foetal heartbeat where
I knew it should be. I pressed my ear flat as a pancake
to her distended abdomen. Not a gurgle or a whisper
could I hear, much less a rhythmic thumping.

'Mr Smith,' I said, 'I must ask you to telephone for
the doctor. Tell him Nurse has been here for three hours
and needs help.'

The doctor lived in the next village, but there was a
telephone at the big farmhouse just a mile away. The
man cycled there with all speed. The doctor arrived in

his car nearly as soon as Mr Smith got back, breathless and soaking wet.

'I don't want no doctor,' Mrs Smith wailed. 'Allus done it on my own afore; what's gone wrong this time?' She was getting frightened now and a little hysterical.

'Nothing has gone wrong, Mrs Smith; we'll soon have you comfortable.' I tried to reassure her.

When the doctor came I explained the situation so far.

'Keep that pot boiling, man,' he said. He was talking about the pan on the stove which was used for boiling jam and never before for surgical instruments. He was jacketless in seconds, with his sleeves rolled up and wearing a rubber apron.

'Give her some more chloroform on the mask, Nurse,' he said. 'Keep her under.'

At long last the ordeal was over. A monster was born, a mongol, chin on chest, evisceration—the midwife's nightmare. It was the creature which our senior lecturer had told us there was only a chance in a thousand we would ever see. I saw it and gasped in horror at the big-headed misshapen thing that had come from the woman's body. We made sure that she didn't see it as she came round from the chloroform. Fortunately husbands were not allowed at births then, so he didn't see it either.

'Wrap it up, Nurse,' the doctor said, turning away. I rolled the hideous thing in an old towel and wrapped it well in sheets of newspaper. The doctor took the bundle out to Mr Smith in the kitchen and had a word with him. I think he buried it like a dead animal in the garden or a field. Mrs Smith was told it was a stillbirth. All she said was, 'I thought it was lazy-like coming. Might all be for the best, thank God.'

That was my introduction to country midwifery and I have never forgotten it.

Some weeks later, a child knocked again at my door.
'Can you come quick, Nurse, as Mother has tipped a kettle of water in the fire and burnt my little brother?'

I pedalled down the lane as fast as any fire engine and went straight into the cottage.

The mother sat over the open kitchen grate, nursing a toddler who was moaning and who appeared to be only semi-conscious. All his visible flesh was blistered and the blisters were covered with grey wood ash. The water had poured out of the overturned kettle into the wood fire, sending a shower of scalding ash over the child. The ash was on his eyelids, up his nose, down his throat. A huge blister hung out of his mouth, caused no doubt when he opened his mouth to scream. His bare arms were one huge blister to his fingertips.

I was petrified; I didn't know what to do. The mother was numb with shock. The doctor, I thought desperately, the ambulance.

I dashed out onto my bicycle and telephoned the doctor and the ambulance. The doctor arrived and gave the child a pain killer. I dabbed gently and I am afraid ineffectually at the tortured flesh with gauze and olive oil, trying to clean off some of the ash; it stuck like glue. The mother sat rocking the child until the ambulance, mercifully, arrived. A big burly attendant carried the child tenderly to the waiting vehicle. It was a nightmare journey of nineteen miles to the hospital.

The boy recovered, but he was scarred and pitted for life. Whilst in hospital he fell from a first floor window out of his cot which had been carelessly pushed, with the side down, near the open window. Fortunately he fell into a flower bed and sustained no more than a broken arm. I wonder if he was accident prone, or whether he bore a charmed life.

Some of the cottages in the village were extremely old and under order of demolition, but people out of necessity had to live in them. In one cottage like that, in a row of similar cottages, lived a young married girl expecting her first baby. Her husband, a farmworker, and little more than a boy, had patched up and repaired the cottage and between them they had made a home of a derelict 'one up and one down' with a privy at the bottom of the garden shared by the neighbours. A bench with an enamel bowl and jug, outside the back door in summer and inside in winter, served as bathroom. A tub of rainwater outside the back door provided a delightful natural soft water supply; soap lathered right up in it. For all culinary purposes there was a small black wrought iron grate, the sling basket type, with a hob at either end; a kettle usually sang on the hob—that was the sole source of hot water. These were the facilities I had to deliver a baby. Not far removed from biblical days.

The lucky ones lived in the few council houses in the village. These boasted a bath in the kitchen with a whitewood lid. The villagers, being both resourceful and not fond of bathing, found innumerable alternative uses for the bath. One family used it as a coal bin, since it was close to the kitchen fire; another stored the winter crop of potatoes in it and still another used it for dry goods like flour and cereals. Those few who used it for its legitimate purpose were considered by some villagers to be very forward-looking; others thought they were taking a great risk with their health, especially in the winter. The whitewood top which fitted over the bath served as a kitchen table and was kept scrubbed miraculously clean and white.

The woman in the broken-down village house had been in labour too long for my peace of mind. I summoned the doctor, an act which always signalled trouble to the villagers; they much preferred the local Gamp, an old woman who did—or more precisely didn't—'do' for them with very little fuss or preparation, much less antiseptic precautions. On this occasion the doctor coped as well as he could with complications; I tried to sterilise instruments in an enamel bowl wedged on the open fire. The ambulance had been sent for. Pray it comes in time, I said to myself between trips up and down the Jacob's ladder which served as a stairway from the bedroom to the kitchen, to fetch the hot water. In anguish I watched the doctor who had one knee and most of his weight on the bed, trying to deal with the situation.

'A little more ether on the mask, Nurse,' he said. I obeyed his instructions; the poor girl welcomed the lapse into oblivion. Suddenly there was an ominous cracking splintering sound and the legs of the foot of the bed went through the ceiling. The bed tipped sideways and downward, shooting the doctor onto the floor. I grabbed the half-conscious girl and stopped her from slipping to the foot of the bed, toward the gaping hole in the floor.

Just at that moment, the ambulance arrived. The attendants swarmed up the Jacob's ladder and in seconds had the terrified patient, now recovered from the ether, on a stretcher and into the ambulance. We were soon on our way with sirens screeching the sixteen miles to the hospital. Thanks to the doctor's delaying tactics, the baby was not born in the ambulance and all ended happily in the hospital shortly after our arrival.

Most of the people were cooperative; they were pleased to have their own nurse. But I could be a hero one day and lose my halo the next. One evening a young farm hand called in at the surgery on his way home from the fields. He had been in pain all day with a foreign body in his eye. His mates hadn't helped by popping corners of screwed-up handkerchiefs into his eye attempting to dislodge the offending object.

'Sit down,' I said, 'and hold your head back.' I stood behind him and bent over and rolled the eyelid back. Then I put a drop of olive oil into his eye. He blinked and a sharp whisker from an ear of corn lay on his cheek, washed out by the oil. He was immediately relieved and I had worked a miracle!

The next day an irate farmer brought a young boy to me with a blue pea as hard as a nail firmly wedged in his ear. His brother, a crack shot with a pea shooter, had hit the bull's eye: his brother's eardrum. I probed and used forceps and succeeded only in pushing the pea farther into the child's ear. 'I don't have anything here that will get the pea out,' I said to the father. 'I'm afraid you'll have to take him to the doctor in the next village.' The father, already extremely irritated, gave me to understand that he didn't think much of me as a nurse if I couldn't deal with a simple operation. So that day my halo was lost.

I recovered my reputation somewhat when my landlady had a painful seizure in the middle of the night. Her husband called me, but he was not particularly alarmed. She had had these attacks before, he said, and had always recovered in a day or two.

She was writhing in pain. I soon diagnosed her trouble: she had a hernia. I told her husband firmly that this time she would not recover unless he called an ambulance to take her to the hospital immediately. It was soon round the village that I had saved my landlady's life. I had safeguarded my reputation once again.

Not long after the episode of the collapsed ceiling, I was hastily summoned to the Vicarage. The Vicar, a man of eighty, had had a heart attack. He was much loved in the village, where he had lived for forty years and where he visited and comforted the villagers, married hopeful couples, christened babies and preached coherent sermons. He had long white silken hair and looked somewhat like Lloyd George. Unfortunately, he did not recover from the heart attack; he was the first person to die in the District while I was there. The funeral cortège was like a mobile flower show. Every man, woman and child in the village lined the route, many openly weeping. Men touched their caps in respect and women curtsied in a strange, old world way which reflected the pace of life in country villages at that time.

The passing of the Vicar put me in a quandary over my weekly bath. The vicarage was one of only two or three houses in the village which had a bathroom, with or without hot and cold water. I had been granted the privilege of bathing at the vicarage on Friday evenings. I was watched with awe as I cycled through the village every Friday evening en route to my appointment with soap and hot water. The people could not believe that I could keep my health, returning in winter from total immersion.

My landlady came to my rescue. Since I was the District Nurse, it was understood that I must keep up my standard of cleanliness at all costs. There was an old wooden wash house at the bottom of the garden with an antiquated brick copper used only on wash days. The fire could be kept going after Monday's washing; I could cleanse myself on Monday instead of Friday. My landlord agreed readily to fill the copper from the soft rain water tub which stood at the entrance and ladle it out into the zinc washtub when it was hot; he fetched the tub in from the hook on the wash house wall where it hung all week. With relish he ladled the hot water from the copper and cooled it with cold water from the tub outside. I don't think his mind was altogether on the job or that his Sunday parishioners would have appreciated his thoughts at the time.

'Will that be all, Nurse?' he would ask, leering and chortling. 'Sure there's nothing else I can do for you?'

I ushered him out, drew the curtains firmly and locked the door. At times, however, my ablutions were overseen by the cat and the odd broody hen who somehow managed to secrete herself in some dark corner on her nest of eggs. The wash house was a not unpleasant bathroom; in the summer there was the scent of honeysuckle and in the winter the glow of the dying embers of the fire up the copper hole. The contented cluck of the hen was company, and so was the silent cat on the warm hearth. The soft rainwater was like pure silk cascading through my fingers in the perfumed air. No artificial beauty aids were needed here; I was close to nature.

Everything moved at a slow pace. Farmers still drove their horses and pony carts. There was one taxi owned and operated by the general grocers and a motorised van for delivering bread. There were very few cars: a few were owned by the handful of Royal Air Force families who lived in furnished rooms or lodgings; the village was about eight miles from the Air Force camp. Even most of these men cycled back and forth to work. In the course of my duties I met these families who, in return for any trivial attention, subscribed handsomely to the nursing funds.

One family introduced me to a young man who was newly home from a tour of duty in the Middle East. He was resplendent with a gold-filled toothy smile and a new Morris Crowley Coupe car. Needless to say, all the village was at his feet. He tried his charm on me without success. He cruised like a lord of the manor through the village in his shiny automobile and addressed me familiarly as I was pedalling laboriously uphill.

Cheek, I thought. I am not to be picked up by any Tom, Dick or Harry, car or no car.

In those days it was a great adventure to have travelled

abroad. Most holidays consisted of a week at the nearest seaside resort, accommodation only. Mum still did the shopping, but the landlady cooked the meal. This was cheaper than boarding since hotels were for the favoured few and too expensive for the likes of us.

My Air Force friends took me as their guest to the village midsummer dance, where they introduced me formally to the hero of the day and the beau of the evening. I learned afterward that this meeting was planned because he was determined to meet me. I went home after the dance in the new Morris Coupe.

Our friendship developed, but my heart was still with Bill; I told him I was practically engaged but it didn't seem to register with him. His name was David and he was Welsh, with a beautiful soft voice and a slight accent which fascinated me.

He asked me to go the following Saturday evening to the cinema in a neighbouring town. 'Jessie Matthews is on in *The Good Companions*,' he said. I loved musicals, and I couldn't refuse. I said I would go, if my duty permitted me. On the Saturday morning I did the usual half-hour visits in the village. There was one expectant mother who seemed on the brink, but she assured me that she was 'lovely'. 'You go, Nurse, and enjoy yourself,' she said when I told her about my invitation to the cinema. 'Never you fear, I'll still be waiting when you get back.'

It was a wonderul show; Jessie Matthews sang and danced her way delightfully through the whole programme. She solved all the problems she encountered and enslaved her lover. I felt relaxed and happy, driving home in the shining new automobile. 'Enjoyed yourself?' David asked. 'It was good, wasn't it?' He wanted to linger on the way home, but I was thinking about my work.

'No,' I said, as he slowed down, 'I've already been

away from the village too long. I must get back. Anyway it doesn't look good for the nurse to be out after midnight.'

'You are a funny little thing,' he said. 'You worry too much, Ann. Nothing's going to happen while you're away for a couple of hours.'

But what was it our lecturer used to say? 'There's nothing so unpredictable as midwifery.'

We arrived in the village and cruised quietly downhill through the main street. At the far end of the village, on the rise of the hill, I saw light streaming from what appeared to be a wide open door, onto a car parked by the roadside. I recognised it: it was the doctor's car, and next to it was parked the Mini belonging to the District Nurse from the next village. She needed a car because her village was much larger than mine.

I leaped out almost before David had time to stop; I had no time to say good-night or to thank him.

'What happened?' I gasped to my landlady who opened the door to me, arrayed in curlers and best dressing gown, holding a lighted candle in her hand.

'Mrs Smith was took about two hours ago. They sent for the doctor and he sent for the nurse from the next village as you was out gallivanting.'

Frantically I pulled off my clothes and climbed into my uniform; never at any early morning roll call had I battled so frenziedly with buttons, buckles and safety pins. Grabbing my medical bag I mounted my bicycle and pedalled up that hill as fast as I could go.

Mr Smith met me at the door with a glowering look. 'Where you been till now, Nurse?' he asked accusingly. I didn't reply, but pushed past him in the doorway. He barely made room for me. I climbed the creaking wooden staircase and entered the bedroom. The doctor was washing up, preparing to leave. I handed him a towel; he looked at me and did not say a word. Nurse, busy attending to Mrs Smith, looked up and gave me an encouraging smile. My heart warmed to her. The baby was wrapped in a napkin, lying peacefully in an improvised cot near the fire. The room was unventilated and heavy with the smell of sweat.

'Can you give me a hand to move her over a little?' Nurse asked, breaking the tense silence. The doctor bade her goodnight and left. I said goodnight too, although I didn't think he was including me in his farewell. I helped Nurse with the mother and bathed the baby who did not seem any the worse for my neglect. In an hour we were both ready to leave. Everything seemed perfectly normal. 'I don't know what to say to you, Nurse, or how to thank you,' I stammered.

'These things happen,' she said. 'You couldn't know the woman would start as soon as your back was turned, or that she would need the doctor, unfortunately. Now don't worry over it, don't fret. Everything will be all right. It'll be a nine days' wonder in the village and then it will be forgotten. You'll see.'

I lay in bed and turned the situation over in my mind. I vowed I would never leave the village again. It was all my fault. All the trust and the good reputation I had painstakingly built up had evaporated for the sake of a few hours at the cinema. I cried myself to sleep in frustration and disappointment.

The Smiths were angry at me; they felt I had let them down. They did not want to cooperate with me and they resented what they saw as my unnecessary fussing round Mrs Smith. She seemed to be doing well for the first three days; and the tension too was lessening. Then on the fourth day, she had a restless night. She had an unquenchable thirst and two bright red spots appeared on her cheekbones. Her eyes were too bright and her hair was limp.

'She's got a chill, 'asn't she, with all that fancy washing of yourn,' said Mr Smith sullenly.

'Well, Mr Smith,' I said, 'give me plenty of warm water now. She is sweating. I must give her a blanket bath and I shall need clean sheets and a clean nightgown.'

He went off grumbling. 'You'll be killing her, that's what, with all this bathing. Get her death of cold.'

A neighbour brought the enamel bowl of hot water and some clean linen. She agreed reluctantly to help me sponge the patient and reduce her sweating and her temperature. I decided the doctor must be sent for—another unpopular move.

'She ain't never been like this afore,' said the worried husband. 'I don't know what's come to 'er.'

Well, I thought I knew, but I was not prepared to voice my opinion. If I was right, we were going to have to battle for her life. While I was waiting for the doctor to come, I gave my feverish patient plenty of fluids.

The doctor came and took her temperature. When he looked at the thermometer, our eyes met. He looked grave and I am sure I looked anxious.

'You know what this is, Nurse? The rash will come out tomorrow. Keep washing her down in tepid water. No solids, plenty of fluids. I will look in again this evening.'

So that was it: the dreaded killer, puerperal fever. We had no antibiotics then and the fever had to take its course. I practically lived and slept at the Smith house, Mr Smith held that I was to blame because of my fancy nursing; he insisted she had caught a chill. He became so hostile to me that I had to enlist the doctor's help to get any cooperation at all. The doctor tried to convince the man that I was only carrying out his instructions but I think if he dared, the worried, ignorant, half-demented creature would have told us all to go to hell, including the doctor.

After weeks of dedicated nursing Mrs Smith miraculously recovered and seemed none the worse for her frightful experience. A less robust woman would have died. I was triumphant but exhausted and my routine work had gotten very far behind. There was no chance for me to take a holiday, which I badly needed. Two weeks a year was my ration; I was often on duty weekends and public holidays; I had no one to relieve me. The only way to get a rest was to drop from sheer exhaustion.

When Mrs Smith was out of danger and convalescing, I cycled to the next village to see my friendly District Nurse. She had never had a case of puerperal fever in her District. 'Why does everything have to happen to me?' I wailed. 'How do you think she got the germ, Nurse?'

'We'll never know. She may have been up to something to bring it on herself because she knew you were out of the village. Maybe she thought she could cope and save herself a lot of bother and it would all be over before you got back. You know they are all very ignorant, poor souls, and haven't a clue about antiseptic procedure. They still have faith in the old wives' tales and the village Gamp. You're the first trained nurse they have ever had. It isn't going to be easy to convert them to your way of thinking, but stick to it. You'll win.'

'It certainly isn't going to be easy, you can say that again,' I said morosely. 'You know her husband threatened to throw me out because I washed her so much.'

'Nurse,' my friend said seriously, 'you saved that woman's life with your care and attention. Stop blaming yourself and wallowing in self-pity. You were away when you were needed and nurses should never be out with boyfriends after midnight. It's not proper. You're not likely to make that mistake again, are you? So now how about a nice cup of tea, and cheer up!'

She made me feel self-confident. As Mrs Smith got better my spirits revived; then too the demands on me lessened. But I told myself that I had finished with men. I did not see David for two months. Then one morning when I was taking my landlady's dog for a walk, David's car pulled up beside me.

'Good evening, stranger,' he said, beaming at me. 'My word, you do look thin. What have you been doing to yourself?'

'Oh I can't go into it. But I'm all right,'

He opened the car door. 'Hop in,' he said. As I sat down beside him he put a comforting arm around me. I couldn't resist his sympathy. I poured out the whole story while Rover scampered across the fields.

'I thought something was wrong when I left you that night,' he said. 'You poor little thing, what a rough time you've had. I'd like to knock that man's block off, the stupid fool.'

This was too much for me. I burst into tears and wept on his shoulder. My firm resolve to have nothing further to do with men melted away; they could be so kind and understanding, I thought. He gave me his large handkerchief and I recovered my composure. I didn't want to get involved with David, as nice as he was. I was still hoping Bill was coming to see me; his was the shoulder I longed for.

'Now look,' David said, 'there's another good film on this Saturday. How about it? Give yourself a day out.'

'Oh, no!' I cried in alarm. 'I couldn't. I shall never leave the village again, not even on my off duty.'

'Well, then on Saturday I will call for you and we will ride back and forth and round the village and Rover can sit in the back and be chaperone and everyone will be able to see that Nurse is not deserting her post and all is prim and proper.'

We both laughed at this ridiculous picture, but he

could not persuade me to leave the village at night. That nightmare experience had terrified me.

I had been working in the village for nearly two years now and all this time Bill and I had been corresponding regularly. Somehow every time he planned to visit me, something turned up to prevent him. I understood: work was difficult to get and men had to hold on to their jobs. The dole was pitifully inadequate. Many poor souls were on the breadlines and nearly starving. I made allowance for that. I planned to visit Bill for one week of my holiday and spend one week at home. I saved carefully; my small salary more than met my small needs. I could afford a few days in a hotel in London.

The holiday was coming near. I wrote to Bill suggesting some arrangements and waited anxiously for his reply. I hadn't realised quite how much I was looking forward to seeing him again. I imagined his huge bulky form striding toward me at Liverpool Street station. He would tuck my arm in his and I would be breathless, trying to talk and keep up with his long steps. He would hail a cab and we would drive somewhere cosy and intimate, to eat. I had so much to tell him.

'Nurse!' my landlady shouted up the stairs, 'There's a registered package here for you. Can you come down and sign for it?'

I ran downstairs in my dressing down and curlers. Probably something important from the Nursing Federation; some new rules and regulations to mark and learn.

It was postmarked London and addressed in an unfamiliar hand. I went upstairs again and sat on the bed. I slit the envelope open; three snapshots fell onto the bed. A woman and children I did not recognise. I pulled a postcard-sized photograph out of the envelope. A man and a woman. A slimmer, younger Bill stared at me from the photograph. A young woman was sitting in a chair in front of him. Bill's hand was on her shoulder. The letter was simple and had an unmistakable air of truth about it:

> We have been married for ten years. I found a letter from you to my husband in his jacket pocket. I enclose a photograph of Bill and me and snapshots of the three children. If you are the girl I think you might be, judging from your letter—you will not write to or even attempt to see my husband again. If he finds out I have written to you he will murder me. Please believe me when I say you are well rid of him.

I moaned in shock. My landlady, who had probably been hovering round the door wondering about my package, came into the room.

'What is it, Nurse?' she asked anxiously. 'Bad news from home?'

Quickly I gathered up the photographs before she could see them.

'Yes,' I said. 'Bad news. It gave me a shock.' I was trembling, but I didn't cry, my usual safety valve. I felt shivery and numb. My landlady went out and returned with a cup of tea laced with Our Father's precious brandy.

Eventually I got dressed, buttoned my uniform with trembling fingers, and did my morning duty in a daze. I was behaving automatically and I could concentrate on nothing. 'Aren't you well, Nurse?' a kindly patient enquired. 'You want a holiday, you do. Always at it you are.' She gave me a cup of tea, 'to buck me up.'

After lunch which, to my landlady's concern, I hardly touched, I decided to cycle to see my friend the nurse in the next village. She was older and more experienced than I was; maybe she could see something in the letter that I had overlooked. Probably it was a cruel joke— some jealous disappointed woman trying to split up Bill and me. 'Well rid of him . . .' How could anyone say such a thing? And 'murder' her! Bill wouldn't hurt a fly. Once when we were in the country he had chased off some boys who were stoning a cat. I knew him.

I arrived at the bungalow at the far end of the village where she lived with her husband who was the local butcher and practically threw myself into her arms when she opened the door.

'Here, steady,' she said, catching hold of my arm. 'What have you been doing to yourself? You look like a ghost.'

At the sound of her voice I broke down completely and wept, handing her the letter and the photographs. She looked at them and read the letter and then went off to the kitchen. While she was gone I sobbed and sobbed. She returned eventually, as my flow of tears lessened and I was gasping for breath. She was pushing a tea trolley laden with cups and saucers and delicious-looking thin sandwiches and a fruit cake.

'I don't suppose you've eaten much today,' she said.

She insisted on my having a sandwich and I must say it did taste good. Nature prevailed over my broken heart.

After a moment I said timidly, 'You don't think it's true, do you?'

'Of course it's true,' she said calmly, looking at me. 'And you've got to accept it. You don't want the whole village to know about it, do you? I'll give you some sleeping tablets so you can get some rest.'

She produced a small vial from the pocket of her uniform.

'What shall I do about the letter?'

'Don't do anything. You can't write to the wife, she doesn't want you to. And whatever you do, don't write to Bill ever again; forget about him. I don't think he'll write to you again but if he does, don't answer him.' She paused a moment. 'Didn't you ever suspect him? Didn't you wonder why he never visited you here? Why he was never free at weekends when you were in London together?' She shook her head. 'You are too trusting. You're going to get badly hurt as you go through life if you can't tell the gold from the glitter. Now don't start in again,' she said hastily as my eyes filled. 'When is your holiday? I think a change would do you good.'

'I don't want a holiday now; I can't go to London,' I said dismally.

And I felt as though I had lost my enthusiasm for everything. I did not even enjoy my work. I behaved mechanically and took little interest in village life. I became lethargic and lost weight, and refused all invitations. By turns I was sullen, cheerful and despondent.

I remember particularly one case that came up at this time.

I was making an ante-natal visit to a woman about forty years old who was not due for another four weeks. She lived in an outlying cottage; I had to cycle some mile and a half and then walk my bicycle across two ploughed fields to get there. All was quiet and still in the cottage. No one answered my knock so I pushed the door open and entered. The remnants of a meal were on the kitchen table. A cat stretched lazily on the hearth in front of the empty grate. I crossed the kitchen and pushed open the door leading to the front room. A faint groan greeted me. My patient, a grossly overweight fifteen stone, was writhing on a feather mattress which was torn and leaking badly. Feathers were wafting around the room; the mattress had no sheet or any other kind of covering. Every time the woman tossed and turned more feathers exploded upward. She was fully dressed and wore a coarse sacking apron over her clothes; on her feet were Wellington boots covered in mud and feathers. There were feathers in her hair, on her face and clothes and bare arms.

'Thank Gawd you've come, Nurse,' she said. 'It won't be long now, it's coming.'

'Where's your husband?'

'In t' field, picking 'taties,' she gasped.

'And the children?'

'In t' field helping their dad.'

Not a creature at hand to turn to for help. I did not dare to leave her on her own. I looked round the room in dismay while feathers settled onto me. Did I wash her or pluck her? I had to get rid of those feathers. I heaved the big lump of a woman to one side of the bed, and drew the mattress from under her, letting it fall to the floor. I pushed it unceremoniously under the bed out of sight, out of the way. Luckily there was an old straw mattress on the bed springs, which the woman could lie on.

I went into the kitchen to look for some sort of kindling to start a fire. Only newspaper was available. Often at home I had coaxed a dying fire with improvised paper rings. I rolled and twisted the paper into rings and laid them strategically in the grate. Matches were to hand and with luck I got the small pieces of coal to glow from the paper. Soon I had a kettle boiling for hot water. I spread clean newspaper all round the room and brushed up the feathers in between sneezes. In a drawer I found clean sheets and a few odds and ends that she had prepared for her confinement. I undressed her with difficulty, and pulled off her Wellington boots. With the mother washed and brushed up and in a clean nightgown and clean bed, the baby made its debut, little knowing it had nearly been born into a feathered world.

'Why, Nurse,' my landlady said when I sat down to supper that evening, 'you've got one or two feathers in your hair.'

I ran into David from time to time on my evening rambles with Rover. He tried to jolly me out of my doldrums. I still refused steadily to leave the village in the evenings. I was dedicated to my job.

'You are becoming a hermit,' said David. 'You can't go on punishing yourself forever; it isn't a natural life for a young girl.'

'It's the life I've chosen,' I said primly.

'Don't tell me all you want out of life is nursing and gathering flowers in the hedgerows.'

We were sitting in the car; Rover was going wild chasing his shadow across the fields.

'Ann, I like you, I like you a lot,' David said suddenly. He tried to take my hand but I snatched it away.

'Can't you tell me what's troubling you?' he asked. 'Why are you so unhappy? You're not still worrying over that woman, are you? She did get better, didn't she?'

'I'm not unhappy. I'm not worrying over anything. I just want to do my job. I am dedicated,' I said, warming to my subject. 'I want to give my life to these village people. Like a nun.'

'Have you spoken to anyone else about this? I mean,' he said carefully not looking at me, 'your doctor for instance? Perhaps he could give you something so that you would be less depressed.'

'I'm *not* depressed, I told you, I'm quite happy. My life is my own and I can do what I like with it. I don't have to ask the doctor or you either and I didn't ask for your advice.'

I called Rover and left David sitting crestfallen in the car, watching us walk away.

I decided not to go home for my week's holiday; work was the best antidote for my unhappiness, I thought. My sister was disappointed; she wrote that she had something important to discuss with me. But I could not go home and answer questions about Bill. I still made excuses for him in my mind. Every night I brushed my hair with the black ebony hairbrush with the silver 'A' on it.

I received an unusually thick letter from my sister

after that. Alice had been engaged for three years, and she wanted to get married that summer. My youngest sister Laura had passed her exams and was now a fully qualified teacher and was taking a post in the Midlands. Who did that leave then to look after my father but me? Alice wrote that Father was, as I knew, very set in his ways and would not take kindly to the only other alternative—a housekeeper. She wanted to know whether I would consider giving up nursing and coming back home to take care of Father.

I read and re-read the letter. I was being asked to give up my dedication to nursing; I was being asked to turn my back on my villagers. They had come to rely on me; they had forgiven and forgotten the time I had let them down over the birth of Mrs Smith's baby. And I had a profession which I had worked so hard to attain.

But I was very young and romantic. The idea of self-sacrifice appealed to me, obviously. I saw my father and myself as two deserted souls together; my father had suffered longer but I was sure that, like his, my wound would never heal. Like my father, I thought, I would be faithful to my grief for my whole life. I was on the brink of enjoying my misery—a dangerous thing for my future.

I told David about my dilemma and he advised me strongly not to give up nursing.

'How can you contemplate spending the rest of your life looking after your father?' he asked dramatically. 'It's like putting the clock back a hundred years; it's like something out of an old novel. You'll end up a lonely old woman yourself. It's not fair of your family to ask this of you. Your sister is taking her happiness as she has a right to do. Your father should engage a woman to look after him.'

'Oh, but David,' I cried, 'my father couldn't stand a stranger living in his house.'

'Well, he could try, couldn't he?' David asked.

I was cross with David; I thought he was very unkind and I was sorry I had told him about it. I made up my mind. I had a duty to my father. I gave in my notice to the Nursing Association and my father paid the penalty for the months I wouldn't fulfil my contract.

I went home feeling both noble and submissive. I was now as committed to my father's welfare as I had been committed a month or so earlier to nursing. My father was delighted to have me, and at first I was happy to be home again.

The wheel had turned full circle . . .

I had not been at home more than a week when I began to realise how self-deceptive I had been. My father treated me exactly as he had when I was fourteen years old; his demands were inflexible.

Because I was at home with a good deal of time to think, and because I was back in my childhood setting, I kept thinking about the things that had happened to me—and indeed to Grannie. I remembered how her last years had been poisoned by her separation from us, and how she had been literally sent away to die by those on whom she had the strongest claim for love and protection.

It began to seem to me that often the weak and helpless fall by the wayside, and that blood kinship did not always protect one from predators. I had tried to break the pattern into which I had been forced when my mother left—the pattern of oldest unmarried daughter sacrificing her life for her family. I had entered a profession, with great difficulty and some suffering. And then I had been summoned back again to take up my old role, and I had romanticised my action and felt noble. But I saw very quickly that I could be thrown aside again as I had when my sister had taken my place or as

Grannie had been when she was too old and sick to be anything more than a nuisance.

I thought about it all and thought about it and corresponded with David about it. After I had been home three months I realised that I was a victim and that I had allowed my family to become victimisers. I told my father firmly that I was going to have to leave and that I would find a housekeeper to take my place. I think my father felt that I had failed him; but I believed that I had better do that rather than fail myself.

I went back to my profession and in the course of time David and I were married. I had two children of my own, a boy and a girl. And I determined that each of my children should be respected as a separate individual with a separate life to live.

Postscript

WE were married on 6 January, 1934, and settled in Heacham, a Norfolk market town. Our daughter Gwyneth was born in January of 1935. Later that year David, who was a maintenance engineer for the Air Ministry, was assigned to Egypt because of the Abyssinian crisis. I took the baby and lived with my father until the following year when we joined David at the Royal Air Force base at Aboukiri. There I was able to put my nurse's training to good effect with health visiting and family care among the RAF community.

In 1938 we returned to England; David was assigned to the RAF base at Mountbatten near Plymouth. We were still living there in 1939 when Germany invaded Poland and war was declared. David was reassigned to RAF Benbrooke, an important Bomber Command base in Lincolnshire. Throughout most of the war years we lived in a cottage in the village of Benbrooke; our son David John was born there in September, 1943. In 1945 my husband was assigned to a small RAF station in Lincolnshire and the family moved once more, this time to our own house in Cleethorpes on the Lincolnshire coast.

We lived happily there until 1948 when David was posted to Palestine. Because of the unstable political situation there I stayed in Cleethorpes with the children for three years until 1952 when David was assigned back to England, as a station engineer to an Air Force hospital at Nocton Hall in Lincolnshire. In 1953 Gwyneth entered London University and in 1955 young David became a boarder at Lincoln School. I worked as a clerk in the x-ray department at the hospital. The time at Nocton Hall was a happy and rewarding one.

In 1956 my husband was once more assigned overseas, this time to the sheikdom of Bahrein in the Persian

Gulf. With Gwyneth grown and, having graduated from London University with a degree in English Literature, working as a copy writer in a London advertising agency, and with young David away at school, I was able to accompany David. I started a kindergarten for Air Force families in Bahrein. To my surprise the Sheik enrolled his son in the school. Each morning the child arrived in a Cadillac, accompanied by his nanny and an escort. I like to think that that kindergarten was a great success.

In 1960 we returned to Lincolnshire where David worked at a number of RAF bases for two years until he was assigned to Cyprus. I took an apartment in Kensington with my son David who was following in his sister's footsteps and reading for a degree at London University. In 1963 I joined David in Cyprus, where we spent two marvellous years. In 1965 David was assigned to the Ministry of Defense in London; we bought the lease of a Georgian house in Bayswater where we lived until 1969 when David retired and we moved once more, this time for the last time, to Kingston-upon-Thames in Surrey.

I remained on reasonably friendly terms with my father until his death in 1950. My mother did not die until she was in her nineties: she remarried, but left her second husband, and settled in Cleethorpes at the same time that we lived there. I saw her on occasion but I could not behave with warmth toward her. I lost touch with her in 1952. My sister Alice died fifteen years ago; she left two children. My brother John is still living. He had difficulty finding a career, but became a temporary officer in the British Navy during the second World War and was offered the opportunity to become a career officer after the war. His wife however, objected to this, so he settled in the West of England and opened a draper's shop. He felt that his wife had interfered seriously with his life, and eventually left her. My closest relationship is with my youngest sister Laura, who is still living in Birmingham; we keep in touch. Laura taught school for many years although she married and had two children.

In 1984 David and I celebrated our golden wedding anniversary in January; in April David died, at the age of eighty.

Now in 1988 I live alone in Kingston; at eighty-two I keep house for myself and enjoy frequent visits from my children. Gwyneth Ann has her own public relations firm in London's West End; she and her husband Clive have a mews cottage in Marylebone. David is a career air force officer; he and his wife Rosemary are the parents of my two grandsons, Julian and Austen, to whom this book is dedicated.